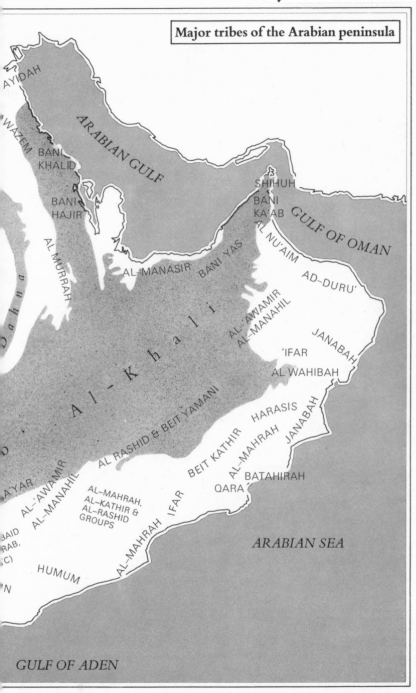

Major tribes of the Arabian peninsula

Arabia Unified

A Portrait of Ibn Saud

MOHAMMED ALMANA

Arabia Unified

A Portrait of Ibn Saud

HUTCHINSON BENHAM
LONDON

Hutchinson Benham Limited
3 Fitzroy Square, London W1P 6JD

An imprint of the Hutchinson Group

London Sydney Melbourne Auckland
Wellington Johannesburg and agencies
throughout the world

First published 1980
© Mohammed Almana, 1980

Set in VIP Sabon

Printed in Great Britain by
The Anchor Press Ltd
and bound by Wm Brendon & Son Ltd
both of Tiptree, Essex

ISBN 0 09 141610 8 cased
ISBN 0 09 141611 6 paper

THE PRAYER OF EVERY MOSLEM

تلبية

(The hajj refrain)

لبيك اللهم لبيك

لبيك لا شريك لك لبيك

إن الحمد والنعمة لك والملك

لا شريك لك لبيك

Here am I, O God, at Thy command,
Here am I.
Thou art the only God,
Thine art praise and grace and dominion.
Thou art the only God. Here am I.

Sunday, December 1, 1985
8:00 pm.
Watched a personal interview of the
author, Mohammed Almana, age 81 -
on Channel 2 - by Elain "Perry" -
Most impressive to hear how a country
was made and unified.   JBC

In memory of my father, Abdullah Almana,
who gave me the education which made it possible for me
to write this book.

Contents

CONTENTS

List of maps

List of illustrations

LIST OF ILLUSTRATIONS

Errata: In the *List of Illustrations*,
the tenth and eleventh captions indicated
on page 12 should read:
'The Sultan's palace at Shibam in the Hadramaut'
'Home of the Zaidi Imam Yahya in Yemen in the 1930s'

Acknowledgements

Mr P. J. S. Bysshe read the original manuscript and corrected my use of English idiom where necessary; Mrs Helen Roberts in Al-Khobar did the initial extensive typing of the first draft; and Ms Jana Gough helped me put the finishing touches to the book. To all these three I owe my heartfelt thanks for their efforts in bringing the book to a successful conclusion.

I should also like to thank *Life* magazine and *The Times* for permission to quote two statements by King Ibn Saud, and the United States' National Archives and Records Service for allowing me to reproduce some of the correspondence between King Ibn Saud and the US government, subsequently published in *Foreign Relations of the United States*. The English translations of the Koran are based on *The Meaning of the Glorious Koran* by Mohammed Marmaduke Pickthall (George Allen & Unwin). The translation on page 39 is taken from *The Seven Odes* by A. J. Arberry (George Allen & Unwin).

My warmest thanks go to Mutlaq Ibn Ba'adi Al Utaiba for permitting me to draw on his scholarly work, *Islamic History in Brief* (Al-Mouttawa', Dammam), and to Dr Abdul Aziz Al-Hulaiby, Deputy Dean of the College of Arts and Literature, Riyadh University. Finally, I should like to record my deep appreciation of the help and encouragement given to me throughout by my friend Othman Himmat of the Sudan and my brother Abdul Aziz Almana.

Preface

At the turn of the century my birthplace, Zubair, was a bustling, prosperous town, lying on the main trade route from Iraq to Najd, in Arabia. For the Arabs, Zubair was the gateway to Iraq and beyond, and the town was almost entirely populated by Najdi merchants. My father, who was himself originally from Najd, dealt in Arab horses; his main customers were Indian maharajas and the British cavalry. When I was ten, he took me to live with him in Bombay. Although I spent the next twelve years of my life in India, first at an English school and then travelling for the family business, I maintained a keen interest in the affairs of my native Arabia, where a great new leader by the name of Abdul Aziz Ibn Saud had arisen. I was fascinated by the exploits of this extraordinary man, and I determined to serve both him and my country.

When I left school, my father tried to persuade me to stay in India and study medicine. However, my mind was made up: I wanted to return to Arabia. Meanwhile, I tried to find a job with the merchant community in Basra, but nobody would employ me; I was told that I was too highly qualified! (In those days, very few people spoke English, with the exception of the Jews and a few Christians.)

During this period, and indeed even when I was in India, I wrote several letters which were accepted for publication by the *Basra Times*. The editor at that time was a young Welshman, and we soon became friends. He offered me a job as a clerk, with a view to writing articles for the paper at a later date. Unfortunately, I lost my job on the paper soon afterwards, due to rivalries within the office. I was very nearly destitute; my father had refused to help me as I had

15

not listened to his advice. That night I prayed hard and long. While I was praying, a visitor entered the house where I was staying in Zubair. He turned out to be a relative of mine. When I discovered that he had come via Basra, I asked him to give me all the latest news. To my delight, it transpired that two men from the Court of Ibn Saud were there at the time.

I went straight to the editor of the *Basra Times* and asked if he would be interested in publishing an interview with one of Ibn Saud's ministers. He agreed enthusiastically, and even suggested several questions I might ask. I left for Basra the next day, and had a long and pleasant discussion with Minister Abdullah Al-Damlujy and Hafiz Wahba. After the interview, upon a sudden impulse, I asked Al-Damlujy if there might be a position for me at the Court of Ibn Saud. I explained that I had received a good education at an English school in India and that I spoke fluent English and Urdu as well as my native Arabic. Al-Damlujy promised to see what he could arrange, and a fortnight later I received a telegram granting me an appointment as translator to the Court of the King. His Majesty was in Mecca at the time. I arrived there on 26 May 1926, still scarcely believing my luck, and started my period of service with the King.

I was to remain in the Court as a translator for a full nine years, during which time I was a constant companion to His Majesty on all his travels and expeditions. It was an eventful period, which saw the meteoric rise and subsequent rebellion and destruction of the religious brotherhood known as the Ikhwan, war with the Yemen and the beginnings of the great Arabian oil story. Naturally, when I eventually left the Court I had many tales to tell of my experiences and my friends urged me to write a book on the subject. I often thought of doing this, but only recently made a start on it. I was finally persuaded after several of my English friends approached me and told me they were tired of reading books and articles about Arabia and the Arabs by Europeans who had appointed themselves experts on the subject after visiting our country for only a few weeks. It was about time, they thought, that a native Arab wrote a book in English, giving an Arabian view of his country's recent history. Thus I set about writing this book, which takes as its theme the unification of Arabia and tells the story of Ibn Saud from his capture of Riyadh in 1902 to the middle of the 1930s, when the oil saga began.

There are already several excellent works in English about the life and times of Ibn Saud, particularly those written by that remarkable Englishman, Harry St John Philby. It was not my intention in writing this book merely to duplicate information which could be read elsewhere. My hope is that I can fill in some of the gaps which history has left; for this reason, I have concentrated on recounting in some detail the events with which I was personally involved during my nine years' service with the King. I have told the story of what happened before then only in outline, for the benefit of those who are not familiar with it. Where I describe events with which I was not connected personally I have attempted to do so, wherever possible, by recording what was told to me by people who actually participated in these events, rather than by referring to written accounts by other authors.

Alas, it is now over forty years since I left the King's Court and with the passage of time my memory is not as fresh or complete as it once was. Nevertheless, I have done my best; I hope the reader will forgive any inaccuracies which may prove to have crept into my text, and also any idiosyncracies of style which may have arisen through my use of a language which is not my own.

Finally, I should mention my principal motive in writing this book, which is to make my own personal tribute to the memory of the man I came to admire above all others, His Majesty King Abdul Aziz Ibn Abdul Rahman Ibn Faisal Ibn Saud.

1

Arabia Frequens

إِنَّ هَذِهِ أُمَّتُكُمْ أُمَّةً وَاحِدَةً وَأَنَا رَبُّكُمْ فَاعْبُدُونِ .

سورة الأنبياء ـ (٩٢)

Lo! this, your religion, is one religion, and I am your Lord, so worship Me.

(Koran, The Prophets 92)

The greatest phenomenon in recent history has been the rise in influence and power of the Arab countries, chief among which is the vast kingdom of Saudi Arabia. All over the world, people are taking a new interest in the Saudi state and have a renewed respect for its wealth, its economic power and the wisdom of its rulers. Yet few foreigners realize that until this century the territory which now comprises Saudi Arabia was a disunited land of small kingdoms, imperial spheres of influence and warring tribes, where boundaries and allegiances shifted as swiftly and erratically as the desert sands. The modern state of Saudi Arabia was created from nothing during the early part of this century as a result of the extraordinary military prowess and statesmanship of just one remarkable man, His Majesty King Abdul Aziz Ibn Saud.

To appreciate the full measure of Ibn Saud's towering achievement, one must have some knowledge of the politics of the Arabian peninsula at the beginning of this century. In 1900 most of Arabia was dominated, if not actually governed, by the waning but still powerful Ottoman Empire. To the east of the country, the Turks physically occupied the area of Al-Hasa on the shores of the Arabian Gulf. They effectively governed Hejaz in the west through Sherif Hussein of the Hashemite family, who, though nominally independent, was in reality little more than a Turkish puppet. To the north, they held the Fertile Crescent – the lands which now comprise Palestine, Syria and Iraq. They also attempted to control the central desert areas by giving support to those tribes and rulers who appeared to them to be strongest. However, this was never more than temporarily successful, for the wandering bedouin were not easy to influence by any method and probably regarded the Turks simply as a convenient source of supply.

For most of the nineteenth century the Turkish rule could not have been described as oppressive. The Turks were Moslems, and Arabia was the birthplace of the Prophet. The Turks tended to treat the Arabian people with the reverence due to the occupants of a Holy Land and they were allowed a good deal of independence. Indeed, it was not uncommon for the Turks to pay regular pensions to local chiefs without expecting anything in return. However, towards the beginning of the First World War, the rule of the Turks became less benevolent as a new wave of young administrators – members of the Young Turks – attempted most unwisely to interfere with the Arab way of life and to introduce Turkish customs. They made the teaching of the Turkish language compulsory in local schools and also tried to force the Arabs to wear the fez rather than their traditional head-dress. This was particularly resented and there were riots all over Arabia in which the demonstrators chanted, 'Rather death than the fez.' Many did indeed lose their lives, for the riots were broken up with considerable violence, in particular by Jamal Pasha, Governor of Greater Syria. By the beginning of the First World War the Turks had succeeded in making themselves quite unnecessarily unpopular and had themselves sowed the seeds for the Arab Revolt organized by T. E. Lawrence in Hejaz.

At the turn of the century there was another important imperial influence in Arabia in the form of Great Britain. Although Britain did not occupy any of the territory in what is now Saudi Arabia, it dominated Muscat, Oman and Aden in the south, and Egypt and the Sudan to the west of the Red Sea. It had also promised by treaty to protect a number of sheikhs in the territories on the Arabian Gulf, in particular Sheikh Mubarak of Kuwait. Not surprisingly, the British maintained a keen interest in the activities of the Turks in Arabia and were always on the look-out for opportunities to undermine their authority.

The land of Hejaz deserves special mention because of its

importance as a religious and commercial centre. Its power was concentrated in the towns of Medina and Jeddah, and of course in the Holy City of Mecca. All faithful Moslems were – and still are – required to make the hajj, or pilgrimage to Mecca, at least once in their lifetime and more frequently if possible. The consequent flow of pilgrims to Hejaz brought in a substantial flow of money to its tax-collectors and merchants, and also a continual flow of new ideas from the outside world. As a result, Hejaz was richer and more sophisticated than the rest of Arabia, and notorious amongst the spartan desert Arabs for the moral laxity of its citizens.

To the people of Central Arabia, empires, nations and fixed boundaries were concepts of little meaning. Their vast land was mostly parched desert or scrub; while some of the population lived in small towns clustered around the few oases, the majority were nomadic bedouin wandering with their families and herds from pasture to pasture. The desert bred proud, fierce, intolerant men, whose loyalty was not to any distant monarch or emperor but first and foremost to their own tribe. The Arabian tribal system was, and indeed still is, one of infinite complexity and subtlety. Broadly speaking, each tribe occupied a roughly defined territory within which it controlled the pastures and water-holes and through which other tribes could pass only with its permission or by force of arms. The names of the tribes are legion but some are so important that they deserve an immediate mention.

Between Riyadh and Mecca and down into the province of Asir, the dominant tribe was the Utaiba. In the area between Medina and Kuwait the principal tribe was the Mutair; a section of this tribe which lived between Medina and Unayzah was known as the Bani Abdillah. In the centre of the country was the Harb tribe, which had sections in Najd and also in Hejaz. Around Riyadh there was the Subai tribe, another section of which lived in Southern Hejaz and Asir. To the south of Riyadh lived the Qahtan tribe, which occupied an area extending down to the Rub' Al-Khali, or Empty Quarter. Members of this tribe were also to be found in large numbers in Southern Hejaz. The Qahtan tribe was traditionally considered to be the oldest tribe in Arabia and the mother of all the other tribes. In the area of Jabal Shammar lived the Shammar tribe, people renowned for their hospitality, strength and courage and also noted for the beauty of their women.

Not only were there many different tribes, but each one was itself divided into at least two main sections. Most tribes were probably formed centuries ago when several powerful families succeeded in establishing their own groups of followers. There might be two sons in a family who on the death of their father would each lead their own half of the tribe; this process of subdivision would then tend to continue from generation to generation. Taking the Utaiba tribe as an example, this had two principal sections, known as the Burga and the Rawaga. Each section had further divisions. For instance, the Burga contained other groups called the Mugata, Nafah, Dahna and Ossuma. There were yet further subsections of each of these groups. All the tribes were structured in this way. Usually, of the two main sections in each tribe, one was notably more powerful and successful than the other and was thought of as the principal or dominant section. Any man with ambitions to become a great king in Central Arabia needed an encyclopedic knowledge of the structure of every tribe and of the jealousies and rivalries simmering inside it, for the principle of 'divide and rule' could be applied to good effect within a single tribe as well as between the various different tribes. Ibn Saud was not only extremely well-versed in the intricacies of the Arabian tribal system; he also knew how to use the intertribal rivalries to his advantage. He frequently managed to ally the less powerful sections of the main tribes with his forces against the more successful branches of these same tribes.

Amongst the tribes – and sometimes between the different sections of individual tribes – there had for centuries been a state of continual warfare. This was not war of the European kind, with massive pitched battles and hideous casualties. Instead, it mostly took the form of raids on one's neighbours to capture animals and booty, and the inevitable counter-raids and subsequent blood feuds. The raids were indulged in more as a kind of sport than through any genuine hatred of the enemy, and provided a welcome relief to the grinding poverty and boredom of desert life. Battles were usually on a small scale, where honour could be satisfied but few people actually got hurt. One could almost liken desert warfare to a game of chess, in which the most skilled, alert general eventually 'checkmated' his opponent.

The bedouin were impossible material from which to build an empire. Throughout the history of Arabia, many great men had attempted to unite them under one rule. None had succeeded for long. The problem was that the tribesmen were fiercely independent and owed no allegiance to any outsider. They had immense respect for strength, courage, leadership and luck; a man who had all these qualities in abundance might for a time unite several tribes or tribal sections behind him and start to carve out a kingdom for himself. But victory was usually self-defeating because once the great man's followers had won sufficient booty they tended to disappear into the desert with their loot. If a leader was to retain his supporters he had to keep fighting and keep winning; if he lost battles or stopped to draw breath, his followers would vanish through disappointment or boredom. Many notable warriors had won a realm in Arabia: none had found the formula for keeping it.

Since the eighteenth century, two prominent families in Central Arabia had consistently thrown up great leaders. One was the family of Rashid, centred in the northern city of Ha'il in Jabal Shammar. The other was the family of Saud, which for many years had had its headquarters in Riyadh in Najd and could claim a most distinguished history. In 1745 Mohammed Ibn Saud, Amir of the insignificant town of Dara'iyah near Riyadh, had allied himself with the great religious reformer Abdul Wahhab and started a jihad, or Holy War, which swept him to power throughout Arabia. The dynasty he founded lasted until its defeat in 1817 but sprang up once more in 1819 in the person of Turki Ibn Abdullah Ibn Mohammed Ibn Saud, from whom Abdul Aziz

25

Ibn Saud was directly descended. For two hundred years the families of Rashid and Saud had struggled for supremacy in Central Arabia. Their family histories were intertwined; in 1834 a Rashid was appointed Amir of Jabal Shammar by Faisal Al Saud, the grandfather of Ibn Saud. At the time my story begins, the star of the Rashids was very much in the ascendant. In 1890 Mohammed Ibn Rashid, after a series of successful battles, had besieged and captured Riyadh from Abdul Rahman Ibn Saud. In fact, Abdul Rahman Ibn Saud would have been allowed to stay on as Amir under the Rashids, but he decided instead to go into voluntary exile. He took with him a few of his followers and his son Abdul Aziz, who was then only ten years old. So utter was the defeat of the house of Saud that nobody then thought the Sauds likely ever to rise again.

Until his death in 1897 Mohammed Ibn Rashid ruled Najd almost as an absolute monarch. He appointed governors to rule in towns taken over from the Sauds and also received money and arms from the Turks, although he probably never gave much in return. When Mohammed Ibn Rashid died, his nephew Abdul Aziz Al Rashid succeeded him. Abdul Aziz Al Rashid could hardly have expected any further trouble from the family of Saud. It was unfortunate for him that the young Abdul Aziz Ibn Saud was to grow to manhood gifted by God not only with all the talents and bravery of his ancestors, but also with a uniquely inspired brand of leadership capable of forging a permanent kingdom in the desert where all others had failed. Within a mere nine years this young prince was to take from Al Rashid both his heritage and his life, and was to go on to become the greatest monarch Arabia has ever known. This book tells a small part of that remarkable story.

2
The capture of Riyadh

بَكَى صَاحِبِي لَمَّا رَأَى الـدَرْبَ دُونَـهُ   وَأَيْقَـنَ أَنَّـا لَاحِقَـانِ بِقَيْصَـرا
فَقُلْـتُ لَهُ لَاتَبْـكِ عَيْنُـكَ إِنَّمَـا   نُحَـاوُلُ مُلْـكَاً أَوْ نَـمُـوتُ فَنُعْذَرَا

(امرؤ القيس)

My friend wept as he saw the way which lay ahead,
and realized at last that we were bound for Caesar.
I said, 'Do not weep, for we are attempting to gain
a kingdom and none will blame us if we perish in
the attempt.'

(Imrou Al Qayse)

When the family of Saud fled from Riyadh in 1890 they took refuge first in Bahrain, where they were well received by the ruler of the island, Sheikh Isa. The Sheikh took an immediate liking to the young Prince Abdul Aziz and was to remain his lifelong friend and adviser. Although Sheikh Isa's reception was warm and his hospitality generous, there was nothing he could do to assist the Sauds to regain their kingdom, and so after a while Abdul Rahman Ibn Saud decided to move on. The family and their followers went to Qatar, but this too proved useless as a power base. They then spent a time wandering with the Al Murrah tribe in the Rub' Al-Khali. Abdul Rahman had hopes that he might be able to rouse the tribesmen there to open rebellion. In this aim he was thwarted, for the tough and hardy bedouin had enough work to do keeping themselves alive in the barren terrain without worrying about who was in power in distant Riyadh. Apart from some desultory raiding, Abdul Rahman achieved nothing which could seriously disturb the power of the house of Rashid. But the stay was not without profit. The Rub' Al-Khali is one of the cruellest deserts on earth. To survive in it, to navigate around it, and especially to fight in it, requires immense skill. The Al Murrah tribesmen had that skill, and they passed much of it on to the young Abdul Aziz. In the Rub' Al-Khali, the Prince received an education in desert-craft which was to stand him in good stead for the rest of his life.

Eventually the family found a permanent refuge in Kuwait, where they were the guests of Sheikh Mubarak Al Subah. (The Saud family and the rulers of Bahrain, Kuwait and Qatar were all originally from the same tribe, the Aneyza.)

Abdul Rahman and his son were to spend nearly ten years in Kuwait and it was there that Prince Abdul Aziz grew to manhood. No doubt Sheikh Mubarak considered that to be the host of the prestigious, if temporarily humbled, family of Saud was a privilege which raised his standing considerably in Central Arabia. Certainly he was anxious to expand his own influence by helping Abdul Rahman and his son to fight Al Rashid, and for this reason readily provided them with men, camels and provisions for numerous raids into Najd. Abdul Rahman was also able to obtain some small financial assistance in the form of a pension from the Turkish authorities at Basra. This was somewhat ironic in view of the support which Al Rashid obtained from the Turks, but it is unlikely that the Turks were being either devious or stupid. It was simply their policy to offer support to any Arab prince who appeared to require it, and Arabian internal politics were such that they could hardly be expected to know at any one time who was raiding whom in the desert.

By the time Prince Abdul Aziz Ibn Saud had reached his twentieth year it was already plain that God had marked him out for great things. In sheer physical size he towered above his companions, being fully six feet two inches tall, a most unusual and impressive height for a desert Arab. Everything else about his appearance was on the grand scale, from his strong, jutting nose to his full lips and fine beard. He had a natural kingly bearing and was dignified and graceful in his movements; as a horseman and warrior, he was beyond compare. From an early age he had about him a charm and magnetism which those who experienced it found impossible to describe in mere words. In short, he was a born leader, and had already built for himself in Kuwait a substantial personal following.

Eventually in 1900 Sheikh Mubarak was persuaded to assist Abdul Rahman in a full-scale military expedition against Al Rashid. Mubarak was in a strong position because he had access to the Arabian Gulf, while Al Rashid was landlocked in Najd. Indeed, at the time, Mubarak may well have harboured ambitions of ruling part of the Arabian peninsula. He gathered a powerful army, containing various important bedouin chiefs such as Faisal Ad-Dawish, and sallied forth towards Al-Qasim. However, although the expedition was joined by a strong force from the Ajman and Mutair tribes, it proved a disaster. Sheikh Mubarak and Abdul Rahman were defeated by Abdul Aziz Al Rashid at the battle of Sarif, near Buraida, and were hotly pursued back to Kuwait. Sheikh Mubarak was only able to prevent an attack on Kuwait itself by persuading the British to send a gunboat to bombard Al Rashid's camp, following which Al Rashid was forced to withdraw to his capital of Ha'il.

Prior to the battle of Sarif, it had been agreed between Sheikh Mubarak and Prince Abdul Aziz that the Prince should march towards Riyadh while Mubarak and Abdul Rahman were moving against Al Rashid in Al-Qasim. This was partly a diversionary tactic and partly so that the Prince could test his chances of regaining Riyadh, the capital of his forbears. On their way south, the Prince's forces attacked a group from the Qahtan tribe who were in the town of Rowdhat Sudair and killed their chief, Nazhan Ibn Muraih. Next the Saudis attacked another Qahtan group, this time led by Faisal Ibn Shaih Al-A'assem. When the Prince finally reached Riyadh, he encountered no opposition and was able to enter the city with his men. Such was the resentment of the inhabitants of Riyadh at being ruled by the Rashids that they were anxious to receive any member of the Saud family. The Rashidi Amir, Abdul Rahman Ibn Dhubai'an, took refuge in the fortress with his men, where they were besieged by the Saudis. When Prince Abdul Aziz saw that the siege was likely to be protracted, he attempted to tunnel underneath the fortress. However, after three days, he received news of the defeat of his father and Sheikh Mubarak at Sarif. The Prince summoned all the prominent citizens of Riyadh and told them that he was going to gather more support from the surrounding tribes and would then return. (In fact, this merely served as an excuse for him to leave the city, since his position had by now become untenable.) The Amir and his men were to remain bottled up in their garrison 'like rabbits in their warren', as the Prince put it. After leaving Riyadh, Prince Abdul Aziz moved south towards Yabrin, on the edge of the Empty Quarter, travelled from there to Qatar and then sailed with a few companions to Bahrain and finally back to Kuwait. By this time he had decided that he could no longer rely upon Sheikh Mubarak as a general; in future, he would have to devise his own strategy for regaining his kingdom. He resolved to make another expedition to Riyadh in the near future, this time without asking Sheikh Mubarak for his support.

The father of the man who told me of this episode was called Abdul Aziz Ibn Jassir Al Madhi. He was Amir of Rowdhat Sudair at the time. Al Madhi and the townspeople had prevented the Rashidi garrison from firing on Ibn Saud when his forces attacked. The Amir had told the garrison that, if they wanted to fight Ibn Saud, they would have to do so away from the town. Subsequently, Al Rashid sent Suleiman Al Quraishi to punish the Amir and people of Rowdhat Sudair for their disloyalty. Al Rashid also showed his displeasure with Ibn Dhubai'an, the Amir of Riyadh. He was discharged and replaced by a man named Ajlan.

By the time that Prince Abdul Aziz had withdrawn to join his father in Kuwait, it was clear that the fortunes of the family of Saud had reached their lowest ebb. Sheikh Mubarak was not disposed to attempt any further military adventures and, while Abdul Aziz and his father were still welcome in Kuwait, it became apparent that their fund of goodwill was gradually vanishing. In later years King Abdul Aziz said that throughout his stay he had always felt he was imposing on the Kuwaitis, and after the battle of Sarif this impression grew stronger. In Kuwait, as elsewhere in Arabia, it was the custom for men of different families to visit one another in the evenings in their respective *majlis* (an area in each house set aside for that purpose). The Prince had become accustomed to being given the place of honour in the *majlis* of each of his numerous friends, but after the battle of Sarif he noticed that this occurred far less frequently. It was clear to Abdul Aziz that his prestige was waning rapidly, and he realized that this must be happening not only in Kuwait; it must also have been diminishing fast in Najd itself. In order to achieve any victory against Al Rashid, the Sauds had to be able to raise support from the tribes inside the areas controlled by him. Abdul Aziz could not rely upon being able to achieve this for very much longer. He knew that the best, and indeed the only, way to regain his prestige would be a sudden, bold stroke inside Al Rashid's territory which would excite the admiration of the tribesmen and enable him to win the following he needed. Although the idea seemed suicidal, he decided to attempt the capture of Riyadh.

The choice of Riyadh was important, for the town had always been the centre of Saudi power and Abdul Rahman still had much support in the area. To Al Rashid the town was of no special importance. It was administered, like his other towns, by a governor – in this case, Ajlan – with the support of a small garrison. To be fair to Ajlan and Al Rashid himself, it could not really be said that the citizens of Riyadh had been governed in a particularly oppressive or tyrannical manner in the years since the family of Rashid had taken the town. Nevertheless, there were many influential chiefs and tribesmen in the district who resented being ruled by a Rashid and would have been only too happy to see the family of Saud resume their rightful place in Najd.

In 1901 Riyadh must have looked much the same as it did when I joined His Majesty in 1926. It was encircled by an outer mud wall, about twenty feet high, in which were set mighty gates at the north, south, east and west. The city was small, probably not more than a few hundred yards across even at its widest point. Inside it was a maze of twisting streets, some so narrow that it was difficult for two men to walk abreast down them. The only open space was the central market, dominated on one side by a large mosque and on the other by the palace which Al Rashid had usurped. Nearby was a tiny market-place, reserved for the womenfolk. All the buildings in the town were of the same adobe construction as the walls. About half had an upper floor but the

33

rest were all single-storey dwellings. Their walls were completely blank on the outside except for an occasional tiny, protruding window.

Before 1890 the city had been surrounded by elegant palm-groves, but when Mohammed Ibn Rashid laid siege to it he wilfully destroyed most of the trees – an unnecessary and unchivalrous act which had earned him the lasting hatred of the inhabitants. In the course of overrunning the defences, Ibn Rashid had also caused severe damage to the outer walls. Neither he nor his nephew had ever thought it worth repairing them properly, and in many places they were seriously dilapidated. Nevertheless, the town remained a formidable nut to crack. At each gate there was a tower in which were stationed two or three men. Although the walls remained unguarded, they could be speedily manned if necessary. Inside the town was a strong central fort which contained a garrison of fifty or sixty men. As a result of his operations against Riyadh a year before, Abdul Aziz had already decided that he did not have the power to take the town by open force. Instead he planned to capture it by stealth.

The Prince again approached Sheikh Mubarak for his assistance, and particularly for the camels he required. It is probable that he told the Sheikh he was planning a raid, but did not disclose the true nature of the expedition in case Sheikh Mubarak should think it too far-fetched to have any possibility of success. The Sheikh grudgingly let the Prince have the camels he wanted, but not surprisingly he did not feel disposed to hand over his best animals. Abdul Aziz was provided with forty old and sickly beasts which were the dregs of Sheikh Mubarak's herd. The Prince picked a small number of his most faithful followers to accompany him and at the end of 1901, still aged only twenty-one, he was ready to set out on his great adventure. The men who accompanied the Prince are so important to our history that I have set out their names in an appendix to this book. (See Appendix 5.)

It took the raiders about ten days to reach Riyadh. They travelled by night, and rested and hid during the day among the rocks and sand-dunes of the desert. When they reached the outskirts of Riyadh in January 1902, they bivouacked amongst the shrubs until nightfall. Until now, with the invaluable habit of secrecy which was to remain with him throughout his life, the Prince had told nobody about his true intentions. Now, at the dead of night, he addressed the men who had completed the journey with him. 'My good and faithful friends,' he said, 'I intend to enter and take the town tonight and all who wish to accompany me are welcome. Those who are reluctant to follow may stay and if, by the break of dawn, you have not received word from me, you must flee for your lives. Should we be successful, you are welcome to join us.'

So hopeless did the Prince's quest seem to his men that only a handful volunteered to enter the town with him, one of them being his cousin Abdullah Ibn Jelawi. The Prince led this tiny force to a part of the wall which he knew would suit his purpose, and by using grappling-irons and ropes the small party climbed into the town undetected. Many of the houses in Riyadh were built against the town wall in such a way that the wall itself formed the back of the house. When the Prince and his followers climbed over the wall, they landed on the terrace of a house which Abdul Aziz knew to belong to a man who had been a servant in the palace when the Prince's father had ruled there. The man's wife had actually nursed the Prince when he was a baby. From the terrace the Prince and his men climbed down into the courtyard, where they found the woman tending her goats. The sight of ten burly men descending from her roof naturally alarmed her and she cried out fearfully, 'Who's there?' 'Hush,' said the Prince. 'It is none other than Abdul Aziz!' When the woman realized that this was indeed true, she wept tears of joy and welcomed him warmly. 'No more polite words,' said the Prince. 'Tell me all that you know about Ajlan, the Amir of Riyadh.' This information took a little time to extract, since the woman had now recovered from her shock and was anxious to share the milk from her goats with her unexpected guests. However, Abdul Aziz insisted that she answer him first. She told him that at night Ajlan was in the habit of sleeping for safety in the fortress, which was of course locked and heavily guarded. Every day after morning prayer, he would leave the fort by the main gate and enter a house directly opposite which was owned by him and occupied by one of his wives. (She was a member of the Al Hamad family from Riyadh, and it was rumoured that she and the Prince had had the same wet-nurse. In Arab society, two children suckled by the same woman are considered as brother and sister, and cannot marry each other.) This was obviously the moment when Ajlan was most vulnerable and the Prince decided immediately that it was then he must strike.

Abdul Aziz and his men crept unobserved along the silent streets and entered an empty house near the one occupied by Ajlan's wife. Climbing up to the roof, they then jumped from terrace to terrace along the line of houses until they reached the one belonging to Ajlan. Stealthily they entered his unsuspecting wife's room. One of them stumbled and the noise woke the woman. Before she could say a word, the Prince put his hand over her mouth and whispered to her to be silent; he told her that her life would be spared provided she made no noise. The Prince and his men then helped themselves to Ajlan's coffee while they waited for daybreak and the emergence of their enemy from the fortress. The main gate of the fort was of traditional construction. It was sizeable enough to admit large bodies of men and camels, and had a small postern door which was always guarded; this door was so designed that a man could only go through it head first, thus enabling the guard to deal with him without difficulty should his appearance be unwelcome. It was only a few yards from this gate to the door of Ajlan's house.

At dawn after prayers, Ajlan emerged as expected through the postern door into the roadway outside. Abdul Aziz watched his progress through the slits in the door of the house. As usual, there were horses tied up outside the fort and Ajlan, who was a great lover of horses, stopped to admire and pet them. Abdul Aziz had planned to deal with Ajlan after he had entered the house, but the sight of his enemy only a few feet away was too much for the Prince to bear; with a violent war-cry he threw open the door and burst out upon the unsuspecting Amir. Although taken completely by surprise, Ajlan managed to defend himself for long enough to retreat to the gate and attempt to fling himself through the postern door. Abdul Aziz caught him by the leg and tried to pull him back, but Ajlan was able to kick himself free and he scrambled into the interior of the fortress and on into the mosque, hotly pursued by the Prince and his men. Inside the mosque he was cut down by the sword of the Prince's cousin, Abdullah Ibn Jelawi.

The garrison of the fortress was taken completely off its guard. Most of the men were stationed on the first floor of the fort and had no time to come to Ajlan's aid. They were a motley group, consisting of members of the Shammar tribe and some servants and bodyguards. The shock of the assault and the death of their leader completely demoralized them, and the daring of the Prince's attack deceived them into thinking that he had invaded the town with a huge force. Before they had time to react, Abdul Aziz himself bravely walked into the centre of the courtyard and announced himself to them. He shouted to them that resistance was pointless now that Ajlan was dead and he promised to spare their lives if they surrendered. The garrison laid down their arms immediately and were locked in their own dungeons. Only about ten men were killed on the Rashidi side; there was no loss of life among the Saudis.

In the moment of victory one of the Prince's men went to the highest tower of the fortress and proclaimed to the waking city, 'There is none but Prince Abdul Aziz Ibn Saud. All is peace and safety!' After twelve years of exile the Prince had now recovered his capital from Al Rashid. It remained for him to win his kingdom.

3

The fall of Al Rashid

وَمُدَجَّجٍ كَرِهَ الكُمَاةُ نِـزَالَهُ   لاَمُـمْعِـنٍ هَـرَبـاً وَلاَ مُسْتَسْـلِمِ
جَـادَتْ لَـهُ كَفَّي بِعاجِـلِ طَعْنَةٍ   بِـمُثَقَّفٍ صَـدْقِ الْكُعُـوبِ مُقَـوَّمِ
بِرَحيبَةِ الفَـرْغَيْنِ يَهْـدِي جَرْسُها   باللَّيْـلِ مُعْتَـسَّ الذِّئابِ الضُّـرَّمِ

(عنترة بن شداد)

Many's the bristling knight the warriors have shunned to
 take on,
one who was not in a hurry to flee or capitulate,
my hands have been right generous too with the hasty thrust
of a well-tempered, strong-jointed, straightened spear
giving him a broad, double-sided gash, the hiss of which
guides in the night-season the prowling, famished wolves.

(Antarah Ibn Shaddad)

The young Prince could hardly have chosen a more formidable opponent than Abdul Aziz Ibn Mutaib Al Rashid, who was a brave and resolute man with a fearsome reputation as a fighter. It has justly been said (and Ibn Saud would have been the first to agree) that no braver man ever strode the desert wastes. Al Rashid's pride and courage are well illustrated by a story often told about him. One day, when he was entertaining a number of important chiefs in his *majlis*, a small desert scorpion crept into his clothing and began to sting him mercilessly. (The desert scorpion is less ferocious than the scorpion found in towns, but its sting is very painful nonetheless.) Any ordinary man would have leapt up and torn off his clothing to dislodge the animal, but there was nothing ordinary about Al Rashid. For a matter of hours, while the scorpion stung him again and again, he remained in his seat talking amiably to his visitors and showed not the slightest sign that anything was amiss. Only when the last of his guests had left did he retire to his private chamber to remove and crush his tormentor.

From their capital in the northern town of Ha'il, the family of Rashid had long been one of the most powerful in Arabia. Since the Rashids had driven the family of Saud into exile, the area around Riyadh had been regarded by them as just another province of their kingdom. One might have expected Abdul Aziz Al Rashid to have responded immediately to Ibn Saud's impertinent capture of Riyadh by sending a punitive expedition to recover it. Ibn Saud still had only a small following, and the dilapidated defences of Riyadh – which had allowed him to enter the town without detection – could not long have resisted a siege by a large force. Al Rashid had an obvious opportunity to throttle Ibn Saud's infant kingdom at birth. But instead of taking seriously the threat posed by the Prince, Al Rashid was too proud to accept him as a serious rival and made the fatal error of treating him with contempt, as if he were a fly who could effortlessly be swatted at any convenient time. It was not until the autumn of 1902 that Al Rashid decided to march south to deal with the usurper, and this gave Ibn Saud nine invaluable months in which to consolidate his position. The Prince's first action was to set the citizens of Riyadh to work repairing and rebuilding the fortifications of the town, in anticipation of the counter-attack which he expected at any moment. He himself set an example to his new subjects by personally labouring long hours to bring liquid mud to the builders at the walls. Al Rashid's reaction upon hearing about this was to say, 'Let them build to their hearts' content; we shall destroy the walls in no time.' However, he took no action to carry out his threat.

When the walls of the city were in good repair, the Prince brought his entire family to Riyadh. His father, Abdul Rahman, immediately abdicated in Abdul Aziz's favour and handed him the historic family sword which had belonged to Abdul Wahhab himself and had remained in the family of Saud for generations as a symbol of their power. This public ceremony and the return of the whole Saud family to their traditional capital, coupled with the dramatic manner in which Riyadh had been captured, persuaded many wavering local chiefs that the tide of fate had turned against Al Rashid. They came in scores to Riyadh to offer their allegiance to the Prince. Within a few months the young Ibn Saud had a sufficient army to leave his father in charge of Riyadh and take an expedition to the provinces south of the city in order to expand his kingdom. By the time Al Rashid had started to move south from Ha'il with his avenging army, Ibn Saud had re-established his family's control in huge areas of the southern provinces extending from Riyadh down to the boundaries of the Rub' Al-Khali, and was now sufficiently powerful to take on his old enemy on equal terms.

The object of all desert warfare at the time was to attempt to outmanoeuvre the enemy so as either to take him by surprise or to cut him off in the desert without water. Since both sides would be liberally supplied with scouts and guides, it was not easy for one army to conceal its presence from the other. Indeed, it was not unusual for the whole of Arabia to know where each army was located, for news of their movements would be passed with astonishing speed by the wandering bedouin as they went from place to place. In every village the old men would sit together, arguing for hours on end about where the armies would go next, and waiting for the next messenger to arrive to see who had been proved right. The unique kind of warfare which resulted was a cat-and-mouse affair, made up of a great deal of marching and countermarching coupled with frequent small raids and skirmishes; it only rarely culminated in a full-scale battle. Such was the pattern of the conflict between Al Rashid and Ibn Saud, and it was not until the end of 1902 that the first battle was fought between them at Dilam, about fifty-five miles south-east of Riyadh. Ibn Saud succeeded in ambushing the enemy troops. He followed up his advantage with a cavalry charge which forced Al Rashid's men to retreat rapidly northwards in disorder, fortunately unaware that the Prince's men had almost entirely run out of ammunition. Following the battle, the attitude of Al Rashid towards his enemy underwent a rapid change; instead of regarding him with contempt, he now swore never to return to Ha'il until he had liquidated the Prince or died in the attempt.

Desultory fighting continued throughout 1903, when Al Rashid made several successful raids against tribes in the northern areas near Artawiya and the Kuwait border, and appeared likely to attack Ibn Saud's ally Sheikh Mubarak in Kuwait itself. The unfortunate Sheikh Mubarak found himself in a terrible dilemma, being anxious to be seen to have supported whichever side in the conflict eventually won, but not knowing whom it was likely to be. His solution was to send regular letters expressing friendship and support to both Ibn Saud and Al Rashid, and these were usually dictated

simultaneously. One day Sheikh Mubarak's clerk acciden-
tally mixed up the envelopes and each Prince received the
letter intended for the other. Al Rashid's reaction is not
recorded, but Ibn Saud, far from being angry, was hugely
amused to see his old friend's duplicity so comically exposed.

In any event, wherever Sheikh Mubarak's allegiance lay,
Ibn Saud was certainly not prepared to see Kuwait taken
over by the Rashids, so he immediately moved his forces
north to counter the threat. Al Rashid promptly doubled
back and attempted for the first and last time to make a
surprise attack on Riyadh. Unfortunately for him, Abdul
Rahman, the Prince's father, had taken the fullest possible
precautions to protect the city and through his scouts had
ample warning of the enemy's advance. By the time Al Rashid
arrived, the city was so well defended that he could not even
try to assault it and was obliged to retreat northwards again
for fear of being caught in the rear by Ibn Saud. So precipi-
tous was Al Rashid's withdrawal that a force sent from
Riyadh by Abdul Rahman to pursue him was able without
difficulty to capture the town of Shaqra, about eighty miles
to the north-west. Ibn Saud himself followed with reinforcements and had soon taken the towns of Majma'a and Zilfi,
with virtually no loss of life, thereby extending his kingdom
in the north to the borders of Al-Qasim. Thus, in little more
than a year, the young Prince who had been considered by
Al Rashid almost too trivial a nuisance to merit his attention
had captured half the Rashidi domain and appeared poised
to take the rest.

In the summer of 1903 Ibn Saud advanced in Al-Qasim
with the assistance of Sheikh Mubarak of Kuwait. By the
beginning of 1904 he had captured Unayzah and Faidhat As-
Sirr. In June 1904 Buraida also fell to him, after a siege of
several weeks. The Prince now controlled large parts of Al-
Qasim and was getting too close to Ha'il for the comfort of
Al Rashid who, realizing that his situation was now becoming desperate, appealed to the Turks for assistance. The
Turks had always supported Al Rashid and so far in the
conflict had aided him with arms and supplies: now they

sent him men. No less than eight battalions of disciplined, well-trained and fully equipped Turkish soldiers were sent into the desert to aid the Rashidi cause. Unlike the bedouin, they were armed with modern rifles, had plenty of ammunition, and were also equipped with artillery. No doubt they expected to crush Ibn Saud's lightly armed and undisciplined irregulars; and they would very likely have done so had the Prince tried to engage them in a full-scale conventional battle. But the Turks were not used to desert warfare and conditions and they lacked mobility. They died in their hundreds from disease without the necessity for Ibn Saud to fire a shot. By skilful manoeuvre and by repeatedly cutting their lines of supply, the Prince could and did outfight them. In the months of September and October 1904 a series of engagements were fought in the area of Bukairiya between Ibn Saud on the one side and Al Rashid and his Turkish allies on the other. The result was a total victory for the Prince: the Turkish force was annihilated, their equipment and artillery were captured, and Al Rashid was forced to retreat back to Ha'il, having himself lost to his enemy large numbers of camels and a substantial quantity of supplies. However, he did not lose his pride, and obstinately encamped outside his capital so as to honour his vow never to return to it until Ibn Saud had been crushed.

After this overwhelming success, Ibn Saud was obliged to leave Al-Qasim abruptly in order to deal with a rebellion in the area of Qatar. For about a year there was no further conflict between the two rulers. Then in 1906 Al Rashid decided to strike once more and began to raise an army of more than twenty thousand men. The whole tribe of Shammar was gathered from the northernmost part of the Jabal Shammar region, together with members of many smaller tribes. The force included no less than two and a half thousand of the best Shammar horsemen. When Ibn Saud heard of his enemy's preparations, he immediately gathered his own forces in readiness for war.

At about this time Al Rashid wrote a letter to the Prince, saying that it was a shame for two faithful Moslems to cause unnecessary bloodshed by perpetual warfare, and suggesting that the issues between them should be settled by a personal duel, with the winner taking all. To a man of Ibn Saud's skill as a warrior this offered a tempting solution, but the Prince could not trust Al Rashid, so with his usual tact he declined the offer. In his reply the Prince praised Al Rashid's courage but commented that Al Rashid was a man who had, by his reckless bravery, often shown a desire for death. Ibn Saud on the contrary wanted to live; and a man who wanted to live had left the path of wisdom if he fought a man who wanted to die. In any event, the whole issue was in the hands of God and it was for God alone to decide the result of the conflict.

The Prince's next move was to march into the north of Al-Qasim, where he soon became involved in the usual preliminary skirmishes with small parties of Rashidi troops. Al Rashid had deployed his forces to the west and north-west of Al-Qasim and, on one of the rare occasions that he was able to outmanoeuvre the Prince, made a rapid march east and crossed the Al-Qasim escarpment just to the south-east of Unayzah, thereby placing his army between Ibn Saud and Riyadh and effectively cutting off Ibn Saud from reinforcements and supplies. When the Prince's followers realized their predicament, most of them prudently melted away into the desert, leaving Ibn Saud with only a handful of loyal soldiers. It is reported that he had left not more than two hundred men with only a hundred camels and ten horses. His plight could hardly have been more desperate.

Many stories have been written about the battle of Rowdhat Muhanna which ensued. The following account was told to me personally by Ibn Saud's standard-bearer, Abdul Rahman Ibn Muttrif, who was present at the battle, and I have every reason to believe it to be accurate. The Prince held council with the ten or so tribal chiefs who had remained with him although their men had disappeared. It was decided that they should attempt to slip through the enemy lines by travelling at night and hiding by day. The following night the small group set off on their journey, trusting in their desert skills and the mercy of God to escape detection. Although Ibn Saud had hoped to steer clear of any large body of enemy troops, he suddenly found himself on the edge of Al Rashid's encampment with only a sand-dune separating him from the Rashidi army. The Prince climbed the dune and stopped at the top to survey his enemy. His friends bade him hurry away but it was as if his feet were stuck in the sand and he refused to move. Increasingly desperate, his friends begged him to leave at once, whispering urgently, 'O Prince, if you are lost everything will be lost.' They even tried to pull him away from the dune but he pushed them off and, with a gleam in his eye, said to them, 'Look! The enemy are completely off their guard and unaware of us. I shall not move from here until I have had a go at them.' 'But it is suicidal,' pleaded his followers. The Prince replied, 'It is too great an opportunity to miss,' and he told them of a plan he had been able to devise on the spot. The chiefs agreed to try out the plan on condition that they and the Prince withdrew immediately to a safe distance. Ibn Saud at first refused to do this, as he was determined to be involved personally in the coming battle. However, the chiefs were adamant and the Prince eventually agreed with reluctance to withdraw. After giving instructions as to how the attack was to be conducted, he and his companion chiefs galloped off to a safe distance.

The force of two hundred men was divided into two sections. Each section made its way carefully to sand-dunes on opposite sides of the great encampment, avoiding the few guards posted by Al Rashid. There they waited for the enemy to fall asleep. By midnight most of the camp-fires had died down and all was quiet. The first party crept silently and stealthily towards the camp. There was only one small flicker of light, and they headed towards it like a moth in the dark flying towards a flame. As they approached the light it became clear that it was a candle inside a tent. Suddenly a figure came out of the tent, followed by a servant carrying a kettle. The raiding party immediately froze in their tracks, but in the excitement the soldier who was carrying the

Prince's standard let it slip in his hands and there was a jangling noise from the metal balls and ornaments attached to the flag. The man who had come from the tent called out in their direction, 'That is not the way, Al-Fraikh.' Al-Fraikh was known to be Al Rashid's standard-bearer, and the imperious tone of voice used by the man who had called out was obviously that of a master addressing a servant. The figure by the tent could only be Al Rashid himself, who had obviously mistaken the Prince's standard-bearer for his own man. It took the Saudis a moment to realize their amazing luck. Then one of the soldiers cried out to his companions, 'O you who seek Al Rashid, here is your man!' The raiders fell upon Al Rashid who, despite his brave attempt to defend himself with his drawn sword, was instantly overpowered, cut down and killed. The uproar immediately roused the entire camp and the raiding party seemed doomed to annihilation. Just at that moment the second section of the Prince's men, who had stationed themselves on the dunes around about, began an intense rapid fire into the camp, blazing away all their ammunition as quickly as they could. The raiding party inside the camp did the same. It was a brilliantly successful ruse; to Al Rashid's bemused soldiers, roused precipitously from their slumbers, it seemed as if their camp was being attacked from all sides by an overwhelming force. Deprived of a leader to rally them, the Rashidi troops degenerated into a disorganized rabble. Thinking that their enemy was already amongst them in force, they started shooting indiscriminately inside the camp, thus inviting return fire from their own men. Soon the encampment echoed with furious gunfire from end to end as groups of terrified soldiers fought desperately with each other in the darkness, unaware that the enemy existed only in their imagination.

In the resulting confusion, the Saudis managed to escape from the camp almost without loss. They withdrew with the utmost speed, taking with them Al Rashid's signet ring as proof of his death. The Prince was waiting for them at a pre-arranged hiding place. Since he had travelled on horseback, and the rest of the Saudi force had perhaps a hundred camels among two hundred men, it took them three or four days to catch up with him. When the Prince heard of their success he was delighted, but the killing of Al Rashid seemed to him so unlikely that he refused to believe his men even when they produced the ring. He ordered them to return for the body, saying, 'I cannot believe this until you bring back his head.' His men duly returned with extreme caution to the battle-field, where they found nothing but dead men and animals. The slaughter in the camp had been tremendous and the survivors had fled back to Ha'il. They had made no attempt to bury their chief, and Al Rashid's head was severed and brought in triumph to the Prince. Thus died the greatest of the Prince's enemies. After his death at Rowdhat Muhanna, the survival of Ibn Saud's kingdom was never again seriously in doubt.

4

The consolidation of a kingdom

فِي بِضْعِ سِنِينَ لِلّهِ الأَمْرُ مِنْ قَبْلُ وَمِنْ بَعْدُ وَيَوْمَئِذٍ يَفْرَحُ اَلْمُؤْمِنُونَ . بِنَصْرِ اللّهِ يَنْصُرُ مَنْ يَشَاءُ وَهُوَ العَزِيزُ الرَحِيمُ .

سورة الروم ــ (٤ ــ ٥)

Within ten years — Allah's is the command in the former case and in the latter — and in that day believers will rejoice
In Allah's help to victory. He helpeth to victory whom He will. He is the Mighty, the Merciful.

(Koran, The Romans 4/5)

In the seven years after the battle of Rowdhat Muhanna, Ibn Saud's territory expanded no further. It is unlikely that he himself could have said exactly where the boundaries of that territory lay because it was defined, not by lines on a map, but rather according to the loyalties of the bedouin tribesmen who had come to accept him as their ruler. The area north of Riyadh he controlled as far as the northern boundaries of Al-Qasim. Beyond that lay Jabal Shammar, which was still under the control of the family of Rashid and remained hostile to Ibn Saud. However, after the death of Abdul Aziz Al Rashid, his sons engaged in a long and vicious struggle for the control of Ha'il, resulting in the assassination of three Rashidi monarchs in seven years as well as the deaths of numerous lesser members of the family. While this feud was going on, the Rashids were too busy fighting each other to present any threat to Ibn Saud. To the south the Prince controlled all the territory up to the natural boundary formed by the Rub' Al-Khali. To the east was Al-Hasa, occupied by the Turks, who had no cause to be friendly to Ibn Saud. While they now knew better than to attempt any further military expeditions into the desert, they could still be relied upon to support the Rashids and obstruct the Prince as much as possible. Furthermore, while they held Al-Hasa they also held the ports in the Arabian Gulf and thus ensured that Najd remained landlocked. To the west lay Hejaz, which was for all practical purposes a Turkish province governed by the puppet ruler, Sherif Hussein. Hussein had no cause as yet to be actively hostile to Ibn Saud, but he harboured dreams of ruling the whole Arabian peninsula and an eventual clash between the two rulers seemed probable. Even

Sheikh Mubarak in Kuwait had shown that he could not be trusted entirely, and he was known to be jealous of Ibn Saud's sudden and spectacular rise to power.

Although the Prince was surrounded by enemies, both actual and potential, most of his problems in the period after Rowdhat Muhanna originated inside his own domain. Ibn Saud could count on the loyalty of his tribesmen as long as there were battles to be won and booty to be gained; but as soon as the pace of warfare slackened, the very same tribesmen were likely to revolt and attempt to overthrow him. The Prince had to deal with several such revolts, including a serious rebellion of the Mutair tribe under Faisal Ad-Dawish in May 1907. Ad-Dawish was defeated at the battle of Majma'a and pardoned. Thereupon he rebelled again, only to be defeated once more by the Prince at a battle near Buraida.

The rebellions, large and small, with which the Prince had to deal all had two things in common. First, all of them were crushed (though not always without difficulty). Secondly, in every case the rebel leaders were treated with mercy and often pardoned and restored to their positions of authority. In doing this Ibn Saud was displaying more than simple generosity and mercy; he was also showing great wisdom. The traditional penalty for treason was death. If the Prince had executed each tribal chief who rebelled, he would have had to replace him with a man of his own choosing. It is unlikely that any man would have come forward for such a task, for the resentment of the tribesmen at the presence of an interloper would be likely to take such a murderous turn that he could not have expected to live long. Furthermore, the execution of a tribal chief might itself start an endless blood feud with the tribe in question. By defeating and then pardoning the treacherous sheikhs the Prince was more likely to earn their eventual loyalty and respect. In most cases this policy proved remarkably successful, although there were a few notable exceptions such as Faisal Ad-Dawish. Another persistent turncoat was the Governor of Buraida, Mohammed Aba Al-Kheil. He rebelled in 1908 and was defeated, pardoned and restored to his position by the Prince, only to do exactly the same thing again. Even on the second occasion, when Ibn Saud had every reason to execute him, Aba Al-Kheil escaped with his life and was merely banished to Iraq.

In 1909 there was further trouble in Ha'il when, after another outburst of murderous infighting, Zamil Ibn Subhan of the house of Rashid became the new ruler of Jabal Shammar. Shortly after establishing himself, Ibn Subhan attempted a large-scale raiding expedition into Ibn Saud's territory, where he suffered a resounding defeat at the battle of Asha'alan. Although on this occasion the Rashids had been easily dealt with, they continued to be a thorn in the Prince's side. It was obvious that sooner or later there would have to be a final reckoning with Ha'il.

Sherif Hussein of Mecca also started to make his presence felt. In 1911, encouraged by the Turks, he sent a strong military expedition into the west of Ibn Saud's territory. At Quai'iya, about a hundred and ten miles south-east of Medina, this expedition was fortunate enough to kidnap Ibn Saud's brother Sa'ad. In order to ransom his brother, the Prince was obliged to recognize Turkish sovereignty over Al-Qasim and had to agree to pay a nominal tribute to them. The recognition of this non-existent Turkish power was always an absurdity, and the tribute was never paid. Nevertheless, it was an insult which Ibn Saud could not easily forget.

As has already been seen, one of Ibn Saud's greatest difficulties in building up a stable kingdom was the same problem that faced any desert leader, namely, the fierce independence, belligerence and rapidly shifting loyalties of the desert tribesmen. In 1912, partly in an attempt to ease this problem, the Prince initiated a revival of the puritan, fundamentalist religious movement started by Abdul Wahhab in the eighteenth century. The revival aimed at uniting the tribesmen in the service of God; the Prince's great innovation was to encourage them to form permanent settlements. Out of this revival sprang the fearsome religious movement known as the Ikhwan, or Brotherhood, which provided a core of fanatical warriors ready to fight to the death for God and the Imam against the infidels. Of the formation, growth and eventual destruction of this movement, more will be told later. For the moment it need only be said that within a year of the birth of the Ikhwan, Ibn Saud found himself with a large, ferocious and powerful army of men who regarded him as God's chosen instrument and could be relied upon to remain loyal and rally round him whenever he gave the call to arms.

The first victory for the Ikhwan came very quickly. In 1913 the Prince decided that the time was ripe for him to take the initiative against the Turks in Al-Hasa. On 8 May his army, including a number of Ikhwan detachments, made a sudden night attack on the town of Hufuf, which had a Turkish garrison of about twelve hundred men. The Turks were taken completely by surprise and offered almost no resistance. With his usual magnanimity, Ibn Saud allowed them to leave the town after they had surrendered their arms. They were escorted to Bahrain from where they eventually sailed back to Turkey. The rest of Al-Hasa contained only a few Turkish troops; they surrendered as soon as they heard of the débâcle at Hufuf. In less than a month, and with very little bloodshed, the Prince had gained a large new province and access to the Arabian Gulf from the south of Kuwait right down to the north of Qatar. In Hufuf he installed a new governor – none other than Abdullah Ibn Jelawi, whose spearthrust in the mosque at Riyadh eleven years before had heralded the beginning of the new Saudi kingdom.

The outbreak of the First World War in 1914 brought one immediate benefit to Ibn Saud in that the commitments of the Ottoman Empire elsewhere made it impossible for the Turks to attempt the recapture of Al-Hasa. During the war Najd became something of a backwater. The famous Arab Revolt (in which Lawrence of Arabia played such a prominent part) took place in Hejaz, which unlike Najd still contained Turkish troops for the Arabs to revolt against. However, the Turks managed to cause some trouble for the

Prince by continuing to support Jabal Shammar. This area was now ruled by Saud Ibn Abdul Aziz Al-Mutaib Ibn Rashid, who engaged Ibn Saud in sporadic fighting, particularly in 1915. In January that year a fierce but indecisive battle took place at Jurrab, near Zilfi.

The battle is now chiefly remembered because, strangely enough, one of the casualties was an Englishman, Captain W. Shakespear. He had previously been Political Agent in Kuwait, and had managed to build up a strong personal friendship with Prince Abdul Aziz. Shakespear had been sent back to Arabia with the title of Political Officer on Special Duty. He had insisted upon accompanying Ibn Saud on the expedition against Ibn Rashid, and had been determined to take part in the battle even though the Prince urged him to stay out of danger. The Najdis had with them one of the Turkish cannons captured eleven years before at Bukairiya. Shakespear was directing its fire during the battle when his position was overrun by Rashidi cavalry and he was cut down and killed. His death was much regretted by Ibn Saud; it was also a considerable blow to the British, who lost their only representative in Najd. This proved significant towards the end of the war when the British, who were concerned that the Rashids with Turkish support might interfere with their operations in Palestine, wanted to commence negotiations with Ibn Saud to persuade him to attack Ha'il. They had nobody to do this in Riyadh, so a mission had to be sent especially for the purpose. The British offered as inducements substantial sums of money, ten thousand rifles, plentiful supplies of ammunition and no less than four field guns – in all, quite sufficient resources to enable the Prince to overwhelm the defences of Ha'il. Ibn Saud accepted the offer, but the weapons were never delivered. This was because the man in charge of the British mission, Harry St John Philby, made (on his own initiative) a journey to see Sherif Hussein in Hejaz. The Sherif, who was anxious to obstruct Ibn Saud in any way he could, prevented Philby from returning. There was therefore no British representative in Riyadh to conclude the agreement and make the necessary arrangements. By the time another British representative reached Ibn Saud, the Turks in Palestine had been defeated and the British no longer had any need of assistance from Najd. Nevertheless, Ibn Saud attempted an attack on Jabal Shammar and laid siege to Ha'il. The siege failed for lack of the British guns to bombard the walls of the town and the Prince was forced to retire to Riyadh.

Despite this setback, Jabal Shammar had only three more years of survival as an independent state. In 1919 Saud Ibn Rashid was shot dead during a picnic by his cousin Abdullah Ibn Talal. Abdullah was instantly cut down by Saud's loyal servants. Abdullah's brother Mohammed Ibn Talal, who was also involved in the plot, was imprisoned. The eventual successor to the throne was Abdullah Ibn Mutaib. (See Appendix 3.) He was the grandson of Ibn Saud's old enemy Abdul Aziz Al Rashid, but he had none of his grandfather's courage or ability. Under his rule Jabal Shammar became weak and divided; Ibn Saud was able to invade it with ease and persuade many of the Shammar tribesmen to join his army. In one of many desperate moves Abdullah Ibn Mutaib released his cousin Mohammed from prison, whereupon Mohammed rebelled against him, forcing Abdullah, ironically enough, to seek refuge with Ibn Saud. Mohammed now took over the defence of Ha'il, to which Ibn Saud again laid siege. This time the Prince brought with him the Turkish guns he had captured at the battle of Bukairiya seventeen years earlier. By now the guns were very dilapidated and it is not certain whether they were still serviceable. However, the threat of bombardment was enough to demoralize the occupants of the city. One of the gates of Ha'il was guarded by men of the family of As-Sabhan, who were related to the Rashids. The As-Sabhan had good cause to be disgruntled with the state of affairs in Ha'il, for a number of their close relatives had been butchered in the recent family strife. Certainly they had no desire to be deluged with high explosive for Mohammed's sake. Secretly they made a pact with Ibn Saud to allow the Najdi army into Ha'il under cover of darkness. Once the Saudis were inside the walls, the garrison surrendered with little resistance. After nineteen years of struggle the Prince was at last master of Jabal Shammar.

As always, Ibn Saud was chivalrous in victory. The Rashidi army was absorbed into his own and several young Rashidi princes, including Mohammed Ibn Talal, were taken, not as prisoners, but as honoured guests to his capital of Riyadh. In time, many of them were to become Ibn Saud's loyal and devoted subjects. In fact, in the 1920s I came to know Abdullah Ibn Mutaib personally. He was living in Riyadh on a pension provided by Ibn Saud, and seemed happy and content. He was always ready to talk and we discussed everything under the sun – except for his experiences in Ha'il, about which he was reluctant to say anything at all. Sadly, he died in the 1950s in Riyadh, in very unhappy circumstances.

Mohammed Ibn Talal was kept under guard in a room at the palace for some time, but later he was put under house arrest, with some servants and bodyguards to look after him. After a while, he managed to sneak out of his house, disguised in women's clothes. By pretending to be a poor woman with a petition, he somehow slipped past the guards at the royal palace, ascended the staircase to the first floor and stood by the open door of the mid-morning general *majlis*. From here, he would have had to push past the throngs of seated bedouin, which would have been most unusual for a woman. The King immediately became suspicious. He strode towards Ibn Talal and disarmed him, tying him up in his billowing skirts. He was taken off by the guards and again imprisoned in his house, this time under a tighter guard. Later on, he swore his loyalty to the King and gave an undertaking not to repeat his behaviour. Subsequently, he was given a little more freedom; he even came with the King's troops to the battle of Sibillah, although still closely guarded. Ibn Talal stayed under house arrest for the rest of his life. In the end, he was killed by one of his own servants, who immediately committed suicide.

In recognition of the fact that Ibn Saud now ruled the whole of Central Arabia, the sheikhs and *ulemas* (religious leaders) of the kingdom decided to honour him with a title; at a public ceremony in Riyadh the Prince was proclaimed Sultan and Imam of Najd.

5
Hejaz and Asir

قُلْ جَاءَ الحقُّ وَمَا يُبْدِىءُ البَاطِلُ وَمَا يُعِيدُ .

سورة سبأ ـ (٤٩)

Say: The Truth hath come, and falsehood showeth
not its face and will not return.

(Koran, Saba 49)

By the end of the First World War it had become apparent that it was not only with Ha'il that there would have to be a final reckoning. Sherif Hussein of Hejaz, having thrown off his Turkish yoke and overlords with the aid of the British, appeared to suffer increasingly from delusions of grandeur. He began to make empty claims to suzerainty over all the states in the peninsula, including Najd. Nobody knew where he got his authority from, as all these countries were now independent and owed no allegiance to him. The Sherif wrote letters in an imperious tone to a number of rulers in Arabia, including Ibn Saud, to the effect that he had decided to establish an Arab state, of which he would naturally be the head; he requested everybody to acknowledge his sovereignty. In the circumstances Ibn Saud's response was a masterpiece of restraint. He replied as an equal, politely pointing out that Najd was independent and therefore he could not comply with the Sherif's request. However, he trusted that Najd and Hejaz would continue to coexist peacefully as neighbours and friends. On receiving this most diplomatic of letters, Sherif Hussein is said to have flown into an uncontrollable rage.

The friction between Najd and Hejaz became focused in 1919 at the oasis of Khurma, some one hundred and ten miles east of Mecca. The Sherif considered Khurma to be part of his domain, but the inhabitants thought otherwise and had declared themselves loyal subjects of Ibn Saud. In 1918 two punitive expeditions had been launched from Hejaz against Khurma, but on each occasion the oasis had been successfully defended. Sherif Hussein was determined that there should be no mistake the third time. In 1919 he gathered a force of thirty thousand men from the remnants of the army of the old Turkish regime and from parts of his own army that had fought the Turks with Lawrence. At their head he put his own son, Amir Abdullah. Not only did he order his son to crush the revolt at Khurma; it is reported that, in an expansive moment, he also ordered Abdullah to sweep through Najd and spend the summer in the gardens of Al-Hasa.

Abdullah had an army which was exceptionally well-equipped by desert standards, for most of the supplies and weapons donated by the British towards the Arab Revolt were still in his father's possession. Nevertheless, he appeared to be in no hurry to carry out his instructions. He ordered his forces to gather on the outskirts of the town of Turabah and, having fortified the camp, simply remained there while his soldiers kicked their heels and yet more men and weapons were gathered. He had obviously decided that the gardens of Al-Hasa could manage without him for a few more weeks.

Abdullah's delay was to have severe consequences for Hejaz. While he dallied at Turabah, news of the gathering of his army sped to Riyadh and reached the ears of one of Ibn Saud's guests, Sheikh Khalid Ibn Luway, of a tribe related to the Sherif. Ibn Luway was a bedouin chief of Southern Hejaz who had been a prominent member of the Sherif's army. One day Amir Abdullah had roundly insulted Ibn Luway, who had immediately left Hejaz to take refuge with Ibn Saud in Najd. Upon hearing about Abdullah's activities, Ibn Luway lost no time in asking his host for permission either to raise an army to defend Najd or actually to mount an attack on Abdullah with whatever men of the Utaiba tribe he could gather together at short notice. This proposal to use only the Utaiba tribe for an attack was by no means as foolhardy as it might at first have seemed, for the entire region between the centre of Najd and Mecca was inhabited by almost no other tribe. If they could be mobilized against the invaders, Abdullah would have to advance into Najd through territory which was wholly hostile to him; he would be subject to continual harassment and likely at any time to have his lines of supply cut behind him. When Ibn Luway

Left: Sheikh Isa Ibn Ali of Bahrain, who first gave refuge to the Saud family when they fled from Riyadh in 1890 after the Rashidis had captured the city. *Royal Geographical Society*

Below: Sheikh Mubarak Al Subah of Kuwait (seated, centre) with Ibn Saud (seated, left), Ibn Saud's brother Sa'ad (standing, centre) and other members of the Saud family. The family found refuge with Sheikh Mubarak until Ibn Saud recaptured Riyadh in 1902. *Royal Geographical Society*

Above: Ibn Saud with some of his brothers and sons near Thaj, in Eastern Arabia, where the Prince camped with Captain Shakespear. *Royal Geographical Society*

Opposite: Prince Sa'ad Ibn Saud, in a photograph taken by Captain Shakespear in 1911. *Royal Geographical Society*

Outside the Old Palace, Riyadh. *Popperfoto*

The outer mud walls of Riyadh, showing the Al-Hasa gate, 1912. *Royal Geographical Society*

Left: Postern door in Riyadh fortress, where the Rashidi Governor Ajlan was trapped by Ibn Saud and a handful of his followers when they recaptured the city in 1902. *MEPhA*

Below: Members of Ibn Saud's puritanical Ikhwan brethren

Left: Ikhwan at Kuwait, 1926. *Royal Geographical Society*

Right: Typical Ikhwan dress, 1923. *Royal Geographical Society*

General view of the city of Unayzah, captured by Ibn Saud in 1904.
Popperfoto

The market-place at Hufuf, the capital of Al-Hasa, which fell to Ibn Saud
in 1913. *Popperfoto*

The Governor of Abha, the capital of Asir, on his way to the mosque. Abha fell to the Saudis in 1921. *Popperfoto*

Jizan, on the Red Sea, annexed by Ibn Saud in the late 1920s. *Keystone Press Agency*

Left: Sherif Hussein Ibn Ali of Mecca. This photograph was taken in Amman in 1924, after he abdicated in favour of his son Ali. *The Times*

Below: Amir Abdullah Ibn Hussein, who was defeated by the Utaiba chiefs, Ibn Bijad and Ibn Luway, at the battle of Turabah in 1919. *Magnum Photos*

approached Ibn Saud, the Sherifian army had not actually moved into the Prince's territory but was merely a potential threat. Ibn Saud therefore did not feel that he could afford at that stage to be directly involved in any attack against the Sherif. He told Ibn Luway that he could plan and do what he wanted on his own; if the Utaiba tribe chose to join him, that was their own affair. This was a scheme of a sort commonly used by the Prince to excellent effect, for it enabled him to take advantage of any successes scored by Ibn Luway while still being able to disown him if he failed.

Sultan Ibn Bijad, another chief of the Utaiba tribe and a prominent member of the Ikhwan, joined forces with Ibn Luway. The two set off in secret from Najd, unproclaimed except by the secret communications of the desert, and made their way towards the main force of the Sherif at Turabah, gathering warriors from the Utaiba tribe as they went. By the time they reached the boundaries of Hejaz, they had raised a force of three thousand men which included several Ikhwan contingents. Nevertheless, they were still outnumbered ten to one by the Sherif's army, and clearly could not have engaged the enemy in a conventional battle. Instead Ibn Luway and Ibn Bijad decided to attempt a surprise attack at night.

In the hands of a competent commander the well-equipped Sherifian army, in their fortified camp, should have had little difficulty in beating off such an attack. But it had been apparent from the outset that Abdullah was no soldier. Both he and his father were novices at desert warfare; they had no real knowledge of the tribes of Najd or of their methods of fighting, and neither man appreciated the importance of having scouts constantly on the alert to guard against just such an attack as was now being planned against them. The Sherif and his son were rulers of the city, not the desert, and in dealing with the bedouin chiefs and tribesmen they tended to be disdainful and aloof. Furthermore, they were thoroughly tight-fisted when it came to making gifts to visiting bedouin, in marked contrast to Ibn Saud, whose generosity was renowned throughout Arabia. In consequence most of the desert tribesmen were openly or covertly hostile to the Sherif, and there was little chance that any wandering bedouin would consider it worth informing his son about the approach of the enemy. Even so, Amir Abdullah did receive a warning about the forthcoming assault. A story is told that, on the evening before the attack took place, an old woman stopped Abdullah as he was about to enter his tent. She urged him to take care and be alert as she had had a dream which had warned her that some danger was lurking not far from the Amir's army. Abdullah's response was to fly into a rage and order his soldiers to drive her away.

Even as Abdullah's troops were ejecting the old woman, the Utaiba tribe were silently surrounding his camp. The plan devised by Ibn Luway and Ibn Bijad was similar to that carried out by Ibn Saud himself thirteen years before at the battle of Rowdhat Muhanna. Their force of three thousand men was divided into two groups each of three hundred men and a third large group containing the rest. One of the smaller groups worked its way round to the north of the camp; the other skirted the huge encampment and positioned itself to the west. The main group remained in the east. At midnight, when all was quiet, all three groups opened fire simultaneously upon the slumbering inmates of the camp, who awoke to find bullets flying at them from all sides. Just as at Rowdhat Muhanna, the bemused soldiers were deceived into thinking that they were being assaulted by a huge force, and started firing in all directions. Once again, this haphazard cross-fire from the defenders caused furious battles to break out inside the camp between groups of Abdullah's men, each of which was convinced that the others were enemy formations. The two smaller attacking contingents then wheeled round and joined the main force in the east, whereupon the whole Najdi army charged into the camp, turning the confusion inside into outright panic. They then disengaged abruptly and retreated into Najd as fast as they could, letting the inferno burn itself out. The Sherifian troops were routed and fled in disorder towards Mecca, leaving behind hundreds of dead and all their guns, rifles, ammunition and equipment. Amir Abdullah himself, rudely aroused in the middle of the night, was so bewildered and distracted that he had scarcely any idea what was taking place. All he knew was that somehow he had been defeated and must flee for his life. He was able to sneak out of the camp on a mule and, accompanied by a few loyal servants, scampered away to Ta'if, which he reached three or four days later.

The telephone operator at Ta'if post office was a man called Abdul Nassif. He told me the following story. When he heard that the Amir had appeared with a handful of his servants and followers, he telephoned Sherif Hussein in Mecca to tell him of the ignominious arrival of his defeated son on a mule. The Sherif was enraged at the news and, after making a number of comments which could hardly be repeated here, quoted a famous Arab saying:

ذَهَـبَ الحمـارُ بِأمًّ عَمْرٍ   فَـلاَ رَجَعَـتْ ولاَ رجـعَ الحِمَارُ

To hell with the old witch and her donkey. Pray that neither she nor the donkey returns.

After the resounding defeat at Turabah in 1919, Hejaz was obviously vulnerable to further attack. Khalid Ibn Luway came to Ibn Saud urging him to attempt an immediate invasion. The Prince refused outright as the Sherif still received British support and any move against him would be a most dangerous and hazardous venture. In any event, Ibn Saud was about to move once more against Ha'il and could not have spared the time or resources for any other military operations. Even after Ha'il had fallen, Ibn Saud, now Sultan of Najd, was too busy elsewhere in his kingdom to concern himself with Hejaz. As always, his prudence paid dividends. Events in the west of Arabia now seemed to move inexorably in his favour, and it was not long before the Western Province of Asir was to be added almost effortlessly to his dominions.

Asir lies on the Red Sea, to the south of Hejaz. At the beginning of the 1920s it enjoyed a kind of semi-independence under the control of an amir named Hassan Al-Aidh who ruled from the capital town of Abha. Al-Aidh had recently strengthened his position by the military defeat of a rival group in Asir, led by the family of Al-Adrisy. The victory had been achieved with assistance from Sherif Hussein. Subsequently, Al-Aidh became both arrogant and overconfident; he began to ally himself increasingly with the Sherif and attempted to suppress and persecute all those who opposed him.

In linking himself so strongly with the Hashemites, Al-Aidh gravely misjudged the mood of his people. The tribes of Asir were predominantly from the Shahri, Shahran, Qahtan and Asir groups, although there were also some members of the Subai and the Utaiba. These tribes were all puritanical in their religious beliefs. They viewed with suspicion and distrust the worldly town-dwellers of Hejaz, and were sympathetic to the Wahhabi movement. With the rise of the Ikhwan and the expansion of the realm of Ibn Saud, it was inevitable that they would look for leadership and guidance towards Riyadh rather than Mecca. In 1921 a group of tribal chiefs from Asir arrived in Riyadh and complained to Ibn Saud of the ill-treatment that they were suffering at the hands of Al-Aidh. The Prince agreed to mediate on their behalf. However, Al-Aidh refused to have anything to do with any Saudi deputation, claiming that the whole idea amounted to unjustified political interference in his internal affairs. He then redoubled his persecution of the dissenting tribal chiefs, many of whom had to flee Asir in fear of their lives.

Al-Aidh's actions were intended to be the clearest possible rebuff to Ibn Saud, and represented an insult which he was not prepared to overlook. At the end of 1921 a strong Saudi force, under the command of Abdul Aziz Ibn Mussaud, was dispatched to Asir. Ibn Mussaud reached the area of Bishah, where he encamped. From there he sent a letter to Al-Aidh requiring him to confirm his allegiance to Ibn Saud. Al-Aidh's reply was simple and direct. He sent a messenger back to Ibn Mussaud with a small package; it contained a clip of bullets. No clearer invitation to battle could be given, and Ibn Mussaud was not the man to turn it down. With his army he

immediately advanced into Asir. At Wadi Hajlah he found
Al-Aidh's army entrenched in defensive positions under the
command of Mohammed Ibn Abdul Rahman Al-Aidh. The
battle which followed resulted in the complete defeat of the
Asiri forces. They withdrew in disorder to Abha, where Hassan Al-Aidh was hastily improving the fortifications. The loss
of morale amongst the Asiri troops was so great that as the
Saudi forces approached the town much of the army fled,
taking all their arms and equipment with them and leaving
only a frightened skeleton force to defend the town. By this
time the tribal chiefs in the area scented a Saudi victory.
Preferring, as always, to be on the winning rather than the
losing side, and anxious to share in any booty that was
going, they threw in their lot with Ibn Mussaud. Abha was
taken with little difficulty, and shortly afterwards a very
deflated Hassan Al-Aidh was compelled to surrender. Ibn
Mussaud treated his captive with courtesy and sent him and
others of his family to Riyadh. There he was received by Ibn
Saud with the magnanimity and generosity which the Prince
always displayed towards the vanquished. Ibn Saud even
offered to appoint Al-Aidh as his Amir of Asir. Al-Aidh was
too proud to accept the offer but was nevertheless allowed
to return to Asir, where he retired with his family to his old
mountain stronghold of Hamalah.

The saga of Asir did not quite end there. Ibn Mussaud
appointed an amir named Fahd Al-Ughaily to govern Abha.
Al-Ughaily proved unpopular and it was not long before the
fickle bedouin were urging Hassan Al-Aidh to rebel against
him. Al-Aidh eventually agreed and, with a powerful force
of tribesmen, laid siege to Abha. The town was stoutly
defended by the Saudi garrison but it eventually fell; it was
then the turn of Al-Ughaily to be taken captive. Ibn Saud
reacted swiftly to these events by sending his son Faisal to
Asir with a powerful force. The rebellion collapsed on his
arrival and Abha was reoccupied with little resistance. Faisal
wisely appointed a new amir named Abdul Aziz Ibn Ibrahim,
who proved much more popular than his predecessor with
the local population. The unfortunate Hassan Al-Aidh and

his family found themselves once more on the journey to Riyadh as prisoners. With his boundless patience and generosity, Ibn Saud again received Al-Aidh warmly and pardoned him for his part in the rebellion. This time, however, the family were not permitted to return to Asir. Like the Rashids, they were allowed to live in Riyadh under a very mild form of house arrest so that the Prince could keep a firm but kindly eye on them. When I came to Riyadh I often saw Al-Aidh and his son in the market-place, where they were accepted on equal terms with all the other subjects of Ibn Saud.

Asir was to prosper under Saudi rule and the province became a favourite with Prince Faisal, who found that he could always rely upon the friendship and loyalty of its people. The tribesmen of Asir were given full freedom to travel and set up business in any part of the Saudi domain; being an energetic and enterprising people, they took full advantage of their new privileges. As the Arab proverb says, 'A new farmer is good news for the field.'

Coming so soon after the battle of Turabah, the annexation of Asir was a bitter blow to Sherif Hussein. He now found the Saudis encroaching upon him from both east and south. One might have expected the Sherif to be extremely careful to do nothing further which might offend Ibn Saud. But Hussein continued to harbour inflated ideas of his own power and importance and still saw himself as the natural leader of Arabia. In 1924 he made the calamitous error of judgement which was to result in his overthrow. For centuries the Ottoman Sultans had been recognized as Caliphs, the successors of the Prophet Mohammed and the spiritual leaders of Islam. The new Turkish government which had taken over at the end of the First World War saw no purpose in continuing the Caliphate and abolished it. Sherif Hussein immediately filled the vacancy by having himself proclaimed Caliph with great pomp and ceremony. This preposterous action was resented by Moslems everywhere, and particularly by the Ikhwan, who already regarded Hejaz as a sink of iniquity and heresy.

70

On his own initiative Sultan Ibn Bijad raised an Ikhwan army, mostly from the Utaiba tribe, and led them across the desert to attack the Sherif. This perilous expedition did not have the open support of Ibn Saud but it probably had his blessing. Once again the Sherifian army was taken by surprise. One morning in September 1924 an advance scouting contingent of tribal warriors was to be found looking into the heart of Ta'if, the pleasant hill town about forty miles from Mecca which was the summer capital of Hejaz. The unsuspecting populace did not even notice the warriors, assuming that they were members of a local tribe grazing their animals in the hills. In fact they were only waiting for an opportunity to seize the town and occupy it. Ta'if had a military garrison led by one of Hussein's sons Sherif Ali, but most of the soldiers were encamped at the nearby village of Al-Hadda. The old Turkish fortress in Ta'if probably only contained a token force to keep law and order among the local citizens. The Ikhwan swept down upon the unsuspecting town with terrifying speed, occupied it without any opposition to speak of and passed on to Al-Hadda. There they mounted a ferocious assault on the garrison, which was routed with heavy losses.

The account of the loss of Ta'if given by the Sherifian government to the outside world included allegations that the Ikhwan had behaved with the utmost barbarity and had brutally murdered women and children. Foreigners writing on the subject have repeated these allegations as if they were undisputed fact. For my part, I believe them to be entirely false. The Amir of Ta'if himself told me that nobody was killed in the town except members of the garrison, and some of the townsmen who tried to resist. The atrocity stories were probably spread by Sherifian officials anxious to discredit Ibn Saud and the Ikhwan and divert attention from the calamitous defeat of the Hejazi forces. The very success of this ruse was disastrously counter-productive, for the lies were believed by the citizens of Hejaz and utter panic spread throughout the Sherif's domain. (Such is the power of rumour that some religious leaders in India even forbade the pilgrimage to Mecca for a time.)

It was not long before Mecca itself had fallen to the same stalwarts who had taken Ta'if. Mecca offered no resistance to the invaders, for Sherif Hussein had himself abandoned it and gone to Jeddah. Shortly after Mecca had been occupied in October 1924, Ibn Saud himself arrived there for the first time in his life.

إِذَا جَاءَ نَصْرُ اللَّهِ وَالفَتْحُ . وَرَأَيْتَ النَّاسَ يَدْخُلُونَ فِي دِينِ اللهِ أَفْوَاجًا . فَسَبِّحْ
بِحمدِ رَبِّكَ وَاسْتَغْفِرْهُ إِنَّهُ كَانَ تَوَّابًا .
سورة النصر

When Allah's succour and the triumph cometh
And thou seest mankind entering the religion of Allah in troops,
Then hymn the praises of thy Lord, and seek forgiveness of Him.
Lo! He is ever ready to show mercy.

(Koran, Succour)

He entered the Holy City, not as a conquering monarch, but with bared head and dressed in the simple robes of a pilgrim. He brought with him substantial reinforcements, including a large contingent of the Mutair tribe under the redoubtable Faisal Ad-Dawish, who was now a member of the Ikhwan and was for a change fighting on the side of his Prince.

In the meantime the vanguard of the battling tribesmen pressed on in pursuit of the remnants of the Sherif's fleeing army. They took Raghama and laid siege to the city of Jeddah, in which the remaining forces of Hejaz had taken refuge. There were several confrontations between the defending garrison and the invading army; most were stalemates fought between the fringes of Raghama and the outskirts of the city. There were even a few primitive tanks in Jeddah, for which the defenders had high hopes; but when the tanks ventured outside the walls they were soon either disabled or captured.

Eventually Ibn Saud himself arrived at the battlefield and

assumed command. He could undoubtedly have crushed Jeddah quickly and easily had he chosen to do so; instead, he wisely refrained from causing the unnecessary bloodshed which would have resulted from an assault on the city, realizing that it would inevitably fall to him in the end. Right at the start of the siege, Sherif Hussein was approached by a group of notables from Jeddah and asked to abdicate in favour of his son, Ali. In reply, Hussein quoted the poet Al-Mouttanabi:

مَشِيْنَاهَـا خُطّـاً خُطّـاً عَلَيْهِ كُتِيَـتْ وَمَـنْ كُتِيَـتْ عَلَيْنا خُطّـاً كُتِيَـتْ مَشِيْنَاهَـا

We have walked along the path of life that was laid down for us, as needs must men whose steps have been ordained.

He then fled the country from the port of Aqaba, never to return. Ali was immediately proclaimed King of Hejaz in October 1924. Sherif Hussein went to Cyprus, where he died. His body now lies in the Al Aqsa Mosque in Jerusalem.

The siege of Jeddah was a peculiar affair. The Najdi forces were stationed in the low foothills to the east of Jeddah; this enabled a close watch to be kept on the port while affording an excellent defensive position in the event of a counter-attack. The hills were just out of range of the artillery in Jeddah. The garrison tried to overcome this problem by mounting their cannons on the highest roof-tops of the city, and from these positions they pounded away at the Saudi forces day and night. Unfortunately for them, their efforts merely weakened the fabric of the buildings and kept the citizens of Jeddah awake at night, for all the rounds still fell short. The siege was by no means complete; ships of all nations continued to come and go at the port. Ibn Saud wisely made no attempt to stop them, as to do so might have led to international complications. In the circumstances it is not surprising that the siege lasted for eleven months. During this time there were several approaches from mediators for a cease-fire or a surrender on terms. One of the mediators was none other than St John Philby, who was again sent to negotiate with Ibn Saud on behalf of the British authorities in Egypt.

While Ibn Saud was besieging Jeddah his forces also had Medina under siege. A small contingent of the Saudi army at Medina was led by Prince Mohammed Al Saud, but it was Ad-Dawish and his Mutair tribesmen who made up the main body of the force. Medina fell easily, in December 1925, while Jeddah still showed no signs of surrendering. It seemed to Ad-Dawish that Ibn Saud was in dire need of reinforcements, and the wily Ikhwan chief sought to turn this situation to his advantage. He went to see Ibn Bijad, who was encamped outside Mecca in an area known as Alma'bida, where part of the Utaiba tribe dwelled. There he suggested to Ibn Bijad that they should approach Ibn Saud and demand to be made Amirs of Mecca and Medina respectively, in return for their continued support in the war against the Hejazis. Ibn Bijad readily agreed to this scheme and the two chiefs lost no time in seeking an audience with Ibn Saud in his tents at Raghama, where they placed their proposal before him. Ibn Saud flatly refused them. Even if the support of the Mutair and the Utaiba was to be lost, he knew better than to give two such impulsive and ambitious men positions of power in Hejaz. To do so would be merely to invite a rebellion in the future. Bitterly affronted, the two chiefs immediately withdrew with their forces into Najd and took no further part in the conflict.

This brief contretemps at Raghama was to have considerable significance for the future. Ibn Bijad did not take the whole of the Utaiba tribe with him when he departed. His support was mainly among the Burga section of the Utaiba, whereas the smaller Rawaga section owed their allegiance to Chief Omar Ibn Rubaian, who remained stoutly loyal to Ibn Saud. Within a few years this tribal rift was to become very important. The Rawaga remained staunch supporters of Ibn Saud, while the smouldering resentment of the Burga under Ibn Bijad was destined before long to blaze up into the Ikhwan revolt.

At the end of December 1925 the desultory campaign at

Jeddah eventually came to an end and the city capitulated. Other parts of Hejaz, such as Yanbu and the northern towns, fell like dominoes and it was not long before the whole of the country was in the undisputed possession of the Sultan of Najd. After the city of Jeddah had fallen and Ibn Saud had entered in triumph, he implemented a wise policy of tolerance and mercy. The inhabitants were told that their affairs could revert to normal, with everybody carrying on business as usual, and the employees of the old government were ordered to remain at their posts. This saved Ibn Saud the trouble of destroying the Sherif's administrative machinery and replacing it with his own; at the same time it earned him the gratitude and loyalty of the government employees, who retained their jobs and livelihood.

After settling matters in Jeddah, Ibn Saud returned to Mecca, where he had the joy of being able to perform the hajj for the first time in his life. By 1925 Ibn Saud was known by his formal title of Sultan of Najd and also by various names such as the Imam, the Sheikh and the *Asheukh* (meaning Sheikh of Sheikhs). On 10 January 1926, at a moving ceremony in Mecca, he was also proclaimed King of Hejaz.

6
The rise of the Ikhwan

... مَنْ يَهْدِ اللَّهُ فَهُوَ الْـمُهْتَدِ وَمَنْ يُضْلِلْ فَلَنْ تَجِدَ لَهُ وَلِـيّـاً مُرْشِدا .

سورة الكهف (١٧)

... He whom Allah guideth, he indeed is led aright,
and he whom He sendeth astray, for him thou wilt
not find a guiding friend.

(Koran, The Cave 17)

The Ikhwan movement had its origins in the puritan, fundamentalist reformation of Abdul Wahhab in the early eighteenth century. Mohammed Ibn Abdul Wahhab Ibn Suleiman Ibn Mohammed Ibn Ahmad Ibn Rashid Al-Tamimi was born in 1703 in the town of Uwainah. He acquired his religious knowledge at the hand of his father, the Qadhi (or religious judge) of Huraimleh, who died in 1740. As Abdul Wahhab grew up he became increasingly disenchanted with the abuses he saw around him in the way the Islamic religion had developed. In particular he deplored the widespread growth of superstitious ritual, the worship of shrines and saints, and the belief in spirits to whom prayers for miracles could be made. He preached that the faith should be returned to its true purity, without any trappings or additions which had not been sanctioned by the Prophet himself. Any object of worship other than God Himself he deemed to be false, and any knowledge other than that gleaned directly from the Koran was thought by his followers to be evil.

In 1740 Abdul Wahhab approached Amir Mohammed Ali Ibn Muammar for his support. This was granted at first but later withdrawn when the movement drew criticism from the Amir of Al-Hasa, Suleiman Ibn Mohammed Ibn Uraiar. Abdul Wahhab found himself banished from Uwainah. After a period of wandering he came to the town of Dara'iyah where he was welcomed by its Amir, a man named Mohammed, of the little-known house of Saud. The two men made a pact whereby they agreed to attempt a reformation of Islam by force of arms. Sheikh Abdul Wahhab was to have complete control of religious life in Arabia in return for his support for Mohammed Ibn Saud in secular matters. The Holy War which followed was spectacularly successful, and much of Arabia was forcibly converted to the Wahhabi doctrine. It was not until the beginning of the nineteenth century that the movement was finally crushed by the power of Egypt, and even then it lingered on in the desert areas, especially in Najd. The Wahhabi tradition remained strong in the house of Saud and was passed from father to son. Ibn Saud himself was brought up and educated as a Wahhabi. On his sudden rise to power, the stage was set for the Wahhabi revival which took shape in the form of the Ikhwan brotherhood.

By 1912 Ibn Saud had won a kingdom for himself in the desert, but its survival rested entirely upon the fickle loyalty of the bedouin and, like so many Arab kingdoms before, it would be bound to disintegrate in time unless some method was found of securing the permanent allegiance of the tribesmen. To achieve this, Ibn Saud conceived the brilliant idea of creating settlements around the oases in his kingdom where the bedouin would be able to cease their nomadic ways and grow regular crops. The Prince realized that once such settlements were well established, their members would have every reason to support a strong and stable central government which would enable them to farm in peace. In this way, he aimed to counteract the anarchy which had so often prevailed in the past. In the settlements Ibn Saud hoped to cultivate the Wahhabi faith so that the settlers would be bound to him, not only in a common desire for peace, but also in a common religious creed.

Each tribe had water wells in the desert which it regarded as being under its exclusive control. By means of generous subsidies and gifts, Ibn Saud encouraged the tribal chiefs to build solid dwelling places around the wells. Despite Ibn Saud's painstaking efforts to establish successful settlements, the bedouin proved reluctant and there were many setbacks. These were overcome mainly by the King's unstinting generosity; with large subsidies of money and gifts of camels and other animals, Ibn Saud was eventually able to gain the support of the recalcitrant tribesmen by making co-operation so obviously worth their while.

The first permanent village established under this scheme was founded in 1913 at Artawiya. It was the inhabitants of this settlement who first called themselves by the name of the Ikhwan, or Brotherhood. Soon the movement had spread all over Central Arabia, being particularly strong in Najd. Religious leaders, known as *ulemas*, were appointed to each settlement and instructed the inhabitants in the Wahhabi faith with such success that the Ikhwan soon became renowned for their religious fanaticism. Although the creation of the settlements is one of the most fundamentally important events of recent Arabian history, I find that no details of them have been given in any of the English histories which I have read. As it has always been my intention in writing this book to fill in some of the gaps which history has ignored, I have included a list of the more significant settlements, accompanied by details of the tribes who lived there and the chieftains who governed them. (See Appendix 6.)

The Ikhwan settlements were intended to do more than just create political stability. They also had a military purpose, for Ibn Saud now possessed for the first time a reserve of men whose whereabouts were known, and whose loyalty could be relied upon. A further advantage was that the Ikhwan were always ready to fight. Despite the material benefits to be gained by staying in one place, the tribesmen did not give up their nomadic way of life without regret. There was a saying among them that the pleasure had gone out of the bedouin life when Faisal Ad-Dawish (the chief of the Mutair) first built a mud hut. In particular, they missed the traditional raiding of each others' sheep and camels which was so entrenched in the bedouin way of life as to be more a sport than genuine warfare. This restlessness, coupled with their religious intolerance, made them eager to make war upon the infidel. Since an infidel in their eyes was almost anyone who was not a member of the Ikhwan, the movement became a weapon in the hands of Ibn Saud which he could unleash at will against his enemies.

The Ikhwan had no fear of death in action, for to die in battle was a certain road to paradise, where they knew with utter conviction that they would find cool streams, pleasant breezes, beautiful women and everything else which the heart of a bedouin could desire. They struck terror into the hearts of all the tribes which did not subscribe to the Wahhabi doctrine. When they moved north-east into Iraq, the tribes would flee before them across the Euphrates; if they struck north-west, the Jordanian tribes fled into Syria; and if they moved south, the tribes of the Yemen took refuge in their impregnable mountain strongholds. It was largely as a result of the Ikhwan that Hejaz and Jabal Shammar fell to Ibn Saud with such ease. There came a time in the late 1920s when they dominated the whole of the Arabian peninsula, and could have annexed any part of it at will, had Ibn Saud directed them to do so. Between 1922 and 1924 the famous British historian Arnold Toynbee wrote several articles about the Ikhwan movement. He predicted that, if its rapid growth continued, it would soon encompass the whole penisula and beyond, and might even repeat the early history of Islam by exploding into the surrounding states of Asia and North Africa. (He naturally expected this to take place after the unification of various Arab states.) But this was not to be, for instead of exerting their might against foreign infidels, the Ikhwan became so intoxicated with their own power and strength that they turned inwards and rebelled against the authority of their ruler, Ibn Saud.

The Ikhwan had always been something of a double-edged weapon, and from its very beginnings the movement had been a source of trouble of one sort or another. Indeed, it was only a short time after the capture of Mecca that the Ikhwan caused a serious diplomatic rift with Egypt. By custom, it had always been Egyptian craftsmen who made the Kiswah – the ornate and beautiful cloth which covers the Kaaba in the centre of the Holy Mosque at Mecca and which is woven anew every year. In the summer of 1925 the first hajj took place with Mecca under full Wahhabi control, and the city was full of Ikhwan tribesmen making their first-ever pilgrimage. The Egyptians were anxious to make a good impression on the new ruler of the Holy Land, and arranged that the traditional ceremony which accompanied the bringing of the Kiswah into Mecca would on this occasion be one of particular pomp and splendour. A rich and colourful caravan bore the Kiswah through the gates of the Holy City, preceded by a lively band of musicians and escorted by the Egyptian Guards of the Mahmal. ('Mahmal' means 'the burden borne by a camel', and symbolizes sovereignty.) The Ikhwan were outraged, for under their strict religious code the public performance of music of any kind was considered sacrilegious. They demanded that the music should stop. The offended musicians refused and carried on playing, whereupon the Ikhwan immediately took up weapons and opened fire upon them. This incident not only caused the Egyptians to break off diplomatic relations with the new regime; they also refused ever again to weave the Kiswah. It is for this reason that the Kiswah has ever since been made by Saudi and Indian craftsmen in Mecca itself.

The puritanism of the Ikhwan was so intense that they regarded any form of modern technology as evil. For example, a wrist-watch was considered to be the work of the Devil, as there was no mention of one in the Koran and it was regarded as impossible for such a device to work other than by sorcery. The same applied to cars, telephones, wireless sets and almost every other modern tool which the King needed in order to bring progress to his kingdom. When I joined His Majesty, the government and public services in Mecca were mostly equipped with electricity and modern machines. There was a well-developed post office and telephone service. In Riyadh there was nothing at all. The only official postal service consisted of a servant with a camel who would take important letters from the King to the amirs of the principal towns and return with their replies. If caught in the right mood, he could occasionally be persuaded to take the odd private letter as well. This could scarcely be described as satisfactory, and it was obvious that modern communications were urgently needed. Ibn Saud often expressed the view that not everything about Western culture was evil, and it was always his aim to take what was good from the West and reject what was bad. But the Ikhwan were not easily convinced and Ibn Saud was continually obliged to find different ways and means to persuade his subjects to accept useful innovations. Sometimes a simple ploy would suffice, such as the occasion when he arranged for passages of the Koran to be read over a telephone. The listeners at the other end were forced to agree that a machine which carried the word of God along its wires could hardly be the work of the Devil. A harder line was necessary, however, when wireless telegraphs were introduced into Riyadh. Howls of protest were raised, and were only stifled when the King curtly invited anyone who did not approve to leave.

Such matters were trifles compared to the deadlier forms which could be taken by the Ikhwan fanaticism. The case of an Ikhwan tribesman who slaughtered a member of his own family because he did not conform to strict Wahhabi teaching was by no means unusual. Furthermore, the Ikhwan had an unhappy reputation for disregarding the chivalrous conventions of tribal warfare which had existed for centuries. The allegation of the murder of women and children at Ta'if was a typical example of the type of atrocity of which the Ikhwan were regularly accused. The reputation for brutality in war was in fact quite undeserved; there were never more than a few isolated incidents, which were exaggerated out of all proportion by the King's enemies. But because the Ikhwan were so zealously intolerant in all religious matters, many people believed the stories put about by their opponents to be true, and Ibn Saud often found it an embarrassment that his best soldiers were generally thought of as callous butchers.

I have already mentioned that the seeds of the Ikhwan revolt were sown when, after the capture of Hejaz, Ibn Saud refused to appoint Ibn Bijad and Ad-Dawish to positions of power in Mecca and Medina. The two men, sullen and disappointed, withdrew with their followers into the heart of Najd, where they lost no time in plotting the overthrow of the King. From bitter experience they knew better than to attempt an armed revolt. Instead they decided on a more subtle method. Without warning, they started raiding the borders of Iraq and Transjordan, descending suddenly and mercilessly from the desert upon isolated camps and border posts, seldom striking twice in the same place and leaving havoc and destruction in their wake. One of the first Ikhwan attacks against the Iraqi border was launched by one of the groups which had withdrawn from the Saudi forces besieging Jeddah. Under the leadership of Faisal Ad-Dawish, the group attacked the border at a place called Ichlawa, where the Bani Hussein bedouin of Iraq had an encampment. Ichlawa is near my village, Zubair. I happened to be in Zubair on a short visit home from India at the time. The British military authorities at the Shaibah base wanted to go and investigate the damage caused by the raid. They begged the Amir of Zubair to let me go with them as interpreter. However, I refused to accompany them, saying that I would take no part in any action against the Ikhwan.

The Ikhwan could point to a genuine grievance to justify their raids. The Iraqis had started to restrict the entry of Najdis into their country and had built a line of forts along the Iraq–Najd border. The first two forts were at Sabwa and Sabai'ah; a third was later added at As-Salman. The bedouin regarded these steps as an infringement of their traditional rights of free pasturage and unobstructed passage over the borders. In any event, the Iraqis were regarded as infidels and were therefore 'fair game'. But the true reason for the raids was that the Ikhwan hoped that the British authorities in Iraq and Transjordan would believe the raids to be directed by Ibn Saud himself and so would take steps to overthrow him. In this strategy the Ikhwan achieved a measure of success. For three years they kept up the raiding. Each season they would sortie across the borders of Iraq, Kuwait and Transjordan, attacking whatever tribes or groups of bedouin they came across, plundering their cattle and killing anybody who resisted them. The Iraqis, and the British on their behalf, protested vehemently about the raids to Ibn Saud. He was held to be responsible for the actions of the raiders because the Treaty of Jeddah in 1927 had recognized him as King of Hejaz and Sultan of Najd. (The treaty had been negotiated by Sir Gilbert Clayton on behalf of the British.) The King in his turn protested quite truthfully that he had not ordered the raids and they were nothing to do with him. Nevertheless, the incidents continued. Ibn Saud publicly disowned the raiders on several occasions but the Iraqis and the British regarded this with suspicion, insisting that the King must be tacitly supporting the raids or at the very least failing to make any effort to stop them. I remember that even the members of the King's Court believed he was preparing to conquer Iraq; as we later discovered, he had no such intention. At about this time the Iraqi press printed a great deal of belligerent propaganda directed against the Najdis, and pointed references were made to a previous battle in which the Najdis had been defeated by the Iraqis. The King admitted this, but replied, 'Let the British stand aside and we will fight it out.' The Iraqis balked at this, but angry delegations were sent by Iraq to the Court at Riyadh and there was a general air of sabre-rattling.

It was by now quite clear that something would have to be done to stop the raids. The King tried to influence the tribesmen by making lavish gifts in his usual way but this had little effect. Proclamations were posted in all the towns and villages in the country making it clear that the raids were in direct contravention of the King's orders, but this too proved useless. Eventually in 1928 it became apparent to the King that drastic action was required. He decided to call a meeting at Riyadh of all the influential religious and tribal leaders in his kingdom, with the aim of persuading them to reassert their loyalty to him and thus isolate the rebellious Ikhwan.

The meeting took place in Riyadh and became known as the 'Big Gathering'. Indeed, the year of 1928 is still remembered in Arabia as 'the year of the Big Gathering'. All the principal tribal leaders were invited, including many who were sympathetic to the Ikhwan or who were themselves Ikhwan members. The principal *ulemas* of the kingdom were also present, as were the amirs of all the bigger towns. In all, about two hundred and fifty of the most important men in the kingdom attended the gathering. For about two weeks before the final meeting, the Ikhwan chiefs arrived with their followers in small parties. They were the cream of the fighting men of the desert – fierce, robust warriors with an air of determined independence about them. The King was kept busy in preliminary negotiations with each delegation and the tribesmen were in no mood to compromise. Ibn Bijad's first name was Sultan and his followers walked through the streets and markets of Riyadh boasting, 'A new Sultan has arisen for the faith.' The townspeople were shocked and replied, 'You claim to be devout Moslems but no Moslem should be as arrogant as you.' The Ikhwan were not at all ashamed but retorted in typical fashion, 'A faithful man who is strong is better than one who is weak!'

When the time came for the gathering itself there was not enough room at the palace in Riyadh for so many dignitaries. The meeting, which I had the privilege of witnessing, was therefore held in the palace courtyard. The *ulemas* sat on the King's right, the amirs of the towns and provinces on his left, and in the middle of the courtyard sat the tribal chiefs and representatives. His Majesty opened the assembly by delivering a vehement speech castigating the dissident tribes and taking them to task for trying to disrupt the kingdom by their unwarranted acts of violence. He criticized them by observing scornfully, 'They accuse me of bringing infidels into my homeland, Najd.' He made it clear that he deplored the border violations and wanton attacks of which the Ikhwan had been guilty, not to mention the raids on the caravans and property of those tribes which did not belong to the Ikhwan. The Ikhwan sympathizers who were present at the gathering did not take this criticism lying down. They argued that they were doing no more than carrying out their religious duty by attacking infidels and bringing them back to the true faith. They also raised the usual protests about the Iraqi border forts. After a lengthy debate, the King asked them outright what it was they wanted. The Ikhwan replied that they required the frontier posts on the borders of Iraq to be eliminated, that the use of the telephone and other satanic gadgets in the kingdom should be abandoned, that tribes such as the Juhaina and Bali – who were considered to be unbelievers – should be punished and brought into line, and that the injunctions of the Koran should be enforced on all with the utmost strictness and without exception.

At this point, in a masterly piece of bluff, His Majesty declared that although there was not a single province, tribe, township or acre of land in the whole kingdom which he had not won with his sword on the battlefield, nevertheless he proposed forthwith to abdicate his crown and relinquish all his powers in favour of anyone they might choose to replace him. At this the whole gathering was taken completely by surprise and overcome with bewilderment. After a stunned silence, the assembled chiefs all joined in a chorus of loyal protest at the very idea of the King's resignation. Taking advantage of the confusion he had created, Ibn Saud turned to the *ulemas* on his right and asked each one to his face what opinion the *ulema* held of the King, good or bad, and whether he was for or against him. Not surprisingly, he received a unanimous vote of confidence from the *ulemas*, all of whom agreed that they were for him and would not countenance any other in his place. The King then repeated this process with the amirs of the towns and finally with the tribal chiefs, each time achieving identical results. Having established that all in the gathering were loyal to him, the King demanded that each man should swear a new oath of allegiance. The King's family swore the oath first, followed by the *ulemas*, then the amirs and finally the tribal chiefs. Some of the prominent amirs of Al-Qasim protested that they had given their allegiance from the beginning and one of them, Abdul Aziz Ibn Slaim, the Amir of Unayzah, said, 'I gave it to you in Kuwait.' The King persuaded them that this was a new allegiance and everybody eventually swore the oath. In this outburst of loyalty, the demands of the Ikhwan were forgotten and received no further discussion.

After the assembly had dispersed, the amirs and tribal chiefs returned to their homes, having been lavishly entertained. They were laden with generous gifts of swords, incense, money, food, and even in some cases jewellery for their wives. The King followed up his success at the gathering by travelling to Al-Qasim where he again met representatives of the dissident tribes, made further gifts of arms and supplies, and persuaded the tribes to agree not to indulge in further raiding or create any more disturbances. Then, having done all he could to subdue the Ikhwan by peaceful means, His Majesty set off on his annual journey to Mecca to perform the hajj.

Everybody now hoped that the Ikhwan would be appeased for a time. But they had become too powerful to be quelled for long by gifts and speeches. As soon as Ibn Saud's back was turned, the border raids started again, this time assuming greater and more dangerous proportions. The Iraqis were provoked into taking strong punitive measures. With the help of the RAF they started using aeroplanes to strafe and bomb the raiding tribesmen, sometimes following them into Najd itself and bombing their camps and wells. One such air attack on the Mutair tribe at Al-Lisafah caused numerous casualties among the women and children, and His Majesty felt obliged to make a strong protest to the British government. The King persevered in his attempts to negotiate with the tribesmen, but they became increasingly intransigent and frequently refused even to answer summonses to attend his Court. It was not unusual to see large bodies of armed Ikhwan tribesmen stomping in and out of Riyadh, openly proclaiming their might and their disregard for the King's authority.

As the Ikhwan became more and more powerful, their influence came to be felt increasingly in the everyday lives of the ordinary people of the kingdom, to an extent that those who did not actually experience it would find hard to imagine. As early as 1926, just before I arrived in Riyadh for the first time, no less a person than the Chief of the Court had been publicly whipped by the Ikhwan on the mere suspicion of having failed to appear at prayers. Vigilante groups of Ikhwan roamed the streets, acting as self-appointed religious police and meting out harsh punishments to anyone who did not comply with their strict teachings. The Ikhwan themselves went to extremes of self-denial, sternly avoiding any pleasure or luxury, however slight. They deplored music (as was graphically illustrated in the episode with the Egyptians at Mecca) and distrusted poetry. They would insist upon wearing coarse cloth next to the skin as they considered silk to be a sinful indulgence. No kind of jewellery was permitted, and many went so far as to unstitch the traditional gold braid woven into their cloaks. Anyone who appeared in public with an untrimmed beard, or a robe worn a little longer than usual for the sake of fashion, was likely to be pounced upon by zealous tribesmen and held down while the offending hair or cloth was cut off. Ibn Saud himself was not immune from attentions of this kind. A story is told that he once visited the camp of Faisal Ad-Dawish at Artawiya. His hosts greeted him by declaring that his robe was too long. A pair of scissors was fetched and the garment cut to the regulation size while the King was still wearing it!

For a newcomer like myself, unused to this kind of strict puritanism, it could be very difficult to stay out of trouble. Unfortunately, before I came to Arabia I was a heavy smoker, and to be caught with a cigarette by the Ikhwan meant a sound thrashing at the very least. In Jeddah cigarettes were available on the black market and, with a little discretion, I was able to indulge in my vice easily enough. But things were very different in Riyadh, where the eyes of the Ikhwan were everywhere and tobacco was absolutely unobtainable. I still had a few precious cigarettes which I had managed to scrounge from an Indian driver. I hid them down a hole in one of the rafters of the palace and furtively smoked one when I thought nobody was about. Despite all my efforts to expel the smoke, the sensitive nostrils of an *ulema* who worked in the palace detected the odour, and I narrowly escaped discovery. After that I became a confirmed non-smoker, which was no doubt very good for my health but very hard on my nerves.

By the beginning of 1929 the Ikhwan had become ungovernable. At about this time they committed a blatant outrage when an Ikhwan force raided a large camel caravan owned by a prominent merchant, Ibn Sharida, who was on his way from Buraida to Damascus. Ibn Sharida and a number of his men who tried to resist were killed and the caravan was pillaged. Worse was to come: on the twentieth day of Ramadan, when the King was on the point of leaving for his pilgrimage to Hejaz, news came that two of the most powerful Ikhwan tribes, the Utaiba and the Mutair, were assembled north of Al-Qasim, poised to make their most massive incursion yet over the borders of Iraq. Ibn Saud realized the futility of further attempts at peaceful persuasion. The movement which he had founded to bring peace and stability to his kingdom had come to be an instrument of violence and anarchy. It was clear beyond doubt that the Ikhwan would have to be crushed and that force must be met with force. With a heavy heart, His Majesty began his preparations for war.

7
The battle of Sibillah

فَإِذَا لَقِيتُمُ الذينَ كَفَرُوا فَضَرْبَ الرِقابِ حَتَّى إِذَا أَثْخَنْتُمُوهُمْ فَشُدُّوا اَلوَثَاقَ فَإِمَّا مَنًّا بَعْدُ وَإِمَّا فِدَاءً حَتَّى تَضَعَ اَلْحَرْبُ أَوْزارَهَا ذَلِكَ وَلَوْ يَشَاءُ اللهُ لانْتَصرَ مِنْهُمْ وَلَكِن لِيَبْلُوا بَعْضَكُمْ بِبَعْضٍ وَالذينَ قُتِلوا فِي سَبيلِ اللهِ فَلَنْ يُضِلَّ أَعْـمَـالَـهُمْ .

سورة محمد (٤)

Now when ye meet in battle those who disbelieve,
then it is smiting of the necks until, when ye have
routed them, then making fast of bonds; and after-
ward either grace or ransom till the war lay down its
burdens. That (is the ordinance). And if Allah willed
He could have punished them (without you) but (thus
it is ordained) that He may try some of you by means
of others. And those who are slain in the way of
Allah, He rendereth not their actions vain.

(Koran, Mohammed 4)

Ibn Saud's first action on hearing about the gathering of the Mutair and Utaiba tribes was to dispatch a letter to the amirs of each town and village requiring them to come to Riyadh with their jihad flags. These were Holy War flags which would be followed by all the warriors loyal to the King. As hastily as he could, His Majesty assembled his forces, though matters were complicated for him by the fact that this was the period of the Ramadan fast. As was his right under Islamic law, he ordered all his troops to cease observing the fast. This was a well-established practice in time of war, and to continue fasting once the order to cease had been given was punishable by stoning to death. Despite this, some of the troops refused to stop fasting. The King ordered that they should be stoned, but with his usual wisdom and mercy decreed that the stoning should be merely symbolic so as to shame the disobedient soldiers rather than kill them.

At least one of His Majesty's old allies stood by him in his time of need. Abdullah Ibn Jelawi raised an army of local tribesmen in Al-Hasa and dispatched it to the north of the area under the command of his son Fahd, in order to keep in check elements of the Shammar and Ajman tribes who were known to be gathering against the King. His Majesty could therefore campaign to the north of Riyadh, confident that his eastern flank was secure.

As soon as the King had raised a sufficient force he set off from Riyadh via Shaqra, the capital of the province of Al-Washim, to Buraida, the capital of Al-Qasim. Wherever he went, even in wartime, he was accompanied by most of his Court staff, so it was taken for granted that I would go with him. Most of the force travelled by camel, but some, including the King himself, travelled by car. The King had come to consider cars a most useful aid in wartime; provided they did not break down or get stuck in the sand, they were much faster than a camel, and very handy if one wished to make a surprise attack or a hasty withdrawal. Nevertheless, the cars were left at Buraida because the desert ground after that was so rough that it would have been foolish to risk taking them any further.

At Buraida I remember His Majesty holding several audiences attended by large numbers of loyal bedouin. He talked and joked freely among them, giving encouragement and advice wherever it was needed. Each tribesman to whom he talked might give an opinion about the strength and whereabouts of the enemy or the allegiance of a particular tribe or tribal section. In this way the King gained a mass of information, although much of it was contradictory. It was a pleasure and an education to watch the meticulous way in which His Majesty simultaneously raised morale and gathered intelligence, and the skill with which he sifted and weighed up all the reports and rumours to obtain an accurate picture of the overall military situation.

Shortly before we left Buraida there was a day of heavy rain. The desert burst into colour as flowers and grasses sprang up to take advantage of the short-lived moisture. As we rode off to battle the whole of nature seemed to be wishing us well. While we travelled, His Majesty continued to speak to as many of the chiefs and tribesmen as he could. This was in order to keep up the continual process of encouragement at which he was so expert, and also to satisfy his own voracious appetite for news.

From Buraida we proceeded to Nabjiyah, where it had been arranged that we should await the arrival from Riyadh of two of the King's sons, Crown Prince Saud and Prince Mohammed. Prince Faisal had already been dispatched to guard Hejaz. I later discovered that the Ikhwan were aware of our movements during this time and that Mutlaq Ibn Al-Jaba, one of the chiefs of the Mutair, suggested that an attack should be made on Riyadh before Prince Saud left. 'In Riyadh they only have servants to guard them,' he said. 'Let us go and finish them off. That would leave the King cut off in the desert.' Such a plan might well have been successful, but fortunately for us it was never attempted. Prince Saud and his brother arrived safely, accompanied by their servants and a large number of bedouin and townspeople who had joined them on the way.

We stayed for about a week at Nabjiyah. This was an interesting area with a very fertile, mud-like red soil, from which sprouted a wealth of rich desert vegetation. However, there were few in our camp who were in any mood to appreciate the wonders of desert flora. The atmosphere became increasingly tense, for we all knew how important the coming campaign was to the future of the kingdom. A small incident occurred one night after evening prayer, when gunfire was heard in the distance. Everybody was instantly alert. The King himself dashed out of his tent shouting war-cries and demanding to know what the shooting was about. Several bedouin chiefs had to restrain him from running towards the firing. Servants were sent to investigate the disturbance, and it turned out that the gunfire was just a signal for the benefit of some bedouin from the Shammar tribe who had gone in search of water and had lost their way. The shots had been fired by their friends to guide them home. The incident illustrated how easily débâcles like those at Turabah or Rowdhat Muhanna could occur; even though there had only been a few shots in the distance, everybody in the camp was nervously staring into the darkness ready to fire at anything which moved, and we could easily have started shooting at each other.

The following morning we set off for the town of Zilfi, first crossing a series of huge sand-dunes. Zilfi was peopled mostly by members of the Utaiba tribe. As we approached the town, news reached us that the Ikhwan had sent a small detachment of Utaiba tribesmen there, who were attempting to incite the townspeople to rebel against the King and allow their town to be occupied by Ikhwan forces. This is a good example of the tactics of desert warfare in operation, for if the Ikhwan had succeeded in holding Zilfi against us, we would have been stranded in the sand-dunes without water. Instantly realizing the danger, His Majesty sent five hundred men ahead in the hope that they might capture the Ikhwan emissaries and occupy the town. The townspeople reluctantly allowed this advance guard to enter Zilfi and the Ikhwan emissaries, who were only about thirty in number, fled for their lives. It was a close thing. The townspeople were in a delicate position, torn between their conflicting loyalties to their King and to their tribe; it was only the timely arrival of the royal forces which persuaded them that the more prudent course lay in supporting their monarch. Even so, the reception His Majesty received was less than enthusiastic. Instead of the whole town turning out to greet him, as would normally have happened, we were met by a small, rather nervous deputation comprising a handful of the town's prominent citizens.

Zilfi is a town made up of two linked villages, and His Majesty set up camp between the two. There is a mountain nearby with fertile grassland at its feet where the camels were sent for pasturing. We had only just settled in when the camels in one big herd came trotting back towards our camp. They had obviously been frightened by something and we soon found out what it was. Two messengers (one from the Mutair tribe and one from the Utaiba) had descended from the high plateau where they were camped; they had left word with some local grass-cutters working on the slopes to say that they would come to our camp the following day.

The next morning Abdul Aziz Ad-Dawish (the son of Faisal Ad-Dawish) representing the Mutair tribe, and Majid Ibn Huthlain on behalf of the Utaiba, came to our camp and delivered this message to the King: 'We have been sent by the chiefs of each tribe. We ask from you a pardon. We wish to settle our differences peacefully and we do not want war.' The rebels knew that the raid on Ibn Sharida's caravan had particularly offended the King, and as a gesture of goodwill they offered to pay tribute for the camels which had been captured. His Majesty answered, 'We can sit in the Sharia'h court, and between us see what the court decides.' The Sharia'h court is formed in accordance with the rules laid down in the Koran and presided over by an *ulema* appointed by the King. It has the power to judge criminal matters, and the King meant by his remark that the Ikhwan leaders should submit themselves to the judgement of the court to establish whether or not their actions were criminal under Islamic law. Since they would stand accused of multiple murder and robbery, and the inevitable penalty for such crimes was death, it is perhaps not surprising that the idea did not immediately commend itself to the Ikhwan messengers. Before they left, the King with his usual generosity made gifts of money to them. Then he called together the chiefs of the tribes who were with him to ask their opinion of the rebels' petition. I watched as the chiefs gathered solemnly around the King, and I remember that I had at that moment the sudden feeling that what I was witnessing was like a great drama, except that it was not played as fiction in the narrow confines of the theatre but rather for stakes of life and death in the vast expanse of the open desert.

Abdul Mohsin Al-Firm, chief of the Harb tribe, was the first to speak. He was plainly very angry and cried out, 'Imam, these people are out to cheat you and play on your sympathy. I want nothing to do with this conference. I will go to battle myself, alone.' With that, he leapt onto his horse and was about to ride off towards the enemy. Crown Prince Saud jumped to his feet and caught him, shouting, 'Don't go. You will not live to see the sun set.' After a light scuffle, Abdul Mohsin realized the foolishness of his action and the conference resumed on a more sober note. All were agreed that the rebels' proposals for a peace settlement were quite unacceptable, but Ibn Saud, who unlike Abdul Mohsin was not prone to impulsive gestures, realized that there was perhaps a possibility that his problems with the Ikhwan might be resolved without resorting to a full-scale battle. He sent letters to the chiefs of the Mutair and Utaiba tribes, again requesting their presence at the Sharia'h court and declaring that he would abide by the decision either way. As a gesture of goodwill he also sent one of his *ulemas* to the enemy camp, with instructions to do all he could to effect a settlement. The man entrusted with this task was Abdullah Al-Anqury, who was one of the most distinguished *ulemas* in the kingdom. As religious leaders, the *ulemas* were regarded with total respect and were exempt from molestation even in wartime. This was a convention which the Ikhwan could be relied upon to observe scrupulously, particularly since Abdullah Al-Anqury was in charge of religious affairs in the area around the Ikhwan stronghold of Artawiya.

Without waiting for a reply to his letters, the King ordered his men to strike camp. He instructed his army to make its way to Sibillah, a wheat-field at the top of the Twaiq mountain, about four miles from Zilfi. ('Sibillah' means 'a stalk of wheat'.) The move was a sensible one as our position in Zilfi was not tactically sound, being in a plain overlooked by this high mountain. If the rebels had occupied the heights, they would have been very difficult to dislodge. The King decided to get there first. The journey to Sibillah involved climbing up the steep hillside of Jabal Twaiq, which was sometimes difficult for us, and particularly hard for our camels. We finally camped in a small wadi near the mountain top. Enemy scouts were never far from us, and we could see some of them stationed on the other side of the wadi on the crest of a small hill.

We spent two days camped at Sibillah while the King waited for a reply to his letters. The tension was considerable, and there was another near panic caused by members of the loyal Rawaga section of the Utaiba tribe who got lost and started firing into the air to attract attention. There was no response to the King's message so another was sent. This time the enemy responded by sending an emissary who said to the King, 'If you wish the court's decision, come to our camp and sit with your own *ulema* and have the matter judged.' His Majesty had the gravest doubts about this suggestion but nevertheless called a meeting of his chiefs to discuss it. Their unanimous and adamant decision was that this was merely a trap and that if the King went to the enemy camp he would never return. Heeding their advice, His Majesty sent word to the Ikhwan that their proposals were not acceptable. The enemy then proposed a compromise to the effect that the King should erect a tent between the opposing camps and that two of their representatives should meet him there. This too was considered very dangerous and firmly rejected. Eventually, after much hard bargaining and coming and going by messengers, it was agreed that one of the Ikhwan chiefs would meet the King in His Majesty's camp, subject to strict guarantees of safety.

The following day we learnt that the chief was to be none other than the indomitable Faisal Ad-Dawish himself. This news was greeted with great excitement; everybody was anxious to catch a glimpse of the great man. Although Ad-Dawish was our enemy, he had a charisma about him which was second only to that of the King himself. His bravery, perseverance and endurance were legendary, and his selfless courage inspired unquestioning devotion among the men he led. When he arrived in our camp he came unarmed but with eight Mutair warriors accompanying him on horseback as his personal bodyguard. One of these was his cousin Faisal Ibn Shiblan. An important stipulation which Ad-Dawish had made before agreeing to meet His Majesty was that the King's tent should be empty, apart from the King himself. My own tent was near to the King's so I was well placed to observe the proceedings. The King's tent had four openings, one at each corner. Two men from Ad-Dawish's bodyguard went to each opening; with military precision, they lifted all four tent flaps simultaneously so as to satisfy themselves that the agreement had been kept or, if it had not, to dispose of any potential assassin. The King was alone in his tent, as had been agreed, and both men then gave oaths to do the other no harm. His Majesty gave to Ad-Dawish the traditional bond of safety, saying, 'You are under my protection,' and both men went into the tent. The talks in the King's tent lasted for over an hour, after which Ad-Dawish came out and ordered his bodyguards to surrender their arms because a temporary truce had been agreed. He was then invited to eat with the King and was entertained in a manner befitting an honoured guest.

A traditional martial parade was ordered by the King in honour of his guest, although His Majesty no doubt also intended it as a reminder of his military prowess and strength. First to march past were the cavalry, with members of each tribe shouting out their age-old war-cries. The uncompromising Abdul Mohsin Al-Firm had composed a new war slogan for the occasion, and as he passed Ad-Dawish he shouted out, 'Armed with my belief in the one, true God, I am the comrade of those who respond to His call. Woe to the enemies of the Sharia'h; let them beware of our wrath.' In case the rebels should miss the point, one of our tribesmen shouted to Faisal Ibn Shiblan, 'That means you.' Amidst these displays one of the horses had to be destroyed after falling into an ant-hole and breaking a foreleg. The horseman took the reins from his dead beast and approached His Majesty, saying in the blunt manner of the desert, 'My Lord, I want compensation for my mare.' The King replied, 'You will get it.' One of Ad-Dawish's bodyguard who was standing nearby muttered, 'Prepare its reins,' which was taken by the King's servants as a jeer meaning, 'You will get nothing.' They were furious and immediately set upon the man, intending to tear him apart for his rash words. An ugly incident was avoided only by the King's personal intervention and he immediately had a heavy guard posted to protect Ad-Dawish and his men from further violence.

In the evening, as the desert sun slowly sank below the western hills, His Majesty and Ad-Dawish turned towards Mecca and prayed. There is nothing which can compare with the glory of a desert sunset, with the sand-dunes sharply silhouetted against the golden light of the setting sun. It was an important and moving moment for us all, and especially for His Majesty, as it was his fervent prayer that war would be avoided. Ad-Dawish spent the night in the tent next to the King's own which was normally occupied by His Majesty's personal servants. This was partly for Ad-Dawish's own protection but also enabled Ibn Saud to keep a careful eye on him. Talks continued throughout the following day, and as night approached the King again sought to persuade Ad-Dawish to settle their dispute by taking the whole matter to the Sharia'h court. Ad-Dawish replied, 'I will speak with Ibn Bijad and tomorrow we may return. But I warn you that if we do not come, our absence will mean war.' Then at sunset the rebel chief and his bodyguard mounted their horses and rode away. When Ad-Dawish returned to his camp, he is reputed to have told Ibn Bijad that the King's army was full of fat townsmen who would be of no value if it came to a real battle. He was heard to say to Ibn Bijad, 'They are about as much use as camel-bags without handles!'

There followed another tense night in the King's camp as we all waited to see what morning would bring. His Majesty was concerned about the possibility of a surprise attack and posted an advance guard (the members of which were known as *dhahurs*) between our camp and the enemy. He also ordered that single shots should be fired periodically throughout the night in order to keep his soldiers alert, although he took the precaution of having everybody warned about this beforehand.

The following day was 30 March 1929. At the first light of dawn His Majesty dressed for battle. After morning prayers, men were sent to fetch water; a plentiful supply was important in case we should be drawn away from our watering-holes during the progress of the battle. Over the previous three days the King's army had gradually grown in strength as loyal tribesmen and townsmen arrived from the surrounding area, anxious both to increase the size of His Majesty's forces and to diminish the resources of his treasury. Each tribal chief who arrived was paid six gold pounds, and each common tribesman and townsman received three pounds. It is difficult to say exactly how large the royal army had become but I would estimate that it was between thirty and forty thousand strong. The Ikhwan force was considerably smaller; it could not have numbered more than fifteen thousand, and was possibly not more than ten thousand. But the Ikhwan troops were fierce, hardened and experienced warriors, fanatically brave and determined. The King's force had been hastily gathered together, and contained many men with little or no experience of desert war. Hence our apprehension at the possibility of battle, for the issue was far from certain and the following evening could well have found us all dead, or fleeing before a victorious Ikhwan army.

Early in the morning, it was usual for the *dhahurs* who had been sent out in the night to be relieved and return to camp for their breakfast. Although breakfast usually consisted only of dates and a cup of water (or coffee for the more fortunate), the tribesmen placed great store by it. They considered dates to contain all the nourishment they required. Dates were known as *masamir al rikab*, which can be roughly translated as 'joints of the knees', meaning that the bedouin thought that they gave great strength. But since Ibn Bijad and Ad-Dawish showed no signs of appearing, His Majesty sent out messengers to the *dhahurs* telling them to hold their positions for the time being, and breakfast would be delivered to them. In a last effort for peace, the King dispatched an emissary to the Ikhwan camp, asking for a final answer to his demands. Then he ordered his army to proceed to a wadi known as the Wadi of Ibn Jurallah, which was about twenty minutes' march away and had until now been a kind of no man's land between us and the enemy. His Majesty was mounted on a splendid war-horse; the members of the Court, including myself, followed directly behind him on foot. During the events of the next hour I was able to see and hear clearly everything which the King did.

As we moved forward, a messenger from the enemy camp rode towards us, shouting, 'Where is the King? Where is the King?' He was directed to His Majesty and said to him, 'Imam, we ask you to spare the heads of our people and whatever compensation you want us to pay for our deeds we shall pay it, be it camels or whatever else you ask – just spare the lives of our people.' Ibn Saud replied calmly, 'It is not only a question of camels. You have also killed men and your chiefs must answer to the Sharia'h court and abide by its decision.' There was a convention in the desert that the

chief of a tribe was held responsible for any murder committed, until the real culprit could be found and brought to
justice. In this case, neither of the chiefs had come forward
to accept responsibility for the ambush and murder of Ibn
Sharida's caravan *en route* for Damascus.

Our emissary then returned, saying, 'My Lord, I could not
get to them. As soon as I approached they began firing.' His
Majesty paused for a moment and then cried out, 'Trust in
God and prepare to fight.' Then, just as generations of warrior kings had done before him, he bent down, took up
handfuls of sand and began to throw them in the direction
of the enemy. This is an act which, according to tradition,
had been performed by the Prophet Mohammed prior to
battle. The symbolic meaning of the action is, 'O God, con-
fuse and confound the enemy.'

As the King's army approached the enemy, heavy firing
broke out on both sides and lasted for about ten minutes.
The enemy had an advantage over us because they had taken
up positions on the higher side of the Wadi of Ibn Jurallah
and had built a makeshift wall of large, loose stones for
cover. At this moment the King was aided by a piece of good
luck. From their higher position, the enemy saw a large
number of Ibn Saud's men returning swiftly to camp. The
Ikhwan jumped to the conclusion that their initial fusillade
had thrown the King's forces into retreat. This was quite
untrue, for what the Ikhwan were actually witnessing was
the return of the *dhahurs*, who were exhausted after a long
spell of duty in the open and had at last been relieved and
ordered by His Majesty to return to the rear of the firing-
line in order to receive their dates and water. Mistakenly
thinking victory to be in their grasp, the enemy abandoned
their well-fortified positions and ran down towards the lower
ground to pursue the King's men.

Amongst our forces was a sizeable machine-gun detachment, equipped with about a dozen guns, under the command of Ibrahim Ibn Muammar. The King had suspected
that the Ikhwan were ignorant of the existence of his
machine-guns, and so he had given Ibn Muammar strict

instructions not to throw away the advantage of surprise by using them too early. Ibn Muammar's orders were to hold his fire until a suitable opportunity arose for the machine-guns to be used to maximum effect. His men had therefore sat behind their weapons in mounting frustration during the opening stages of the battle, without firing a single shot. Their patience was rewarded when the Ikhwan suddenly presented a perfect target by leaving their cover and advancing towards them in bunched groups. Ibn Muammar gave the order to fire. The result was devastating, and within seconds almost all the advancing tribesmen had been killed or seriously wounded. When the surviving Ikhwan saw what had happened, they immediately started to withdraw. At that moment the King ordered his sons Prince Saud and Prince Mohammed, who had been waiting on the right flank, to charge with their cavalry in pursuit of the retreating army. As the cavalry approached them, the retreat of the Ikhwan became a rout. Many of the Ikhwan were slaughtered by the Princes' exultant horsemen as they overran the fleeing foot-soldiers of the enemy. When he realized what was happening, Ibn Saud sent word to his sons to pull back. Ever merciful, he abhorred pointless slaughter, and in any event there was a danger that the cavalry would go too far and find themselves cut off. The horsemen reluctantly obeyed the King's command and broke off their engagement, allowing the Ikhwan to retreat without further molestation to Artawiya.

So ended the battle of Sibillah. The whole affair had probably lasted no more than half an hour. It may seem strange that the Ikhwan, who were renowned for their fanatical bravery, should have chosen to flee rather than stand and fight; but it should be realized that fighting to the last man had never been a convention of desert war. It was considered quite acceptable and usual to retreat from the field once the fortunes of battle had turned in favour of the enemy. One lived to fight another day, and it was a simple matter for a defeated force to regroup. Anyone who chose to remain behind and make a stand would have been considered stupid rather than brave. As a result, the number of casualties in desert warfare was not normally severe. Although many thousands of men had been involved in the battle of Sibillah, the King lost only about two hundred dead and two hundred wounded. Thanks to Ibn Muammar's machine-guns, the Ikhwan suffered more heavily and lost about five hundred dead and a similar number wounded. These casualties were in fact considered unusually high for a desert battle.

After the battle, the cavalry returned to our camp in high spirits and a mood of festivity prevailed. It was obvious that the King had won a major success, for this was the first time that the Ikhwan had ever suffered a military defeat. It was an ancient tradition dating back as far as Roman times that after a battle, when blood had been shed, all old loyalties were terminated and new ones had to be made. Accordingly, all the tribal chiefs and amirs in the camp came to the King's tent to offer their allegiance anew. Another tradition was that warriors were entitled to compensation for any losses in battle. Outside His Majesty's tent a long queue formed, consisting of tribesmen claiming reimbursement for camels, horses and arms lost in the battle. No doubt many of the claims were exaggerated or entirely false, but the King was generous by nature and this was no time for financial prudence. All the claimants were given written notes authorizing them to collect money from the Treasury in Riyadh.

The King had one unexpected visitor. Ad-Dawish's cousin, Faisal Ibn Shiblan of the Mutair tribe, entered the camp carrying a large bundle of grass over his shoulders so that nobody could see his face. When challenged, he asked for the tent of Crown Prince Saud, saying, 'It is grass for his horses.' He was directed to the Prince's tent, left his bundle of grass outside and walked in. The Prince's first thought was that Ibn Shiblan had come to assassinate him. But Ibn Shiblan was unarmed. 'I am at your mercy,' he said to the Prince. 'Please take me to your father; I wish to speak to him.' He was taken to see the King, and informed His Majesty that the womenfolk of Ad-Dawish would come to his camp the following day. This was another tradition of desert war, representing the symbolic acceptance of defeat by a

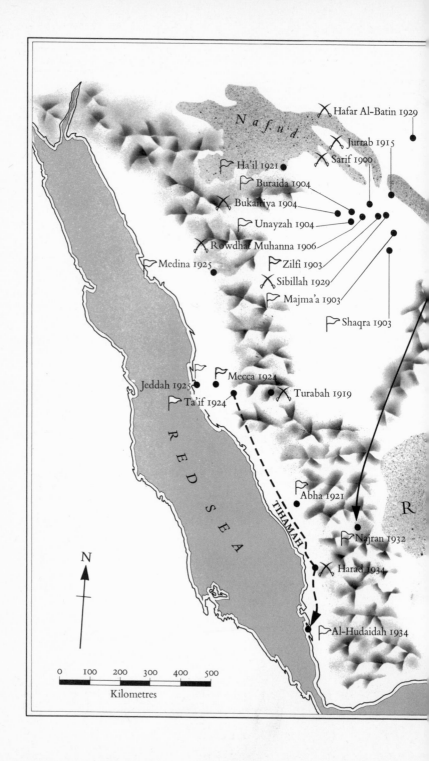

Hafar Al-Batin 1929

Jurrab 1915

Sarif 1900

Ha'il 1921

Buraida 1904

Bukairiya 1904

Unayzah 1904

Rowdhat Muhanna 1906

Medina 1925

Zilfi 1903

Sibillah 1929

Majma'a 1903

Shaqra 1903

Jeddah 1925

Mecca 1924

Ta'if 1924

Turabah 1919

N a f u d

R E D   S E A

TIHAMAH

Abha 1921

R

Najran 1932

Harad 1934

Al-Hudaidah 1934

N

0   100   200   300   400   500

Kilometres

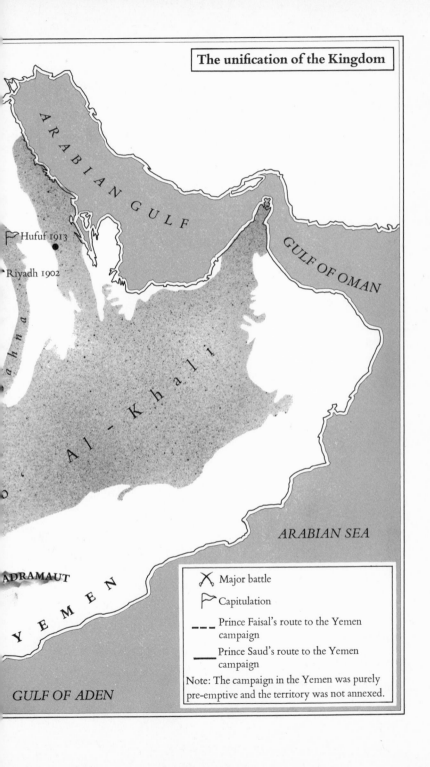

The unification of the Kingdom

ARABIAN GULF

GULF OF OMAN

⚑ Hufuf 1913

• Riyadh 1902

Al - Khali

ARABIAN SEA

ADRAMAUT

YEMEN

GULF OF ADEN

⚔ Major battle

⚑ Capitulation

--- Prince Faisal's route to the Yemen campaign

— Prince Saud's route to the Yemen campaign

Note: The campaign in the Yemen was purely pre-emptive and the territory was not annexed.

vanquished chief. By convention, the women of the beaten tribe would be given food and a tent by the victors and would remain in their camp for three days. They would not be molested in any way and would be under the protection of their hosts. When the three days were up they would return to their home. After delivering his message, Ibn Shiblan was given safe conduct back to his village of Artawiya, which was not very far from where the King was camped.

There was an unfortunate occurrence after the battle, when a band of rebel tribesmen, who had come to see if there was anyone still alive on the battlefield, were mistaken for a raiding party and killed by servants of Prince Mohammed. The King was furious and threatened to execute the servants, but he relented when he realized that there had been a genuine error. Apart from this incident, all the usual chivalries were observed and the wounded on both sides were treated by the King's own doctor, Midhat Sheikh Al-Ardah. Unfortunately, there was not a great deal the doctor could do as his facilities were very limited, but it was quite a novelty in desert warfare to have a doctor available at all. One of the enemy wounded was put in a tent next to mine. He was a giant of a man who had been shot in both legs and one arm. He made no complaint and just sat in the tent as if nothing had happened. Such hardiness was not uncommon among these tough, resilient desert warriors.

After the King had spent about three days at Sibillah, the womenfolk of Ad-Dawish were sent home and His Majesty prepared to leave. He realized that further fighting might be necessary, for the rebel troops who had fled at Sibillah could easily regroup and challenge him again. He decided to march to Artawiya, which was only a few miles to the east of Sibillah. Artawiya had been the first Ikhwan settlement and was now a town of some size. It was governed by Ad-Dawish himself, and was the centre of his power. The defeated Ikhwan had chosen it as the obvious place to which they should withdraw. The only way in which the King could be sure of ending the revolt would be by capturing the Ikhwan leaders, particularly Ibn Bijad and Ad-Dawish themselves. Ad-Dawish was now known to be in Artawiya, and to get to him the King was prepared to take the settlement by force if necessary.

On our way to Artawiya we came to a small pass where we were confronted by a group of about fifty horsemen led by Abdul Aziz, the son of Ad-Dawish. Showing great audacity, Abdul Aziz rode up to the King and said to him, 'O Protected, what is it that you want?' 'I want Artawiya,' said the King bluntly. 'What do you want with Artawiya?' asked Abdul Aziz, to which the King replied, 'I just want your father and nothing else.' Abdul Aziz pleaded with His Majesty not to assault the town and promised that he would bring his father to the King. His Majesty readily agreed, for there were about seven thousand people in Artawiya, and to take it by force would have involved much bloodshed. He ordered his army to march round the town and make camp at a place called Zibda, where it was agreed that we would meet Ad-Dawish.

Before we left, His Majesty made his camel sit and invited me to eat with him. His cook brought the meal of rice and meat, and after we had both eaten we mounted our camels for the ride to Zibda. His Majesty had a thoroughbred camel which had a natural ability to give its owner the smoothest possible ride over rocky ground. It was a remarkable animal and appeared to have the suspension of a Cadillac. Any ordinary camel would jerk its rider up and down with every bump it crossed, but if one watched the King while he rode his camel over rough ground, he appeared to be travelling in a perfectly straight line. There is a breed of pure Arab horse which gives this smooth ride, but it is very rare in a camel. My own camel was obstinate, bad-tempered, uncomfortable and slow. I had a most frightening experience on the way to Zibda because my beast was travelling so slowly that I became separated from the rest of my group and found myself lost in a desolate area strewn with huge boulders. The camel was acting wildly, throwing me about as it struggled to gain a footing on the rocky ground. I was afraid it would break a leg and leave me in the wilderness with no means of escape. Suddenly I saw two bedouin. This did not relieve my anxiety but rather increased it, for if they had been hostile they could easily have killed me for the sake of my rifle and provisions. Fortunately they ignored me and my camel stumbled on. Eventually, after what seemed an eternity, I came to an open space and saw the others and their camels. Needless to say, I received little sympathy as everybody seemed to think it a great joke that I had managed to get lost in the first place.

Later that day, we reached Zibda and made camp. A meal was prepared, consisting of boiled rice with meat and butter oil. Here we awaited the promised arrival of Abdul Aziz Ad-Dawish and his father. They came the next day, when to our surprise we saw that Faisal Ad-Dawish was being carried on a stretcher. During the battle of Sibillah he had received a somewhat bizarre stomach-wound. He had been shot from the side and the bullet had entered one side of his sizeable paunch and gone out of the other. The wound was obviously very serious and everyone was astonished that he was still alive. Abdul Aziz's first action on entering our camp was to request that the King should have a bath and change his clothes before meeting Faisal Ad-Dawish, in order to ensure that His Majesty's clothing should be fresh and free from any possible scent. (The bedouin have a fixed idea that scent can infect wounds.) His Majesty naturally complied with this request, and meanwhile ordered his doctor to attend to Faisal Ad-Dawish. When the two men finally met, Ad-Dawish was reprimanded severely for his wrongdoings. Then the King said to him, 'You are no match for me. I am too powerful. I pardon you; you may go wherever you like and I will give you whatever you need. But your future actions and behaviour, good or bad, will be judged by me and dealt with accordingly.' Ad-Dawish expressed his gratitude for the King's mercy and said he would like to go to Kuwait. He requested money, water-bags, arms, and equipment for drawing water. The King immediately wrote out letters addressed to his agent in Kuwait, Abdullah Al-Niffisi, asking for these supplies to be granted and graciously handed the letters to the rebel chief.

We were all most surprised that His Majesty let Faisal Ad-Dawish go so easily. But the King was always at his most compassionate in victory, and at the time it appeared he had little to lose by letting Ad-Dawish go free. The stomach-wound was very bad and seemed certain to prove fatal. There was another, perhaps more important, reason: His Majesty was anxious to catch Ibn Bijad, and realized that Bijad would be more amenable to surrendering himself voluntarily when he heard of the treatment Ad-Dawish had received. There was one further consideration, of which His Majesty may have been aware but I certainly was not. Some years later I was speaking to a bedouin who turned out to be the son of Faisal Ibn Shiblan, the man who had come disguised to Prince Saud's tent at Sibillah. He told me that, although Ad-Dawish had come to our camp accompanied only by a few servants, five thousand of his men had secretly surrounded us ready to attack if their chief was not released.

After the meeting with Ad-Dawish, His Majesty sent word to Ibn Bijad requesting Ibn Bijad to meet him in the town of Shaqra. The King and his entourage then left for the town of Majma'a, in the province of Sudair, where we rested for two days. Here the King stayed with Sheikh Ibrahim Al-Ungary, who was an *ulema* and the Qadhi (religious judge) of Sudair. We then proceeded to Shaqra, which was about fifty miles to the south, and waited patiently to see whether or not Ibn Bijad would answer the King's summons. Ibn Bijad was the chief of the Utaiba tribe, whose territory extended from Riyadh all the way to Mecca. It was a much larger tribe than the Mutair, and in terms of the number of men he commanded, Ibn Bijad was much more powerful than Ad-Dawish. However, the King had always regarded Ad-Dawish as the more dangerous man because he was uncommonly shrewd and clever. Ibn Bijad, despite his undisputed bravery and fortitude, had never been renowned for his intellect. He rose to the bait and came to Shaqra with about fifty of his tribesmen, no doubt expecting to receive

113

the same lenient treatment as Ad-Dawish. But this time there were no enemy troops surrounding the King's camp. His Majesty chastised Ibn Bijad with the words, 'You are nothing, Bijad. You thought you were someone, but it is Ad-Dawish who was clever!' Ibn Bijad and two of his followers were then promptly imprisoned and sent to Riyadh in chains.

Leaving Shaqra, we went to Ha'il via Buraida and Ar-Rass. While in Buraida the King left suddenly to go to Unay-zah, where he married a girl from one of the prominent families there, the Ash-Shubaily. This was intended as a mark of his gratitude and respect for the people of Unayzah, who had given him strong support against the Ikhwan. He had instructed his retinue to proceed to Ar-Rass and await him there but two of his clerks disobeyed orders and followed the King to Unayzah. They were simply curious to visit the town, and had not thought that His Majesty would object. That evening, they entered the *majlis* of the Amir. Unfortunately, the King himself arrived at the Amir's house soon afterwards and caught the culprits red-handed. He gave orders that they should be put in prison. They were only released when the Amir himself appealed to the King on their behalf, saying, 'As you are all guests in my town, please excuse them.' The King had told nobody about his marriage plans, and it came as a complete surprise to us all when he later joined us at Ar-Rass and informed us that he had a new wife.

When he arrived at Ar-Rass the King was presented with a tricky diplomatic problem. At Sibillah the royal army had been accompanied by Sheikh Saleh Al-Adahel, a very prominent elder who lived at Ar-Rass and was considered to be one of the wisest men in Najd. When Sheikh Saleh realized that the King would be visiting his town, he immediately asked His Majesty to have lunch at his home. Naturally the King agreed. However, after Ibn Saud had entered Ar-Rass, the Amir of the town also extended an invitation to lunch. His Majesty was obliged to decline, explaining that he had already agreed to eat with Sheikh Saleh and that he was only staying one day. The Amir was most put out and declared,

114

'If you do not accept the courtesy that I have extended to you, I will leave the country and never return.' The King decided to resolve his dilemma with a clever compromise. The food for the meal was to be prepared by Sheikh Saleh and eaten in the house of the Amir. Everyone was satisfied with the arrangement. Since the Amir's house was not large enough to accommodate all the King's many followers, we were divided into three groups, following the pattern of the Royal Courts in Riyadh. (The first, and most important, Court was for foreign affairs; the second was for the internal affairs of Central Arabia; the third was for the bedouin, or tribesmen.) Each group was sent to eat at a different house in the town. The rest of the followers were distributed among the other inhabitants. We all dispersed to our various appointed houses.

In the house where I was to eat there was an unfortunate incident. In Riyadh it was the custom for the meat to be served before the rice. Unbeknown to us, the custom in Ar-Rass was different and they served the rice before the meat. When the rice arrived the Chief of the Court flew into a temper, thinking that we were being insulted by not being served any meat. He walked out and ordered us to follow. Just as we were doing so the meat arrived, causing considerable embarrassment all round because it was a custom common to both towns that once one had risen from the table one did not return to it. In consequence we had to leave the house and go without lunch altogether. To make matters worse, our host then complained to the King about our insultingly abrupt departure from his table!

It should be noted here that the amirs were not appointed by the government, but elected by the citizens of each town. Very occasionally – in the case of the death of an amir, for example – the government might appoint a successor, but normally the choice of the citizens was respected and recognized by central government. The amirs were normally loyal to the government, and were considered to be the owners of the towns they ruled over.

Leaving Ar-Rass, the King continued on his journey to the

former Rashidi capital of Ha'il, a stronghold of the Shammar tribe, who were renowned throughout Arabia not only for the superb bravery of their men but also for the beauty of their women. The girls were so beautiful that the Arabs had a facetious joke among themselves: 'As a last resort we'll make do with a Shammar girl.' Such was the reputation of Ha'il that everybody's imagination started to run wild, and the common desire of all was to marry a Shammar girl without delay. Many actually did so, including one of the King's Indian drivers. He was so carried away by the stories of the local beauties that he imagined every Shammar woman to have the features of Cleopatra and he expressed a strong desire to marry such a woman. Some of his Arab friends promised to arrange an immediate marriage for him with a lovely Shammar virgin. A girl was found and the marriage ceremony took place at once. As is usual, the ceremony was performed before the local religious judge, or Qadhi. The girl's father was present but the girl herself, if she was there at all, would have been hidden behind a screen. The man would not see his wife unveiled until the night of the wedding. As darkness fell, the impatient Indian was escorted by his friends to the tent of his new wife and there they bade him good night. The following morning, as dawn broke, a cry of rage issued from the marriage bed and the Indian burst from the tent and divorced his wife there and then. I can only presume that in the cold light of day he saw that the lady his friends had provided for him was not exactly the Cleopatra of his dreams.

On leaving Ha'il, the King and his Court travelled to Hejaz for His Majesty's somewhat interrupted annual pilgrimage. The King made arrangements for his family and new wife to follow after him. While in Hejaz, he ordered the release of some prominent citizens of Mecca and Jeddah who had been held under house arrest in Riyadh on charges of conspiracy. When His Majesty arrived in Jeddah, he received some very bad news in the shape of a telegram from Bahrain informing him that Amir Fahd Ibn Jelawi had been killed by rebellious members of the Ajman tribe. This was a harsh blow for His

Majesty, for he had considered Fahd a valued friend. During the battle of Sibillah, Fahd had protected the King's eastern flank while Abdul Aziz Ibn Mussaud, Governor of Ha'il, had faced Chief Ibn Mash'hur's attack from the north. Without the help of Fahd and Ibn Mussaud (both cousins of the King) the battle might have been lost.

As will be seen, Sibillah certainly did not mark the end of the King's troubles with the Ikhwan. Nevertheless, it broke the backbone of the Ikhwan movement, and made it clear to all that Ibn Saud was determined to be master in his own house and would not tolerate the usurping of his power by others. It also had far-reaching effects which were felt for a long time afterwards, because those tribes or branches of tribes which had joined in the revolt were in disgrace for many years, and the tribes which had assisted the King became favoured. At the time of the King's death, over twenty years later, this division was still an important factor in Arabian politics.

8
The end of the Ikhwan

صبي التوحيد ، أنا أخو من طاع الله ياويل عدو الشريعة منا .

(أنشودة حرب . عبد المحسن الفرم)

Armed with my belief in the one, true God, I am the comrade of those who respond to His call. Woe to the enemies of the Sharia'h; let them beware of our wrath.

(Abdul Mohsin Al-Firm's war-cry
at the battle of Sibillah)

The King's grief on hearing of the death of Fahd Ibn Jelawi was nothing compared to his distress when he learnt of the circumstances in which it had occurred. At about the time of the battle of Sibillah, Fahd had been guarding the King's eastern flank against rebellious Ikhwan from the Ajman tribe in Al-Hasa. When the Ajman heard of the outcome of the battle, they decided that the time had come to negotiate and Dhaidan Ibn Huthlain, chief of the Ajman, sent word to Fahd that he wished to see him. A meeting was agreed and Ibn Huthlain came by arrangement to Fahd's camp at a place called As-Sarar. The two men talked for the best part of the day but by nightfall had not reached agreement. Fahd asked the chief to stay the night but Ibn Huthlain declined, saying, 'Please do not keep me, for I have left word with my people that if I do not return by midnight they are to come for me.' Fahd took this as a threat and lost his temper. He ordered his servants to put Ibn Huthlain in chains and hold him prisoner for the night in a tent. Again the chief warned Fahd that he was acting unwisely, saying, 'The whole Ajman tribe will descend upon you, for they will think something has happened to me.' Fahd replied, 'Let them come.'

Shortly after midnight the Ajman did indeed come. They were in a wild and savage frame of mind, dressed only in loincloths, and were ready to die for their chief. Rudely awakened by the sound of firing as the tribesmen invaded his camp, Fahd dressed rapidly for battle and in a fury gave orders that Ibn Huthlain be unchained and beheaded. The order was instantly carried out. This was the worst possible thing he could have done, for his own force contained a large contingent of Ajman tribesmen whose loyalty to him was

already uncertain. When they learnt that Fahd had treach-
erously killed Ibn Huthlain, they immediately joined the
rebels and turned on the remaining members of Fahd's army,
killing them all. (Fahd himself had leapt onto his horse and
ordered his servant to unchain it. Instead of obeying the
order, the Ajman servant turned on Fahd and shot him dead.)
As a result of this disastrous battle, the King now had nearly
the whole of the Ajman tribe in open revolt against him, and
was without forces in the area to contain them.

It was not long before further bad news reached His
Majesty. Faisal Ad-Dawish had not died of his wound as
everybody had expected. Instead, he had made a miraculous
and speedy recovery and was now up in arms once again,
leading the Mutair in fresh raids against tribes loyal to the
King. He had again been joined by the Utaiba tribe, now led
by Chief Ad-Duhaina. After the battle of Sibillah, Ad-
Duhaina had fled to Iraq and taken refuge with King Faisal.
On his way back to Najd he had conferred with Ad-Dawish,
and it had been agreed that Ad-Duhaina would incite the
Utaiba to revolt against the King; Ad-Duhaina himself was
to guide and lead the tribe. The Utaiba controlled the whole
area between Mecca and Riyadh, so the King was effectively
trapped in Hejaz with no means of returning to his capital.
The situation was extremely serious. Large areas of the country were now hostile to the King, and those tribes and townspeople who remained loyal had neither the strength nor the
inclination to take on the rebels in battle. But His Majesty
was not a man to be overwhelmed or daunted by difficulties
of this sort. By this time he had developed friendly relations
with the British government. He arranged with them that
they would sell him about four thousand rifles and ship them
from Madras to Bahrain in order to supply the few tribes in
Al-Hasa who had remained loyal. The price quoted by the
British was very high, and the King was sceptical. He was
quoted as saying, 'I could get all the necessary arms and
transport them from Jeddah to the Eastern Province on four
hundred camels, at no extra cost.' However, it would have

been impossible for such a convoy to pass through all the tribes in open revolt on the way.

The King decided to gather together what forces he could and attempt to force his way back to Riyadh through the rebellious tribes. His Majesty never lost his confidence or balance. He was poised and relaxed as ever, and although the situation appeared desperate, he was quite confident of victory. He had, of course, a number of advantages over his enemies. With thirty years of successful warfare behind him, he knew that there was nobody who could match his skill as a desert general. He had the benefit of British assistance, access to better arms than the rebels, and money with which to buy the loyalty of the tribes who might not otherwise support him. He also had the major asset of recently installed radio links with all the biggest towns in his kingdom. By using the radio, the King could obtain up-to-date intelligence and speedily direct his forces where they were needed. The rebel tribes were without this facility; they did not know what was happening outside their own areas, and were unable to co-operate effectively.

As His Majesty made his crucial march across the desert from Mecca to Riyadh, he gathered a substantial force of friendly tribesmen and irregular soldiers and supplied them with camels, arms and provisions. The King and his retinue rode in cars, accompanied by a large escort of men on camels. As usual the Court staff, including myself, were with him. We encountered no serious trouble until we reached Afif, a water well which was situated midway between Mecca and Riyadh and was on our usual route. It was a stronghold of the Utaiba and we therefore approached it with caution. We were not attacked, but the Utaiba had polluted the well by the traditional and very effective method of dropping into it a dead man and a dead donkey. His Majesty ordered that his son Mohammed and a group of three or four hundred men should clean the well, and we waited for a period of three days until the water was considered safe to drink. Even so, many suffered serious attacks of diarrhoea after drinking the water, and the King's doctor treated a number of men

123

by giving them injections. Unfortunately, tough as these warrious were, they were quite unused to medication of any sort and the reaction from the injections only added to their discomfort.

Ahead of us, on the direct route from Afif to Riyadh, was a mountain pass which was ideal for ambushes and where a few resolute men could hold off an army. His Majesty was certain that the Utaiba tribesmen from Afif were waiting for us in the pass. He therefore decided to skirt round it and proceed to an oasis called Al-Qaiyah, some one hundred and fifty miles to the north-east. Al-Qaiyah was also inhabited by the Utaiba tribe and the King sent emissaries ahead ordering all the men of fighting age to leave. Only the women, children and old men were allowed to remain. The King travelled to Al-Qaiyah by car and stayed there for four days to allow all his camel force to catch up with him and permit everybody to rest for a time. Then we struck north to the oasis of Dawadimi. The going was slow and troublesome; the cars became badly stuck in the sands of the Wadi Ar-Risha, and extracting them proved quite difficult. At Dawadimi His Majesty met with chiefs of the Rawaga section of the Utaiba tribe, which occupied that area and whose loyalty was to him. The King was well aware that, despite their loyalty, the chiefs were harbouring cousins and other relatives who had joined the rebels. He lost no time in telling the chiefs that he disapproved of the sanctuary being granted and that it should end. After this meeting he went on to Riyadh, having travelled all the way from Mecca unmolested.

During the following few weeks the situation became steadily worse. Riyadh was not under siege but it became an island in a sea of rebellion. The city itself was overrun by bedouin tribesmen, and no one could be certain where their loyalties lay. We were encircled by enemy tribes and it became a risky business to venture far from the town. Ibn Saud had no intention of letting matters rest. As a first countermeasure he ordered his son, Crown Prince Saud, to go to Al-Hasa to take charge of matters there. Saud was to replace Abdullah Ibn Jelawi, the Governor of Hufuf, who had fallen seriously ill after hearing of the death of his son Fahd. Saud and his men immediately set off in a convoy of cars. Unfortunately, the Ajman tribe had anticipated that Ibn Saud might do something of this sort. They were waiting in ambush in an area of soft sand known as the Dahna, about sixty miles to the east of Riyadh.

The Dahna is one of the most remarkable geographical features of Arabia. From the Nafud desert in the north, it runs in a continuous narrow strip down to the Rub' Al-Khali in the south. Never more than sixty miles in width, it is literally a river, for down it the prevailing winds blow fine, powdery sand continually southwards towards the vast sea of the Empty Quarter. For this reason I always describe the Dahna as the 'river of sand', a phrase I think I can claim to have coined personally, as I know of no other historians or geographers who have used it. It resembles a river in another way, too, for a traveller comes across it all of a sudden, and the transition from hard to soft going occurs instantly, just as if he had plunged in from a river bank. The sand near the surface of the Dahna is often found to be damp, but however deep you dig, you will never reach water. For this reason, a man who fails to keep his promise is often described by the bedouin as being 'like the Dahna'.

The shifting dunes of the Dahna made it a splendid setting for an ambush and the Ajman were successful in surprising Prince Saud. They killed a number of the Prince's followers and took many others prisoner. On this occasion the speed of the cars was of little use, for most of them became bogged down in the sand and were easily captured and burnt by the rebels. Luckily, the Prince had borrowed his father's powerful custom-built Mercedes, which was well suited for the sandy conditions, and in this he was able to escape capture and proceed to Hufuf as planned. Those of his men who were captured were taken to Kuwait, which was adopting a neutral position at the time, and they were later released. As it happened, my brother was attempting to make his way secretly to Hufuf with a small caravan at the same time as the Prince was travelling there. The caravan was passed by the Prince and his entourage the day before the ambush, and the following day my brother and his men were the first on the scene. The bodies of the Prince's servants were still lying where the Ajman had left them, and the cars had been stripped of trophies such as horns and lights before being set on fire. In Hufuf, my brother went to see the Prince and told him of what he had seen. He found himself being berated for failing to bury the corpses. Unfortunately, it had been impossible for him to do this as he had brought no tools with him suitable for digging.

Having sent Prince Saud to take charge in the east, the King dealt with the situation in the west by sending from Riyadh a powerful force of bedouin and townsmen under the command of Amir Khalid Ibn Mohammed Ibn Saud to attack the Utaiba on their eastern flank. At the same time he sent instructions by wireless to Prince Faisal in Hejaz to launch an assault from the west, thus subjecting the Utaiba to a co-ordinated two-pronged assault. Although the Utaiba fought bravely, they were for the most part dispersed in small bodies and the King's forces were able to mop these groups up one by one. Within two months the Utaiba were subdued and the route from Mecca to Riyadh was again open.

It was as well that the King had dispatched his son Saud to strengthen the defences of Hufuf, for it was there that the redoubtable Faisal Ad-Dawish was playing his own part in the revolt. With large detachments of the Mutair and Ajman tribes under his command, he was determined to capture Hufuf from the King. But before he could do so, it was necessary for him to overcome the small tribe of the Al-Awazem who inhabited the area and were loyal to the King. The Al-Awazem were not highly rated as warriors, but on this occasion they were fighting to defend their homes and villages, and for once they had an ample supply of arms and ammunition which was part of the consignment shipped by the British from Madras. Ad-Dawish was unable to defeat them, and in the end suffered the humiliation of having to retire from the area of Hufuf altogether.

Before commencing operations in Al-Hasa, Ad-Dawish

had sent his son Abdul Aziz, together with Faisal Ibn Shiblan of the Mutair tribe, on a massive raiding expedition to the north of the country; they had orders to harass all the tribes which were loyal to the King. The raids were successful and the rebels caused a great deal of havoc and damage, as well as seizing large numbers of camels. But when it came to deciding which way to return, Abdul Aziz Ad-Dawish and Ibn Shiblan fell out. Ad-Dawish wished to travel to an oasis called Um Urdhuma (which means 'water well'). Ibn Shiblan had heard that a large detachment of the Shammar tribe, loyal to the King, were heading in that direction. He thought it would be very dangerous to risk an engagement with them, and wanted to take an alternative route. Abdul Aziz Ad-Dawish's temper was as short as his beard was red. He flew into a rage, accused Ibn Shiblan of cowardice and insisted that the force should proceed to Um Urdhuma. Ibn Shiblan, who was a giant of a man, lost his temper too at this point. After a furious argument he left with a hundred and twenty-five of his followers, crossing over the borders of Iraq to the water wells of As-Salman. From there he turned south and returned in safety to Artawiya.

Abdul Aziz Ad-Dawish continued on his way to Um Urdhuma, which was a march of some six or seven days. It was the height of summer and there was no water on the way. His men were near death by the time they arrived and their camels were equally exhausted. The warriors had pushed a kerchief into the anus of each camel. This was a traditional device to prevent air from entering the animal's stomach when its belly was empty, since this was considered dangerous for the camel. As Ibn Shiblan had feared, a large and well-armed detachment of the Shammar tribe, under the command of Nida Ibn Naheer, was waiting at Um Urdhuma grouped in defensive positions around the water wells. (Nida Ibn Naheer had sent for help from Abdul Aziz Ibn Mussaud, who was the Governor of Ha'il and a cousin of the King, but the troops did not arrive until the battle was over.) Although heavily outnumbered, Abdul Aziz Ad-Dawish had no choice but to attack Ibn Naheer's troops, for to carry on without water would have meant a certain and horrible death for him and his men. The confrontation was a total disaster for the Ikhwan. Ad-Dawish attacked with seven hundred men. They managed to kill many of the Shammar group, including Nida Ibn Naheer himself. But in the process Ad-Dawish and four hundred and fifty of his men were killed; the remaining two hundred and fifty, who were too exhausted to continue fighting, were captured. Shortly after the battle Abdul Aziz Ibn Mussaud arrived on the scene. He had the prisoners publicly beheaded on the spot. Ibn Mussaud took a considerable risk in ordering these executions without having first sought the King's authority. In the event His Majesty approved of Ibn Mussaud's action, feeling that the time had come when an example had to be made of the rebels who were hindering the building of his kingdom.

In the meantime Faisal Ad-Dawish, having failed to achieve anything in Al-Hasa, moved swiftly and secretly into Najd. He was hoping to mount a surprise attack on the King's forces, who were camped at the water well of Al-Gaiah, near the town of Majma'a to the north of Riyadh. After crossing the Dahna, Ad-Dawish succeeded in making his way undetected into Najd. The day before the attack was due to take place his men held the war parade which, by tradition, always took place whenever possible before a battle. While the parade was in progress a messenger arrived, bringing Ad-Dawish the news of his son's death at Um Urdhuma. The old warrior was stricken with grief at the news and, in a mood of desperation, ordered his servants to empty his men's water-bags. This was a strategy similar to that made famous by the Moorish leader Tariq* who, having burnt his boats, cried to his men, 'Before you is the enemy and behind you is the sea!' In this case the desert took the place of the sea, but the effect was identical. When Ad-Dawish's men went into battle the following day, they had no alternative but to press home their attack on the water

*Jabal Tariq, the mountain named after Tariq, is known to the West as Gibraltar.

well. The King's men were outnumbered and taken by surprise, and the Ikhwan attack was a total success. Those of the loyal tribesmen who were not killed fled back towards Riyadh. On their way they encountered a convoy of trucks loaded with arms and supplies destined for Al-Gaiah which had unfortunately been dispatched too late to reach the garrison before the Ikhwan attacked it. (Even if it had arrived in time, it would have made no difference, for the garrison was no match for the Mutair.)

Flushed with success, Ad-Dawish crossed the Dahna area and returned to the north of Al-Hasa. Ibn Saud headed north in pursuit about a month later; as always, the Court staff, including myself, went with him. When we came to cross the Dahna, the weather was becoming tolerable as winter was approaching, but water was as always extremely scarce. We headed for the wells of Al-Lisafah and Al-Lihaba, strategically situated and very well-known watering places, which had not long before been heavily bombed during one of the RAF raids against the Ikhwan. I remember well an evening two days later when we were encamped in the Dahna, still many miles from the nearest water. It was approaching sunset, and the King was waiting for the sun to go down so that he could commence his evening prayer. Suddenly a scout appeared from the desert and whispered something in His Majesty's ear. The King took note of what he said but showed no outward sign of emotion. The sun slipped slowly down beyond the horizon, painting fantastic pictures in the sky and sharply silhouetting the dunes round about. His Majesty placed his prayer-mat on the sand and faced towards Mecca, his features calm and thoughtful. I sensed that some matter of great importance was occupying his mind, but as always with His Majesty, it was quite impossible to guess what it might be. After his prayers, the King returned to a carpet which had been laid out for him on a small dune and called some of his soldiers and servants to him. Clearly and confidently he gave the orders which had been forming in his mind during his prayer. His instructions were passed on by his servants to the various tribal groups in his army;

each group was told precisely what it needed to know and no more. This combination of decisiveness and discretion singled out His Majesty as an outstanding general, who gave us all complete confidence in his leadership.

I was soon able to guess what message the scout had brought, for when we got to Al-Lisafah we found that the well had been poisoned with the usual dead man and dead donkey. His Majesty had obviously known this, because he had sent ahead a detachment of five hundred men to clear the wells and empty them of water in order to prevent further pollution. In spite of this, it was two days before the wells started to fill again, and even then the water turned out to be unfit to drink. We had no alternative but to press on, although by now we had been five days without finding water. Further on, at a place called Wafra, we found water in large quantities, but it was brackish and fit only for the camels to drink. That night we camped at a place called Ma'araj Ussoban, at some distance from Wafra. We had about fifteen thousand camels with us, and the King issued an order that they should be sent to drink at Wafra in groups of five thousand at a time. This was typical of His Majesty's attention to detail, for it ensured that it would not be possible for the enemy to make a sudden raid and capture our entire herd while it was watering.

The area around Ma'araj Ussoban is well known for the millions of tiny sea shells mixed with the sand, which points to the area having been under water at some time in the past, although it is now at least sixty miles from the sea. In any event, this was the least of my worries for our thirst was now becoming a real problem. We had stopped drinking water altogether and were making do with small quantities of tea and coffee. That night, as darkness fell, our weary bodies seemed to shrivel in the cold desert air and our mouths were parched and dry. Our very saliva had taken on a glue-like consistency. Not only were the Court staff without water; we had no food either. We asked the Chief of the Court to see what he could arrange. He went through the camp and found that the King's son, Prince Mohammed, was able to give us something to eat. We were invited to his tent, where we found a large plate of rice awaiting us with some meat in the middle of it. The meat was very soft; although I did not recognize the taste, I was too hungry to worry about it. After I had taken a few morsels, Prince Mohammed asked me with a grin if I knew what I had eaten. When I said I did not, he told me it was wild cat. I would greatly have preferred not to know, but I was glad of the food all the same. It would normally have been against our religious rules to eat such meat but it was permissible in time of necessity. In fact, the bedouin are often known to eat wild cat when they can find nothing else.

The lack of water was now becoming very serious, and unless some was found immediately, we were in grave danger of dying of thirst. At the very least our force would have had to split up in search of water, and this would have rendered it ineffective as a military unit for many days. But as dawn broke the following day, our prayers were answered by a sudden cloudburst which awoke us from our restless sleep. The heavens seemed to open up with rain. The downpour filled the wadi nearby with pools of water and the air with a beautiful scent of freshness. The rain lifted everybody's spirits. Since His Majesty had now decided that we should stay where we were for a time, and there was nothing for the Court staff to do, we decided to have a shooting contest on top of a nearby hill. One of the clerks erected a small paper target and we all started shooting at it. Suddenly we found to our alarm that we appeared to have become targets ourselves, for bullets fired from our camp were flying around us and ricocheting off the rocks nearby. We were very frightened and returned immediately to the camp. There we met one of Prince Mohammed's servants, who asked us to come at once to the Prince's tent. The Prince gave us tea and then informed us calmly that it was he who had been shooting at us. He explained that the King did not approve of ammunition being wasted on shooting matches and felt that if his son fired off a few rounds in our direction it would be a suitable method of expressing his displeasure. We protested to the Prince that he might have hit one of us, but he replied that he had been shooting to miss and that he had confidence in his marksmanship even if we did not. I asked him, 'What would have happened if one of us had moved as you fired?' 'Ah,' said the Prince with a reassuring smile, 'the bullet would have gone past by then!'

Two days later we struck camp and continued north. Shortly after we left, the momentous news reached us that Ad-Dawish, whom we had been nervously expecting to encounter at any time, had already been utterly defeated. It appeared that he had been encamped on the banks of the Wadi Hafar Al-Batin, near the borders of Kuwait. There he had been attacked by a contingent of the Harb tribe under Abdul Mohsin Al-Firm, aided by the local Dhufir tribe under Chief Ajmi Ibn Siwait. Al-Firm had achieved total surprise by making his assault when the Ikhwan were fast asleep and their camp was wreathed in an early morning mist. Ad-Dawish's tents had been burned, his supplies and camels looted, and his men killed or scattered. For the old warrior, this was the end. Throwing his bravery to the wind, he had fled the camp on an old camel which the Harb tribe had not considered worth taking. None of us had known that Al-Firm was planning an attack on Ad-Dawish, although I am sure that it had been arranged by the King. This was a good example of the way His Majesty devised and executed his plans in complete secrecy.

After the battle of Hafar Al-Batin there was no more fight left in Ad-Dawish. With a few of his followers, his immediate family and his wives, he fled across the border and into Kuwait. There he sought refuge with the British Consul, Colonel Dickson. Dickson was at first reluctant to help Ad-Dawish, knowing that he would be bound to incur the displeasure of Ibn Saud if he did so. But when Ad-Dawish took off his turban and placed it on Dickson's head, Dickson took pity on him and agreed to help. (This was a custom dating back to ancient times; it symbolized complete helplessness and a request for protection.) Dickson's wife took personal care of Ad-Dawish's womenfolk, who were in a pathetic

state of hunger and misery. As Colonel Dickson had anticipated, Ibn Saud was very angry when he heard that the
British had given sanctuary to his old enemy. The King must
also have been displeased with the Kuwaitis themselves, for
letters taken from the looted camp of Ad-Dawish proved
that the rebels had been receiving supplies and ammunition
from Kuwait. Messengers were sent to Kuwait and Iraq and
it was speedily arranged that His Majesty would meet a
British representative at Ar-Ruqai – a famous meeting- and
watering-place, situated at the point where the frontiers of
Kuwait, Iraq and Saudi Arabia converge.

Our journey to Ar-Ruqai was not without incident. On
the way, our scouts spotted a splinter group of the Mutair
tribe. This group was led by Ibn Ashwan, whose name was
not unfamiliar to me. In 1928 Ibn Ashwan and his bedouin
followers had tried to launch an attack on Kuwait, but were
driven off by Sheikh Ali Al Subah and a few companions in
their cars. During the pursuit, the handful of cars got stuck
in the sand. The bedouin circled back and fought a small
pitched battle, during which Sheikh Ali was killed. Sheikh
Abdullah Al-Niffisi, the King's agent in Kuwait, sent a telegram to His Majesty, giving him the news. Since the telegram
came in Arabic, but in English script, I was asked to translate
it.

At the time we were travelling towards Ar-Ruqai, Ibn
Ashwan's group was known to have deserted Ad-Dawish
and to be moving towards the interior of Najd. Although the
rebellion had now been effectively put down, no treaty or
agreement for safe conduct had been made between His
Majesty and this section of the Mutair, and there was no
way of knowing what their intentions were. His Majesty
therefore ordered that they should be attacked. Prince
Mohammed came forward and asked to lead the attack, but
the King was concerned for his safety and refused.
Mohammed was determined. He took out his pistol and
pointed it at his head, saying, 'Either you let me lead the
attack or I will kill myself.' The King relented and
Mohammed led the assault, which was a complete success.

The Mutair were routed, and forced to abandon their women and children and many of their camels. Their leader, Ibn Ashwan, was killed, although his brother and many of the tribesmen escaped. Among the women who were brought back to the King's camp was Ibn Ashwan's mother, who was prostrate with grief at the death of her son. His Majesty questioned her as to why Ibn Ashwan had joined Ad-Dawish. Wailing and crying, she fell down and cursed Ad-Dawish, saying that he had come to their camp and entwined himself like a serpent around her son, and with lies and false promises had persuaded him to join the rebellion. The King made sure that the captured women and children were treated with the greatest possible consideration, and they were released as soon as we reached a place where they could be left safely.

When we reached Ar-Ruqai it transpired that the British had decided to grant Ad-Dawish political asylum. They had also given sanctuary to two other rebel chiefs, Ibn Lami of the Mutair tribe and Naif Ibn Aba Al-Khalab of the Ajman tribe. This move baffled Ibn Saud, who could not see what advantage the British sought to gain by harbouring his enemies. At Ar-Ruqai the British were represented by Sir John Bagot Glubb (known to the Arabs as Glubb Pasha), Inspector of the Southern Desert and later Commander of the Jordan–Arab Army (better known to the British as the Arab Legion). The King remained camped about five miles south of Ar-Ruqai. He sent Yusuf Yassin, director of the political section of his Court, with myself as translator, to negotiate with Glubb Pasha about Ad-Dawish and the other chiefs. At our first meeting with Glubb Pasha, we greeted him and I spoke to him in English. He responded immediately in immaculate Arabic. We questioned him about Ad-Dawish but it soon became obvious that he would not be able to give us a satisfactory reply. Although he was extremely courteous, he would only undertake to send a cable to London at once, and assure us that the matter would be given immediate attention. While we were at Ar-Ruqai, a number of Iraqi bedouin arrived and Glubb Pasha went to visit them. I was impressed by the close rapport which he immediately established with the tribesmen. He was completely familiar with their customs, gestures and dialects, and joined easily in their conversation, sipping coffee with them in the manner of the desert. When we asked him what the bedouin wanted, he replied, 'These crazy fellows say they want to join the King's flag!'

The next day we had another meeting with Glubb Pasha. He suggested that His Majesty should travel to Khabary Waddaha, where further discussions could take place with the British and the Iraqis. The talks were not only to be about the rebel leaders, but would also cover a number of other disputes between Saudi Arabia and its neighbours, particularly the outstanding issue of the Iraqi border forts. His Majesty agreed to the proposal and we set off south-east on the long journey to Khabary Waddaha. The terrain which we had to cross was particularly harsh. One area which we travelled through was known as *Gara*, or 'bald', so called because it was barren of any type of growth or vegetation. It was covered with very soft, greyish sand, which had a consistency like mud and was very difficult for the camels to negotiate. The bedouin never stayed in this region as there was no grazing for their camels or fuel for their camp-fires. After struggling through it, we rested for a time at Wadi Hafar Al-Batin, an extension of Wadi Ar-Rumma. The river flowing through Wadi Hafar starts at Medina in Hejaz; flows across to Ha'il and Buraida in Al-Qasim; crosses the Dahna; goes on to the Hafar Al-Batin and Ar-Ruqai; turns north-east to Zubair in Iraq; and finally ends in the Arabian Gulf, flowing through Wadi Assba'y near Basra. Wadi Ar-Rumma is also known as 'the wadi of carcasses' because it is prone to fill up very rapidly in times of heavy rain, and many sheep, camels, horses and men have been known to drown there in its strong currents. In the days before the Suez Canal existed, these carcasses were a useful source of food for the lions and tigers which travelled from Africa up into Iraq.

We were all very weary from travel and every part of my body ached. I remember that when I dismounted from my camel and stood on the ground, I was so exhausted that I had the distinct impression that the ground itself was moving under me. Before we set off again, His Majesty asked me how far it was to Khabary Waddaha. Our bedouin guide said that it was about thirty miles, but I had a map with me which had been drawn by Philby on one of his expeditions and which showed the distance to be about eighteen miles. The guide proved to be more accurate than the map, for the journey turned out to be at least thirty-five miles. We did not reach Khabary Waddaha until well after midnight, by which time we were all quite exhausted.

I was only allowed a short time to recover, because early in the morning the negotiations with the British started and I was required to act as interpreter. The British had sent their Chief Political Representative in the Gulf area, Colonel Biscoe, to lead their delegation. Colonel Dickson was also present, as were some RAF commanders from Iraq. Our side consisted of the King himself and two of his advisers, Yusuf Yassin and Hafiz Wahba, later appointed Saudi Ambassador to London. Before discussions began, there was an exchange of courtesies in which the British praised His Majesty and the King responded pointedly by speaking of his regard for British trustworthiness and good faith. Then the talks started in earnest. It transpired that Ad-Dawish and the other chiefs were being held at Shaibah, a military camp near Basra. (It is perhaps worth making the point that neither the Kuwaitis nor the Iraqis had any say in the matter, since both their countries were under British control.) His Majesty insisted that Ad-Dawish was a wanted criminal who should be handed over and brought to justice. The British were politely adamant that he was a political refugee, and refused to surrender him. The subject of Ad-Dawish was not the only matter in dispute. Large numbers of men had been killed, and camels and other chattels captured, in the numerous raids and counter-raids which had taken place over the Iraqi border during the Ikhwan disturbances. It was generally agreed, according to Arab custom, that whichever side had lost more should receive compensation. The Iraqis confidently asserted that they had suffered more heavily than the

Saudis. But Yusuf Yassin had with him files which gave full details of the very severe casualties suffered by the Ikhwan during the attacks and also details of losses caused to Saudi tribes by Iraqi counter-raids and RAF bombing.

The files were regarded with the greatest suspicion by the Iraqis and the British but I know them to have been entirely accurate. His Majesty could always rely upon a steady stream of reliable information reaching him from all corners of his kingdom, for whenever something happened in any part of the country which the local bedouin knew would be of interest to the King, they immediately dispatched a messenger with the news. There was never any shortage of volunteers for the job of messenger, as the King's generosity to those bringing news was well known. It also became common knowledge that His Majesty preferred his intelligence to be as detailed as possible, so whenever a battle had taken place the local tribesmen would record meticulously the casualties which had occurred on each side. The arrival of these messengers at Riyadh was a common sight. If they bore particularly momentous news, they would sometimes fire in the air to attract attention. As they approached the town, the entire population would be waiting for them at the gates to find out what had happened and whether a victory had been won.

Yusuf Yassin did not subscribe to the British idea that negotiations should take place in an atmosphere of courtesy and restrained understatement. He made his points in a direct and forceful manner, and did not mind if this upset the other side. In addition, the wealth of information he possessed and his obvious familiarity with the circumstances surrounding the raids was a considerable embarrassment to the British and Iraqis; it contrasted sharply with the total absence of statistics on their own side. After the first day of talks, Colonel Biscoe took me aside and asked me to request the King not to send Yusuf Yassin to any further discussions. I did not pass on the message. I felt it was an insult to the King that the British should try to dictate who should and should not be in his negotiating team. Furthermore, I knew that

137

Yassin was the only person we had who was familiar with all the details of the losses caused by Iraqi raids, and I was sure that this was one reason why the British wanted him out of the talks. The following day Yassin went with Wahba to the British camp in the usual way and I followed. One of the British spoke to Yassin who instantly became very angry. Wahba came over and asked me if Biscoe had requested that Yassin should not attend. I said that he had, but that I had 'forgotten' to tell the King. I then went to see Biscoe and apologized for my omission. Biscoe was obviously annoyed but seemed to take the hint. Yassin continued to attend the conference. That night the King invited me to eat with him in his tent. Hafiz Wahba was also there. Neither of them said anything to me about the incident, but I am sure that they were making a gesture of thanks to me for my loss of memory concerning Biscoe's message.

The negotiations lasted another week, during which time most of the disputes with Iraq were settled. The fate of Ad-Dawish, however, was not resolved. The British made all kinds of bizarre attempts at a compromise. They suggested keeping Ad-Dawish in Iraq or on a ship in the Gulf, or sending him in exile to India or Ceylon where he would have no chance of causing further trouble. But the King held his ground and refused to make any concessions. He finally became so exasperated with the British attitude that he exclaimed, 'All responsibility rests on your shoulders if you do not do the right thing.' Although the British did not agree immediately to the King's demands, they eventually had no alternative. After a few days, they escorted Faisal Ad-Dawish, Ibn Lami and Naif Ibn Aba Al-Khalab to Khabary Waddaha to be handed over to the King. It is perhaps ironic that in order to save time the British brought the Ikhwan leaders to Khabary Waddaha by means of that supreme invention of the infidel, the aeroplane. Once again Ad-Dawish met his King, but this time His Majesty had no soft words for the rebel leader. 'So,' he said derisively, 'you thought you would scheme your way to safety by hiding with the British!' He harangued Ad-Dawish for several minutes, reminding him of the enormity of his crimes. We all thought that this time Ad-Dawish would be executed, but again the King was merciful. Together with his two comrades, Ad-Dawish was taken in chains and imprisoned in the fortress of Riyadh. The old man's spirit was broken and, surrounded by rowdy common criminals who would steal even his food from him, he did not survive long. Within six months he had died from heart failure, some said of a broken heart. With his passing, his soul at last found peace.

After the King had arranged for Ad-Dawish to be escorted to Riyadh, he asked Hafiz Wahba and me to go back to Kuwait to see if any of the family of Ad-Dawish wished to return to Najd. Our mission was to be accomplished much quicker than we had expected. On our way we met Ad-Dawish's only surviving son, Bandar, coming out of Kuwait with his relatives and womenfolk. They had with them all their remaining camels, including a unique herd of about two hundred jet-black camels known as the Ash-Shurf. These had been Ad-Dawish's special pride and had been reserved for ceremonial occasions. The King had no quarrel with Ad-Dawish's family; they were well treated and permitted to live in Riyadh. Bandar still lives there today. The herd of camels was given by His Majesty to his son Mohammed, who later returned them to the Ad-Dawish family.

During the conference at Khabary Waddaha, the British officials invited His Majesty to meet with King Faisal of Iraq in the Arabian Gulf as a gesture of goodwill and to cement the new friendship between the two countries. The King agreed, and the British arranged for a ship belonging to the Cable & Wireless Company to call at Ras Tanura to collect the King and accommodate him during the talks. The meeting was unusual in that it took place literally in the middle of the Gulf. King Ibn Saud came in the Cable & Wireless vessel; King Faisal in a ship called the *Nearchus;* and Lieutenant-Colonel Sir Francis Humphrys, the British Consul-General for Iraq, in a sloop named the *Lubin.* The three steamers anchored near to each other. The first meeting took place on 27 February 1930 on the Cable & Wireless ship, where the Saudis acted as hosts. As King Faisal came onto the deck of our vessel, he was saluted by Ibn Saud's personal guard. The sight of these magnificent warriors stirred in Faisal old memories of his great desert expeditions with Lawrence of Arabia and his first words were, 'I feel honoured and elated to be among such great soldiers.' With his ever-present quickness of wit, His Majesty replied, 'While our two countries are friends, these soldiers are as much yours as mine.' A lengthy and amicable meeting then followed. When it was over, Faisal invited His Majesty to meet him on the *Nearchus* the following day. The meeting was unexpectedly delayed because a sudden storm blew up, forcing all three ships to take refuge in Iraqi waters at the northern end of the Gulf. The third and final meeting took place on the *Lubin* and the two monarchs parted with mutual expressions of friendship and goodwill.

When the talks were over, Sir Francis Humphrys approached the King and asked if he would meet Glubb Pasha, who had requested permission to come aboard. His Majesty declined because Glubb had provided details of the whereabouts of the bedouin tribes on the Iraq–Najd border, and this information had enabled the RAF to organize their air raids into Saudi territory. The King felt that Glubb exerted an unhealthy influence over the Iraqis and it was also believed that he was working against the interests of the Arabs and frustrating their aspirations to gain independence from the colonial powers. When the King refused, Sir Francis said to him, 'You hear stories about people, good and bad, but unless you meet them personally you cannot form a proper opinion.' His Majesty reconsidered and Glubb Pasha was granted permission to come aboard. The two men spent some time in conversation but I do not think that they ever got beyond the stage of formal courtesies. There was certainly never any real rapport between them.

After this meeting, the ship carrying His Majesty set sail for Al-Hasa. On his way, the King decided that he would visit his old friend Sheikh Isa Ibn Ali Al Khalifa, the ruler of Bahrain (which was at that time still a British protectorate).

Sheikh Isa, it will be remembered, had given help and protection to Ibn Saud and his father during the period of their exile, and he had always been sympathetic to the young King's aspirations. His Majesty therefore gave directions for the ship to sail to the port of Manama in Bahrain. On the way, he instructed me to send two telegrams, one to Sheikh Isa himself and the other to the British Consulate informing them of his intentions. At midnight, just as we were about to anchor, a reply was received from the British Consul to the effect that Sheikh Isa was ill and not in Manama, and therefore could not receive His Majesty. The King decided reluctantly to stay on his ship and proceed to Uqair. But the message proved to be a lie. Early the following morning, the sons of Sheikh Isa heard that Ibn Saud was not proposing to land. They immediately came in several launches to his ship and implored His Majesty to come ashore as their father was waiting at the pier. They said to the King, 'Either you land and see our father or we will all go to Riyadh with you.' As they insisted, the King readily agreed to come ashore, but he said emphatically, 'I have no wish to see the British Consul in Bahrain.' His Majesty greatly resented the trick which the Consul had attempted, although he could easily understand the reason behind it. At that time there was a growing nationalist movement in Bahrain, which was causing considerable trouble for the British. In the circumstances, the Consul had obviously tried to avoid having the greatest independent Arab leader landing on his doorstep, for fear that this would stir up further nationalist demonstrations and riots.

Sheikh Isa was overjoyed at seeing the King again, for it was many years since they had last met. The Sheikh told His Majesty that he had been afraid he might die without seeing him again, but now he could die in peace. Ibn Saud replied, 'Now that my father is no longer alive, I have no one to consult but you.' The two men talked for several hours while the King told the Sheikh of his recent problems with the Ikhwan tribesmen and expressed his desire to establish a united kingdom where all might live together in peace and prosperity. His Majesty then enjoyed a light lunch with

141

Sheikh Isa and his family. Shortly afterwards the King arranged to visit the town of Ar-Rifah on the small island of Al-Muharraq, where he dined with his agent, the well-known Najdi businessman, Al-Gossaibi. When His Majesty came to leave Bahrain, Sheikh Isa's son Sheikh Hamad came to the beach of Az-Zalack, where His Majesty's boat was waiting, and bade the King farewell. Sheikh Hamad was already an old man, but – much to the disapproval of the King – he had never performed the hajj because of the prophecy of a seer that he would die if he were to do so. This was just the sort of idle superstition which any good Wahhabi would deplore, and His Majesty's parting words to Hamad were, 'I will not be pleased until I see you in Mecca.'

After a short voyage, the King landed at the port of Uqair. From there he travelled to Hufuf, where he met his old friend and cousin Abdullah Ibn Jelawi, now recovered from his illness, and Ibn Jelawi's two sons Saud and Abdul Mohsin. (Abdul Mohsin is the present Amir of the Eastern Province.) Finally the King returned to Riyadh, after an absence of nearly two months.

His Majesty did not forget the insult paid to him by the British in Bahrain, and the following year an opportunity arose for him to pay them back in kind. A request arrived from the British government, through their Ambassador in Jeddah, for permission for the Earl of Athlone and his wife Princess Alice to visit His Majesty and cross Arabia from Jeddah to Uqair. His Majesty declined, and ordered me to send a telegram in reply expressing his refusal. The telegram read, 'Regrettably conditions in the desert are not under control and there remain elements of rebel tribes that are still not subdued. At the present time it is neither appropriate nor advisable to cross the desert.' Just in case the British thought that this was the real reason for his refusal, the King asked me to add an Arab proverb which translated as, 'The instigator is to blame,' meaning of course that the British themselves were responsible for his attitude towards them. The British authorities were shaken by this telegram as the King had never dealt with them in this manner before. They now realized the depth of his anger at the Bahrain incident. The whole situation was most embarrassing for them and they hastened to put matters right. A letter was immediately written by the British to His Majesty saying that all their consular officials in the Arabian Gulf, Kuwait and Iraq would like to pay him a visit and apologize for the actions of the British Consul in Bahrain. This meeting did indeed take place, and it showed the extent to which the British government respected the King and valued friendly relations with him. After this meeting, the King's relations with the British were restored to their usual amicable state, and the Earl of Athlone and Princess Alice were given permission to enter the country.

The Earl and Countess came eventually in 1938. After crossing the peninsula, they were to visit various oil company officials at Dhahran. However, they first paid an official visit to His Majesty in Jeddah. The occasion was a memorable one; donning the Arab veil, the Countess of Athlone was the first woman ever to attend an Arabian state banquet. It was also the first time a Wahhabi king had ever dined publicly with a woman. I have always felt that the meeting symbolized the way in which the people of Europe were showing a gradually awakening interest in, and respect for, the new Arabian state. No longer was our desert land an obscure backwater, conspicuous only for its anarchy. Instead it had become almost overnight a great and united kingdom, under the leadership of an inspired monarch who was now clearly and unmistakably in complete control of all his people. The state of Saudi Arabia had now taken its final form. Ibn Saud was ready to put behind him the task of empire-building and take up his position as ruler of a world power.

9
St John Philby

إِنَّكَ لاَ تَهْدِي مَنْ أَحْبَبْتَ وَلَـكِنَّ اللهَ يَهْدِي مَنْ يَشَاءُ وَهُوَ أَعْلَمُ بِالـمُهْتَدِينَ .

سورة القصص (٥٦)

Lo! thou (O Mohammed) guidest not whom thou
lovest, but Allah guideth whom He will. And He is
best aware of those who walk aright.

(Koran, The Story 56)

No book about King Ibn Saud, particularly a book written in English, would be complete without a mention of Harry St John Philby, a strange and eccentric Englishman who became a prominent explorer, map-maker and Arabist, and was probably the only Westerner apart from Captain Shakespear to strike up a true friendship with the King. Philby was born in Ceylon in 1885. In 1908 he entered the Indian Civil Service in the Punjab, where he soon displayed a talent for languages. From 1915 to 1917 he was employed as Political Officer on the staff of Sir Percy Cox in Iraq. Then in 1917 Philby was given the opportunity of heading a British political mission to Ibn Saud. This he accepted with alacrity, first because it gave him an opportunity to get away from his colleagues – with whom he was not always on the friendliest of terms – and secondly because it allowed him to satisfy his ambition to prove himself as an explorer.

Philby's mission has been mentioned previously. Its purpose was to persuade Ibn Saud, by gifts of money and materials, to attack Ibn Rashid and thus prevent Ibn Rashid from interfering with the British campaign against the Turks in Palestine. Philby travelled by camel from Kuwait to Riyadh, accompanied by some of the servants of the Amir of Kuwait. He brought with him approximately one hundred thousand rupees. Having struck a bargain with the King, Philby should have returned at once to Iraq to inform his superiors and gain their approval of the terms of the agreement. Characteristically, he ruined everything he had achieved by making a quite unnecessary and unauthorized journey to see the Sherif of Mecca. The Sherif was glad of an opportunity to obstruct relations between Ibn Saud and the British. By politely stopping Philby from returning to Riyadh, the Sherif was able to prevent the agreement from going any further, thus preventing Ibn Saud from obtaining the arms he needed to attack Ha'il. This did not worry Philby in the least, as his mission to Ibn Saud had enabled him to fulfil his personal ambition: to undertake the forty-four-day crossing of Arabia from Uqair to Jeddah. This journey formed the basis of his first book, *The Heart of Arabia*, published in 1922. Philby's time in Arabia also convinced him that the rising star in the area was Ibn Saud, and not King Hussein of Mecca.

Philby's next visit to Arabia was in 1924. During the last stages of the conflict between the Saudis and the Hashemite dynasty, which culminated in the siege of Jeddah, Philby managed to persuade the British political bureau in Cairo to send him to Jeddah as an intermediary between the warring forces. In fact, he achieved nothing for the British except a certain amount of embarrassment, as the British government had not authorized the journey and had been trying to maintain a strict neutrality between Ibn Saud and King Ali of Hejaz. However, although Philby's mission served little purpose, he was again able to further his own personal ambitions. His visit gave him the opportunity to have several meetings with Ibn Saud, whom he had already come to admire to a point which developed gradually into a sort of hero-worship.

Soon afterwards, Philby decided to give up his work with the British government and settle in Arabia. In 1925 he resigned from the Indian Civil Service and the following year he set up business in Jeddah with, among other things, an agency to sell Ford cars. Philby's real desires were to continue his exploration of Arabia and to become an associate of the King. However, he obviously had to do something in the meantime to earn his living and, in the manner of any good Arab, he was ready to turn his hand to trading of any sort. Some of his ventures were successful, but generally speaking he was not a very good businessman, and certainly the Ford concession never prospered. At one stage in 1926 he was

148

confident that he could sell a hundred Ford cars to the Saudi government at a price of around £300 per car. In fact, the deal never materialized and Philby was left with a large number of Fords on his hands which he had to dispose of locally as best he could.

I first met Philby in Jeddah in 1926. He had heard that there was an English-speaking Arabian translator in the Court and asked to see me. Our first meeting was not a great success. Philby's questions to me were mostly aimed at ascertaining whether or not I did indeed have a good command of English. For my part, I was fresh from India and was so anti-British at the time that I can only describe myself as suffering from extreme Anglophobia. I lost no time in telling Philby how much I disliked the British and how strongly I supported the Indian nationalist movement against them. Not surprisingly, we did not part friends, although this was no doubt just as much my fault as his. Philby did in fact ask me if I wanted anything, and I replied that I would appreciate receiving any English books which he could provide. His response was to write a letter to me through the Chief of the Court, stating that he was regrettably unable to supply any of these items. Although I saw Philby regularly throughout the following nine years, I spoke to him only occasionally and I doubt if I had more than a dozen lengthy conversations with him in all that time. In this respect I probably did better than most other members of the Court, for Philby was a very reserved and taciturn man and tended to avoid company whenever he could.

In 1927, when the King and the Court were again in Hejaz for the annual pilgrimage, it became clear that Philby was finding that his status as a Christian was making it very difficult for him to submerge himself as fully as he would have liked in the activities of the country. In particular, he was of course quite unable to visit the cities of Mecca and Medina, and the other Holy Places. It was also difficult for him to travel, and during the pilgrimage he was only able to see the King in Jeddah. I was present when he had a discussion with the King on the subject. The King suggested to

Philby that if he were to become a Moslem he would be welcome to accompany the King on his journeys, including the pilgrimage to Mecca. This was obviously a most attractive proposition, but Philby nevertheless showed some reluctance, saying that although he himself might be willing, he would have to consult his wife. Later he informed the King that, although he had been ready to consider becoming an Islamic convert, he was unable to do so because his wife was not at all happy about the idea. The King suggested that he might compensate Mrs Philby for releasing her husband by paying her the sum of £40,000. Philby politely replied that he did not think that his wife would be prepared to sell him for that amount, although I do not know if he ever put the matter to the test! There is no doubt that the King meant the offer seriously, which shows that His Majesty already placed considerable value on Philby's advice and services.

Eventually, in 1930, when His Majesty again made the pilgrimage to Hejaz, it was found that the Light of Islam had finally dawned on Philby. He was now not only ready but anxious to be accepted into the Islamic brotherhood. With the King's blessing he declared himself a Moslem, taking, at His Majesty's suggestion, the name of Abdullah Philby. He was generally known afterwards as Sheikh Abdullah Philby, although the term 'Sheikh' was simply a mark of mild respect and was not any sort of title or rank. His Majesty arranged for an *ulema* to attend on Philby at the Islamic Sharia'h court. Here Philby formally declared his credence in the five cardinal doctrines of Islam, namely: to believe in Allah as the one God and Mohammed as his Prophet; to pray five times a day; to fast during the month of Ramadan; to give to the poor an annual tax of two and a half per cent on the value of all one's property; and to perform the pilgrimage to Mecca at least once in one's lifetime, and more frequently if possible. After Philby had made this declaration before a judge and two witnesses at the Sharia'h court, the judge declared him to be accepted in the Moslem religion and he was given a certificate to this effect. Then followed the most severe test of Philby's sincerity, namely, the rite of circumcision, which needless to say is a most painful operation for an adult. Afterwards he was taken to the mosque for his first prayer to God to thank him for his guidance. From there he went to Mecca to pray in the Great Mosque.

Following his initiation into the faith, Philby was taken immediately to Ta'if, a pleasant town in the cool mountain region of Western Arabia near Mecca. There he rested and recovered from the effects of the circumcision. He also received two months' instruction in the fundamentals of the Islamic faith. The King himself appointed the *ulema* who was to teach Philby the doctrines of Islam. The man to whom he gave this task was none other than Mohammed Ibn Ibrahim Ash-Sheikh, who was the foremost *ulema* in the kingdom and a direct descendant of Abdul Wahhab himself. Philby naturally took this as a great honour and the King was happy that he should do so. However, His Majesty, with his usual prudence, was concerned that if a former Christian was to become his adviser and accompany him to the Holy Places, there must be no doubt in anybody's mind that his conversion was complete and his instruction in Islamic doctrine as thorough as could be arranged. At the end of his period of tuition, Philby had to take an examination to satisfy the *ulema* that his conversion and indoctrination were complete. I do not know how he fared in this, but with his considerable powers of application and concentration I do not doubt that he passed with flying colours.

There has always been some doubt as to how genuine Philby's conversion really was. For my own part, I do not think that he had any particularly strong religious convictions. Nevertheless, I believe that he had a passionate desire to be closer to the King and the Arabian people and had decided that he was not prepared to let the matter of religion stand in his way. Philby's own explanation of his decision was that it was a logical choice. My friend Mohammed Dughaither, the telegraph operator at the Court, once asked him outright why he had become a Moslem. Philby replied that he had studied and read books about all the major religions of the world (which was probably true) and Islam stood out as being the only creed which made sense to him. Certainly one could not complain about Philby's outward show of faith, for his observation of the rules and customs of Islam was meticulous and his knowledge of religious literature most thorough.

Following his conversion to Islam, Philby took to wearing full Arab dress. He also took advantage of Moslem law by marrying a second wife, an Arabian girl who was to bear him two fine sons. He became a regular visitor to the King, both in Riyadh and Mecca, and the King naturally kept his promise to take Philby with him on many of his travels. Philby's stocky, bearded figure became a familiar sight to the Court staff and he was in regular attendance at the King's general and special *majlis*. He was accepted by the members of the Court as a friend and adviser to His Majesty, although he was never in any sense the King's servant for he came and went as he pleased. Philby probably understood the working of the King's mind better than most men. Although he would never volunteer advice or information unless asked, once his advice had been requested and given, he was one of the few men who was prepared to argue strongly in support of his opinions even if His Majesty disagreed with him. The King undoubtedly found this a refreshing change from the attitude of most of his other advisers and Philby's fierce independence impressed him. I should like to emphasize here that I do not know exactly what might have taken place between the King and Philby during their private conversations. However, working at the Court, I naturally came to hear reports of these meetings from other people who were present.

There can be no question that Philby's assistance was of great value to Ibn Saud. For example, in about 1929 Philby recommended to the King that wireless communications should be established between the different parts of the kingdom. There was nothing new in this idea. Indeed, before I joined His Majesty, I had myself published an article in the *Basra Times* in which I suggested a similar arrangement to the one proposed by Philby. However, Philby had the ability and the necessary contacts to put the scheme into practice.

Once His Majesty had accepted the idea in principle, Philby organized a contract with the Marconi Company at Chelmsford, England, for the supply of the necessary wireless sets. He also recommended that some Saudis should be sent to England to be trained in the use and maintenance of the equipment. He made the necessary arrangements for the training-course and four youths from the post office at Mecca were selected for training. Philby noted that none of them spoke English and suggested that an interpreter go with them. My brother Abdul Aziz Almana was chosen, and eventually he and three of the operators went to England. The names of the operators were Ibrahim Silsila, Ibrahim Zarea and Hassan Hassoun. After a course of nine or ten months they returned with the equipment, together with an Egyptian engineer who was qualified to install it. Six months later the network was put into operation. It proved such a great success that His Majesty soon purchased more sets, including a portable one which could accompany him on his travels.

Philby was the only Westerner upon whom the King could rely regularly for advice about conditions and attitudes in the outside world. The fact that Philby had managed to manoeuvre himself into this unique position led to a good deal of speculation in the Court about the true nature of his motives. Many people, including myself, feared that he was an agent of the British government and that his aim was to persuade the King to adopt policies which would favour the British. Work of this kind certainly runs in the family. One of Philby's sons by his English wife was Kim Philby, the famous double agent who now lives in Moscow. I recently acquired a copy of Kim Philby's book, *My Silent War*,* and I read it with keen interest in order to see whether I could detect any resemblance between St John's personality and that of his son. I found Kim to be a true replica of his father. I am sure that St John Philby would have made an ideal double agent if he had ever had the opportunity or inclination, but in fact the question never arose. In the first place,

*MacGibbon & Kee, 1968.

Ibn Saud was far too great a judge of men to have been deceived by a political agent. Secondly, I am sure in retrospect that Philby was motivated entirely by his respect and esteem for the King. His Majesty inspired loyalty and devotion in all around him and Philby, like the rest of us, had fallen under his spell. Nevertheless, although nobody questions Philby's devotion and loyalty to the King, it is clear that he was also working in the ultimate interests of his own country.

An interesting sidelight is thrown on Philby's motives when one considers his later involvement in the question of Palestine. I remember Philby having asked His Majesty in open Court in Mecca what he thought about the Jewish question. The King replied that, although the Jews had been their enemies since the time of the Prophet Mohammed, and would continue to be so, he was confident that Great Britain would hold the balance of fair play between the two sides and would not do anything which could harm the interests of the Arabs. At the outbreak of the Second World War, Philby (who was by this time in England) became more directly involved in the Palestine issue. He had come to the conclusion that there was a simple solution to the problem: Palestine should be given to the Jews, and the Arabs resettled elsewhere. The expenses of resettlement were to be borne by the Jews, who were to pay £20 million as a contribution towards these expenses. In return, the Western powers were to give a free hand to Ibn Saud in the southern states of the Arabian peninsula.

In October 1939 Philby met Chaim Weizmann, President of the World Zionist Organization and of the Jewish Agency, and mentioned the plan to him. Weizmann was about to leave for America, where he hoped to raise the proposed plan with President Roosevelt. Philby, meanwhile, was to try to obtain the agreement of Ibn Saud. Weizmann's mission achieved no concrete results, and in 1942 he made another attempt. In March of that year, just before he left for the States, he met Churchill, who referred to the plan. Churchill made it clear that the success of the plan depended upon its acceptance by Ibn Saud, as the leading Arab head of state, but that Britain and the United States were prepared to help Weizmann get the best terms he could. Again, Weizmann's mission came to nothing. Meanwhile, Philby had had no more success in Arabia. He was able to gain a private audience with the King in January 1940, but although Philby was very anxious to interest His Majesty in the plan and gain his consent to its implementation, the King was not prepared to discuss any scheme which was so utterly contrary to the interests of the Arabs. He advised Philby not to mention the subject again, and thus the mission was a complete failure.

One could speculate endlessly on the true reasons behind Philby's backing of such a project. (He later advised the Arabs to accept the partition of Palestine, although this was almost certainly because he feared a worse fate for them if they refused.) However, during my time at the Court, Philby's loyalty to the King and concern for his interests was demonstrated on many occasions. One example occurred when Philby was supervising a shipment of arms to Riyadh for His Majesty's army. Just as the caravan was about to leave, news reached him that a small tribe on the proposed route had risen in revolt. He immediately stopped the shipment until he had satisfied himself personally that the tribe had been driven off the road which the caravan would take. Another of Philby's virtues was that he never sought to gain any material advantage from his association with the King. His Majesty once said that there were only two men who had never asked him for anything; one was Abdul Rahman Subai, the King's agent at Shaqra in Najd, and the other was Philby.

I think there is a danger of overestimating the influence which Philby had over the King. His Majesty was always ready to listen to advice from anybody competent to give it. Philby was often the only source of information and advice about the Western world, so it is not surprising that the King found his assistance extremely helpful. But it is important to realize, first, that Philby never had any real power. His pos-

ition was simply that of an adviser and friend, never a deci-
sion-maker; all the decisions were taken by His Majesty. On
one occasion, while Dame Freya Stark was in Iraq, Philby
approached the King and asked him if he would invite her
to Arabia. The King replied, 'If she comes she will be welcome, but I will not invite her.' Naturally, Dame Freya did
not make the trip. Secondly, Philby's influence was limited
purely to foreign affairs. His Majesty never sought his advice
on internal problems and, indeed, hardly ever discussed such
matters with him.

Yet another of the reasons why I doubt that Philby would
ever have wished to act as a British agent is that he seldom
gave the impression of being a supporter of his own country.
He was often most critical of England, particularly when the
Conservative Party was in power. During the Second World
War, his criticism of British policy was so vitriolic that the
King became angry and ordered him away from the Court
for a while. Philby had at one time considered entering British
politics himself. In 1939 he offered himself as Labour can-
didate at Epping but was rejected. In about 1945 he moved
over to the short-lived Commonwealth Party, but soon afterwards he abandoned his interest in home politics. Once I
asked him if he belonged to any British political party and
I seem to remember him mentioning Mosley.

On an earlier occasion in about 1930, after there had been
an election in England, I met Philby in the Court at Mecca
and asked him what he thought of the new British cabinet.
'Oh,' he replied, 'they are useless.' I asked him why he
despised his own government and he said, 'Because they are
not fit to govern England.' During this conversation he went
on to tell me that there were two schools of thought in
England regarding the Arab countries. One was that of
Allenby and Lawrence. The other – to which Philby sub-
scribed – was that of Hogarth.* Philby explained that the
Allenby school favoured the Hashemite dynasty because they
were thought to be more cosmopolitan and sophisticated.

*Commander D. G. Hogarth of the Arab Bureau in Cairo.

Hogarth's school, on the other hand, favoured the Saudi dynasty, feeling that history showed the Saudis to be better fitted to rule the Arabs.

This was about the longest conversation I ever had with Philby. He must have been in a good mood that day, as generally speaking he was not an easy man to get to know and was always aloof and reserved. Indeed, his reticence in the midst of our hospitable Arabian society verged on the ridiculous. Most people kept him at arm's length and tolerated him only out of respect for the King. Philby had a most effective way of stopping a conversation before it started. For instance, on one occasion when we were returning on camel-back from Arafat after completing the hajj, I found myself riding beside him. I asked out of courtesy, 'How are you?', to which he answered, 'Oh, I am always well,' and rode away from me. On another occasion, my brother had sent me a book on astronomy called *The Mysterious Universe*. I showed Philby the book and asked him what he thought of it. He took one look at it and handed it back to me, saying, 'Don't bother with it. You certainly won't understand it.'

Philby was by nature an uncommunicative man. Even if he had tried, I do not think that he would have been capable of joining in the conversation of the bedouin in the same easy manner that Englishmen like Glubb Pasha achieved so effortlessly. I believe that there were two further reasons why he was reluctant to become involved in discussions with the Court staff. One was that he suffered from a slight speech impediment which he could obviously conceal best by speaking as little as possible. The other was that his conversational Arabic was in fact only moderate. For a man who liked to think of himself as a better Arab than the Arabs, it would have been embarrassing to have engaged regularly in conversations in which his grasp of the language would be shown to be less than perfect. However, he could be very intolerant of me if I seemed to him to be displaying an ignorance of English idiom. One day, shortly after his conversion to Islam, he strutted into the Court office at Mecca and came straight up to my desk, saying 'What's the news?' I replied, 'What news do you want?' and explained that I had news from all over the world on my desk. 'Oh,' said Philby, 'I just said "What's the news?" – it's a common English saying.' I was a little confused and asked him again which country he was interested in. 'Oh, you don't know English,' he said and went off in a huff. After this incident he tended to avoid me, for which I was never very sorry.

Philby regularly wrote articles and stories about Arabia intended for publication in the West. One of the magazines he wrote for was called *The Near East and India*. As far as I know, Philby was never asked to submit his articles to the Court before sending them off. Nevertheless, he chose to do so quite voluntarily and a number of them appeared on my desk from time to time. Presumably I was intended to censor them, although I never had explicit instructions to this effect. There was never anything in the articles which I would have wished to remove. There was nothing of particular interest or significance in them for us; they were just dry reporting of some event, or the comings and goings of the King and his Court from place to place. Only on rare occasions did Philby have anything substantial to report. The articles were all written in his characteristically dry style and all contained factual and favourable comments about the King and his country. Perhaps by presenting his writings to the Court, Philby was hoping to impress His Majesty with his loyalty. If so, the effort was wasted as His Majesty never asked me to translate any of the articles for him.

Philby's dearest ambition was to be known as a great explorer and he would disappear for long periods on various expeditions, sometimes turning up in the most unlikely places. I remember one occasion in about 1929, during the Ikhwan revolt, when I was with the King's caravan as it returned from Riyadh after a successful foray against some rebel tribes in the Eastern Region. All of a sudden, the unexpected noise of an engine was heard and Philby appeared in a Ford car and a cloud of dust. He had been commissioned by the Ford Motor Company to drive the car from the Red

Sea in the west to the Arabian Gulf in the east as a publicity stunt to demonstrate the car's reliability over rough, uncharted tracks. He had heard that the King was present in the area and had made a detour in order to meet him. Philby took the opportunity of joining our group and he drove with the King into the large oasis town of Hufuf where he stayed for a few days.

Philby was very anxious to be the first Western explorer to cross the Rub' Al-Khali from Hufuf in the east to the Arabian Sea in the south. After he had researched the project in some detail, he finally raised the matter with the King. It was essential for Philby to obtain the King's assistance as His Majesty would be able to provide him with camels for the journey and, even more important, some of his own men to act as an escort. Once it became known among the bedouin in the Empty Quarter that the expedition was accompanied by the King's men, Philby would be relatively safe from attack. If he had gone without such an escort his chances of survival would have been slim indeed. His Majesty told Philby that he had no objection to the expedition provided the Governor of the Eastern Province, Amir Abdullah Ibn Jelawi, also agreed to the project. Unfortunately for Philby, the Amir refused to give his permission, saying that a tribe in the region was in revolt and was likely to molest Philby's expedition and not allow it to pass safely. The Amir recommended the postponement of the expedition until the trouble had been settled.

Philby had little choice but to accept the situation and he again accompanied the King and his Court on the annual pilgrimage to Hejaz. On our arrival at Mecca we were greeted by the news that Bertram Thomas had crossed the Empty Quarter from Salalah, a coastal town in Oman on the Arabian Sea, to Qatar in the Arabian Gulf, and had travelled from there to Bahrain. Bertram Thomas had not obtained the King's blessing for this venture, as he had no connection with the King whatsoever. However, he had the assistance of the Sultan of Oman, to whom he was a financial adviser, and this may have been one reason why his expedition was

successful. Thomas had also taken the precaution of including in his expedition one member of each of the tribes he
was likely to encounter on his way, thus taking advantage of
the bedouin custom that a tribe would not attack a caravan
if a member of that tribe was accompanying it to guarantee
its safety.

I was with Philby when he first heard of Thomas's achievement and it was obvious that he was bitterly disappointed at
the news. However, he was not a man given to displays of
emotion and he bore the set-back manfully. He immediately
wrote a telegram to Thomas, who was by now back in
England receiving a hero's welcome. Philby asked me to send
the telegram; it congratulated Thomas on his great achievement and on winning the 'race against time' with Philby
himself. Philby paid Thomas the compliment of quoting to
him an Arabian proverb which says, 'He is not mistaken
who gives the bow to its master,' meaning that Thomas had
well deserved the opportunity given him to attempt the
crossing.

Philby immediately put in hand his own preparations to
cross the Rub' Al-Khali the following year. Thomas had
crossed from south to north; Philby would therefore cross it
in the opposite direction. He was given the King's blessing
and the following winter, at the time of the religious fast in
the month of Ramadan, he was ready to set off. He started
from the north, in the vicinity of Hufuf, with about twenty-
five followers and some Najdi servants who had been hand-
picked by him in Riyadh. In one of our few lengthy conversations, Philby later told me about the expedition. He said
it had taken him about the whole month of Ramadan. As a
traveller, Philby was not obliged to observe the religious fast.
Nevertheless, he chose to do so and ate and drank nothing
between sunrise and sunset. This was confirmed to me by his
personal servants and was no mean achievement for a for-
eigner in the desert. Knowing Philby, I suspect that the hard-
ships of the fast were mitigated by the pleasure of being able
to show his followers that he was a better Arab than they
were. Philby told me that he drank no water at all during

the expedition, only camel's milk, tea without sugar and Arab coffee. This, too, was not strictly necessary as there were tiny springs in the desert which were used by the bedouin. The tribesmen kept these springs secret by placing slabs of stone over them and covering the stones with sand as camouflage. The location of some of these springs was known to Philby's men and the expedition was never seriously short of water. Philby at least had the advantage of a slightly more varied diet than was usual in the desert, as he had taken with him a plentiful supply of biscuits and canned food.

Philby travelled deep into the south until he reached the remains of the ancient town of Wabbra, which had also been passed by Thomas when travelling in the opposite direction. Philby noted two extinct volcanoes there, and also examined a block of iron lying in the sand which was well known to the bedouin and was reputed to have been as large as a camel. In fact, it was only about twenty-four inches long by twelve wide, and was probably a small meteorite. The story of the camel-sized ingot was refuted by Thomas and Philby but both men verified the legend of the singing sands which is also mentioned in the Koran. From Wabbra, Philby did not continue his journey south to the shores of the Arabian Sea and safety. Instead, he struck south-west to the outskirts of As-Saffa and then went north to a point adjacent to Najran. He next returned south-east to the point from where he had started near Wabbra, having then travelled in an almost perfect triangle in the middle of the Rub' Al-Khali. Such an erratic route was typical of the behaviour of this unusual and wilful man. During the time that Philby was in the middle triangle of the Empty Quarter, he searched for the remains of the ancient cities which were reputed to have existed in the region. He reported that in this area he found no trace of animal or plant life whatsoever. Philby finally ended his journey in Najran province and then travelled to Hejaz via Ta'if, expecting to find the King there. However, His Majesty had not yet arrived, so Philby immediately set off in the direction of Najd, finally meeting the King half-way.

During his travels in the Rub' Al-Khali Philby carefully collected, bottled and preserved examples of plant and insect life; he also collected geological specimens. This was his usual practice during all his expeditions and he took justifiable pride in being able to present large and varied collections of specimens to museums in England and to the Royal Geographical Society in London. Probably the most lasting contribution which Philby made to the development of Arabia was his map-making. On all his travels he took the opportunity of making detailed maps. These proved most reliable and form the basis of many present-day maps of the country. Oil prospectors found Philby's assistance invaluable. When I was working for Aramco after leaving the King's service, Philby was a frequent visitor and used to give lectures to the company staff on the geography and culture of Saudi Arabia.

While Philby was undoubtedly a great cartographer, one aspect of his mapping activities revealed his very limited sense of humour. He was most anxious to show on his maps the correct Arab name of every geographical feature. It did not take him long to find out that almost every recognizable lump or dimple in the landscape, however small, had a name given to it by the local bedouin. In consequence, whenever he was on a mapping expedition he would be asking his bedouin guides incessantly for the name of everything he saw. Not surprisingly, towards the end of a long day the bedouin would become more than a little bored and irritated with this constant barrage of questions, and would often try to enliven the proceedings by inventing names of their own. Philby never seemed to realize that his leg was being pulled. Indeed, he commented in one of his books, 'The vagaries of Arabian nomenclature in the mouths of different guides are the bane of the Arabian explorer.' Although the invented names were frequently bawdy, and often positively obscene, he faithfully wrote them all down and had them printed on his maps. The embarrassing positions in which this sometimes put future users of the maps can easily be imagined. I remember that the King was once given a copy of Philby's map of the Dahna, which His Majesty personally knew very well. The map showed Arab names for all the local features, but as the names were written in English script the King asked me to read them out to him. I did so, and found that one of the ridges of the Dahna was shown as 'the ridge of the buttocks'. (This was one of the milder examples of bedouin wit appearing on the map.) I hesitated when I came to this name, but the King ordered me to read it out and so I was obliged to do so. His Majesty then became very angry with me and I had to point out that I was only reading what had been written. The King immediately realized what had happened and burst out laughing.

In this chapter I have not sought to disguise the fact that Philby was not a man whom I personally liked. I was not alone in this for, as I have already implied, his reserved and abrupt manner earned him few friends amongst the Arabs. However, I shared with everyone who met him a great respect for his obvious courage and ability. As a historian and geographer he had the unique advantage of the patronage of the King, and he was the only Arabist at the time who could truly claim to have made all his observations at first hand. During his lifetime he was well known in his own country. This is well illustrated by the fact that on his death in 1960 he merited a two-column obituary in *The Times*. Although he was in fact buried in Lebanon where he died, it was his last wish that he should be buried in Riyadh in an unmarked grave in the manner of a true Moslem.

10

The King's Court

وَالَّذِينَ آمَنُوا وَعَمِلُوا الصَّالِحاتِ لَنُبَوِّئَنَّهُم مِنَ الجَنَّةِ غُرَفاً تَجْرِي مِنْ تَحْتِها الأَنْهَارُ
خَالِدِينَ فِيها نِعْمَ أَجْرُ العَامِلِينَ . الَّذِينَ صَبَرُوا وَعَلَى رَبِّهِمْ يَتَوَكَّلُونَ .

سورة العنكبوت (٥٨ - ٥٩)

Those who believe and do good works, them verily
We shall house in lofty dwellings of the Garden
underneath which rivers flow. There they will dwell
secure. How sweet the guerdon of the toilers,
Who persevere, and put their trust in their Lord!

(Koran, The Spider 58/59)

In May 1926 I arrived in Jeddah to commence my service with His Majesty. It was perhaps as well for me that the King was in Hejaz when I went to join his Court, for life there, although by no means easy, was not nearly as severe as in Najd. I thus had time to adjust from the comparatively soft life which I had led in Bombay and Basra to the spartan conditions of Arabia.

After I had been in Jeddah about a day, cars arrived to collect me and some others who wished to see His Majesty. We were taken to Mecca and I was accommodated at a guest house which belonged to the King. I arrived in the morning and was asked to wait until the afternoon. Following the afternoon prayer, I was taken to see the King by the Foreign Minister's Second Secretary, Fuad Hamza, a man who was himself fluent in English. By this time Abdul Aziz Ibn Saud was already a legend in his own lifetime and I shall never forget my first meeting with him. I was immediately impressed, not only by his physical size but also by the aura which he carried about him of great power, intelligence and wisdom. His Majesty courteously asked me a few questions about myself and my family and then requested the Second Secretary to ask me some questions in English. After a few such questions, the Second Secretary informed the King that my English appeared to be satisfactory and His Majesty immediately invited me to join his Foreign Court. As a civil service examination this may appear perfunctory, but I left the room with the feeling that my abilities had been very thoroughly weighed up by the King. Indeed I am sure that this was so, for after I had been with the King for a while, I learnt that one of his many skills was the ability to assess people rapidly and accurately. After the King had confirmed my appointment we rose and went together to the mosque, where we prayed side by side, a moment I shall always remember as one of the most moving of my life.

During my first few days in Mecca I lived in the guest house where I had spent my first night. The Chief of the Court, Ibrahim Ibn Muammar, showed me great hospitality and invited me to his house on several occasions. As soon as it could be arranged, I was given a rented house in the town. The house was situated conveniently near the palace, and my work at the Court started immediately. My desk was in the hall of the Court and there I worked from dawn until noon, when we had a lengthy break for prayers and lunch. We lunched in His Majesty's dining hall, where the King himself frequently joined us. In mid afternoon we would return to our desks and work until dinner time, which was after sunset. After dinner there would be a short break and we would then return to work until midnight. It was a long working day, about fourteen hours on average, but we enjoyed the work and it was not strenuous. We worked every day of the week and it was not customary to take time off except for religious holidays, during which we often worked anyway.

When His Majesty first came to Mecca he appointed his son Faisal as Viceroy of Hejaz. In keeping with the importance and prestige of the post, the King gave Faisal for his own use the palatial government house of the Sherifs. For his own Court, the King appropriated a substantial private house previously owned by a prominent official in the Sherif's government by the name of As-Saggaf. The family of As-Saggaf had accumulated substantial wealth from their services as contractors for the British government in Singapore. Much of this money had been spent in the erection of fine buildings in Mecca and Jeddah. The King commandeered several of these buildings for his own use, although he paid the As-Saggafs ample compensation, and thus characteristically ensured that they lost nothing by his action.

While in Hejaz, His Majesty moved between Mecca, Jeddah and the pleasant mountain city of Ta'if. During the first few years after he became ruler of Hejaz, he had no fixed residence in Jeddah and often stayed in the comfortable four-storey mansion of Sheikh Mohammed Nassif. Sheik Mohammed, who was to become a valued adviser and friend of the King, was an *ulema* and one of the most prominent citizens of Jeddah. He was also an intellectual and the proud owner of an excellent Arabic library. Before Hejaz fell, he had been instrumental in persuading Sherif Hussein to abdicate in favour of his son Ali. Later he had helped to persuade Ali to flee from the besieged city of Jeddah and surrender it to Ibn Saud. Whenever the King came to stay at his house, Sheikh Mohammed would retire with his family and servants to the top floor of the house and make the first three floors available for His Majesty's exclusive use. Despite the many changes which have taken place in Jeddah, the house and its library are still in existence today.

When not staying with Sheikh Mohammed, His Majesty often occupied the old Turkish garrison building at Jeddah, which also still stands today. Another dwelling where he frequently stayed in later years was a luxurious one-storey house known as Al-Kandara. It was yet another of the prestige buildings erected by the family of As-Saggaf, and was on the site of what is now the Al-Kandara Continental Hotel. Only in the mid-1930s was a purpose-built palace erected for the King in Jeddah and this was constructed, not by His Majesty himself, but by a wealthy Najdi merchant of the city who presented it to the King as a splendid gift. It became known as the 'green palace' because of the greenish hue of the concrete from which it was made. His Majesty was fond of Jeddah. I can remember once or twice seeing him in a moment of rare seclusion and peace, sitting in the hall of one or other of his residences there, serenely contemplating the ever-changing colours of the Red Sea in the glowing sun of late afternoon.

In Ta'if His Majesty appropriated a grand mansion called Shubra which had belonged to Sherif Abdullah Pasha. The house was a copy of a similar building in Egypt which had taken Abdullah's fancy. Abdullah was reputed to have had the thousands of tons of marble and materials needed for its construction dragged piece by piece from Egypt, in order to make sure that his Shubra was an exact replica of the original.

Such were the residences of His Majesty in Hejaz. In my first year I had little time to appreciate them, for after I had been with the King in Hejaz for about a month, he returned with his Court to Riyadh. The contrast was complete and abrupt. Pilgrims from every corner of the globe flooded into Mecca, bringing with them foreign ideas and foreign money and all the latest technology and inventions. In consequence, it was the most cosmopolitan and sophisticated city in the King's domain, and undoubtedly the most worldly. Riyadh was isolated in the middle of the desert and at that time was almost never visited by foreigners. It had little contact with the outside world and possessed none of its amenities. It was a smaller, simpler and much harder place to live in than Mecca, and for this reason was perhaps a more suitable capital for a puritan Wahhabi King. Here there were none of the vices which flourish in the wake of affluence, and the King's pure religious zeal was matched by the spartan faith of his people. I recall being invited after Ramadan to a feast in one of the better houses in Riyadh. When I entered the reception hall I saw that the floor was coated with small white pebbles on which was laid a mat made of reeds. At one end of the hall was a water-bag of goatskin from which one could drink. I remember thinking that this was surely very much the same as things must have been in the time of the Prophet himself.

The King's palace was by far the greatest building in Riyadh and was about eight hundred foot square. Like the simplest dwellings in the town, it was of adobe construction, built of dried layers of mud. Although the palace has long been demolished, one can see to this day the old fortress of Riyadh; it has been carefully preserved and is similar to the old palace in general design and appearance. The palace had two storeys throughout and four wings radiating north, south, east and west from the centre. Each wing was a warren of large rooms, halls, staircases and courtyards. The north wing was the largest; on its ground floor were vast store-rooms piled high with supplies of all kinds, particularly rice and dates, the provisions for the King and his bedouin army. At one end of the wing was a huge kitchen, which catered for the crowds of visiting bedouin as well as for the needs of the palace. It contained cooking-pots eight and ten feet high, each of which was able to hold the meat of a whole camel. Every day the cooks would prepare traditional meals of boiled rice and meat for at least a hundred bedouin guests, who would eat it on the large terrace set aside for that purpose on the first floor just above the kitchen.

The south and east wings of the palace contained offices and accommodation for the Court of Internal Affairs, the army administration and the fifty or sixty Negroes who acted as servants and bodyguards in the palace. Both inside and outside the palace were set many benches made of the same adobe material as the walls. Throughout the day, these benches were always thronged with visiting tribesmen and others who had business with His Majesty or the Court. All the business of the Court was transacted on the first floor of the north wing. Here were the King's courtroom, his general and private *majlis*, a room for his political committee and smaller offices where the Court staff worked. One such office was allocated for my use. A corridor led to the palace mosque in the west wing, above which was a hall where the King could pray privately. Also in the west wing were the King's own personal rooms and the accommodation for the women of his household, most of whom were African girls. The Africans were engaged in the menial duties of the palace and some were married to male servants. Their duties included laundering and bearing the incense urns for His Majesty's clothing. Some of the girls were responsible for the many varied sets of apparel worn by the King at different times. His Majesty liked to change his clothing several times a day, whenever the pressure of state business relented sufficiently to allow him to do so. He usually wore a brown robe in the morning, a grey one in the afternoon and a black one at night. On Friday, which is the Moslem Holy Day, he would wear white.

The most distinctive feature of the palace was its four square towers. The purpose of these was only partly defensive. Each housed one of the King's wives, four being the maximum number permitted under Islamic law. In practice, only three of the towers were occupied at any one time. The fourth was kept vacant in case the King should desire to marry again. Whenever he did so, he always divorced one of his other wives in order to restore the number to three. It is a dictate of the Koran that a man should treat all his wives with equal favour, and His Majesty always spent a night with each of his wives in turn.

When I first came to Riyadh, the palace had much the same primitive facilities as it would have possessed two or three hundred years before. There was no running water or sophisticated drainage, and there was no electricity anywhere in Riyadh. One of the few luxuries which existed in the palace nearly caused His Majesty's death where all his enemies had failed. In the King's personal rooms was a bath-chamber which contained a huge samovar of water heated by charcoal. One day, the charcoal smoke failed to escape properly from the chamber and His Majesty was overcome by the fumes. He would very rapidly have died, had it not been for a quick-thinking servant girl who was alerted by the suspicious absence of sound coming from the chamber and immediately raised the alarm.

Gradually some modern amenities began trickling into Riyadh from Hejaz, despite the opposition of the Ikhwan. In 1926, when His Majesty took over Hejaz, electric power even there had been the exception rather than the rule. Small generating stations had been donated by wealthy pilgrims from India and the Far East and these were used for the lighting of the Holy Places and some of the more prominent buildings. There was a chronic lack of spare parts and skilled engineers to maintain the generators, and such electricity supplies as existed were erratic and unreliable. Eventually in about 1928 a Moslem philanthropist from Burma had the foresight to supply, not only some new generators, but also an Indian mechanic by the name of Mohammed Rafik to operate and maintain them. Rafik was a very competent engineer and under his supervision the generators operated most efficiently. His performance impressed His Majesty, who decided the time had come for Riyadh to have similar facilities. While he was in Hejaz in 1930, he commissioned Rafik to procure new generators and equipment and transport them to Riyadh in order to light the royal palace. Three machines were immediately purchased and sent in trucks to Riyadh, which they miraculously reached more or less intact. Rafik and some assistants followed them shortly afterwards. By the time His Majesty returned to Riyadh, the palace was in a turmoil. Rafik and his men scuttled round like demented spiders, spinning a web of cables and wires all over the Court offices, the harem, the audience halls and various other chambers. Rafik spoke no Arabic, and since I spoke fluent Urdu, I was often required to translate for him in the embarrassing situations which arose as he strung his cables around the private rooms of the palace.

A spacious room had been cleared on the ground floor and given to Rafik for his generators. Finally came the great day when the electricity was due to be switched on. Everybody was waiting eagerly for the big moment but unaccountably nothing seemed to be happening. As darkness fell, I was called by one of the King's servants and told that I was wanted by His Majesty in Rafik's engine-room. I went there immediately and found poor Rafik labouring over his machines, with the majestic figure of the King towering over him, impatiently waiting for the power to be connected. Rafik tried several times to start the engines but each time there was only a tiny flicker of light before the motors spluttered to a halt and darkness returned. My work consisted of translating His Majesty's increasingly terse orders to Rafik to get his engines going, and Rafik's ever more desperate assurances that all would be well in a few moments.

The unfortunate Rafik was never able to start his motors. He left Riyadh as soon as he could, with his tail between his legs, on the rather feeble excuse that he had to return to Jeddah for some spare parts. The rest of the year passed and Rafik was conspicuous by his absence. We then heard that he had managed to persuade Suleiman, the Finance Minister, to allow him to go to Egypt to purchase an expensive new machine. Rafik and his costly equipment eventually arrived in Riyadh in 1931. He was fortunately able to install the generator and get it working without further trouble, and the palace was at last graced by the splendour of electric light. Visiting bedouin who had never seen such marvels before would often ask the King what this electricity was and how it worked. 'Oh, it is nothing,' His Majesty would say dismissively, 'just a machine and some pieces of wire.'

The organization of the Court was devised by the King himself and it worked very smoothly. There were two Courts, Foreign and Domestic, the functions of which were different and separate. There was also a separate, fully-fledged Foreign Ministry. The Foreign Court consisted of the Chief of the Court, the Chief Translator (which was my position), an officer in charge of writing letters, and one or two typists. Even at the time of the King's death in 1953 the Foreign Court was no larger. In the Domestic Court there was one chief and five or six clerks. They divided their work between dealing with the townspeople of Central Arabia and the bedouin tribes. There were also a few minor clerks, and an officer who was responsible for examining petitions sent to the King and pruning any of excessive length. Whatever defects we may have had as a civil service, an excess of bureaucracy was not one of them.

When I first joined the King's service, none of the Court staff received a regular salary. We were paid in the same way as the King's bedouin militia, namely, by periodical gifts of money and clothing. At the end of each year we could expect to receive an extra gift of a lump sum of money. In addition, the families of the Court staff, as well as the staff themselves, could rely upon being clothed at the King's expense. (This system did not apply to the civil service in Hejaz, who received regular salaries, as established during the time of

174

the Sherif and the Turkish regime.) While the King's gifts were always generous, such a method of remuneration made budgeting for expenses something of a fine art. One day, together with others in the Court, I tentatively approached His Majesty and asked him to pay us a regular salary instead. He readily agreed to give a salary to all those who wished to be paid in this way and so the matter was resolved to everybody's satisfaction.

On my arrival in Riyadh, I found that I was to live in a large room in the palace with other members of the staff. This proved uncomfortable even by the standards of Riyadh. I mentioned the matter to the King, who immediately arranged to rent houses for us in the town. Those who were married had a house to themselves and bachelors lived two or three to a dwelling. It was not long before I had cause to regret moving out of the palace. One night I left the palace with the rest of the Court staff to go home. Unknown to us, the King had decided that certain correspondence should be finished that day as a matter of urgency and had told one of his servants to give us this message. For some reason, the servant failed to deliver these instructions before we left and a boy had to be sent out to search for us. He found us only after we had gone some way from the palace. The Chief of the Court was with us and he decided that we had no alternative but to return. This was not as easy as it sounds. The King still had many enemies and there was a constant threat of treachery and assassination. Members of the family of Rashid were in the town and, although ostensibly loyal to the King, remained a likely source of rebellion. His Majesty did not intend to suffer the same fate as that he had inflicted upon Governor Ajlan. The palace was always heavily guarded at night by the King's Negro soldiers, who were not well disposed towards unexpected visitors. We returned very cautiously to the side gate of the palace, which was our usual entrance, but we were prevented from going in by a burly black slave belonging to one of the King's sons. The large scimitar which he was waving discouraged any argument with him, so we all went instead to the main gate. Here we had a long dispute with the gatekeeper, who also refused to let us in. All this time the King was with one of his wives in a tower opposite the gate. On hearing the commotion, he looked through a slit in the tower and saw a number of people milling around the entrance to the palace. Concluding, reasonably enough, that some sort of conspiracy was afoot and that his enemies were trying to break in, His Majesty grabbed his rifle and took aim at us. Had he opened fire, he could certainly have shot several of us with ease, for he had an excellent rifle and was a first-class marksman. Fortunately for us, just as the King was about to squeeze the trigger, he heard the sound of our nailed boots on the stony ground. Realizing that conspirators would hardly be likely to make so much noise, he dispatched a servant to find out what was going on. When he was told what had happened, he immediately sent word that we should leave the correspondence until the morning. The next day he told us with glee that he had very nearly shot us all and this remained a favourite story of his for years afterwards.

A typical working day at the palace would start for the King at about 8 a.m., when the Chief Chamberlain, Ibrahim Ibn Juma'a, would announce to him the names of the people who had come to see him that day with petitions or particular matters they wished to raise with him. Everybody who wished to see the King had first to arrange it with the Chamberlain, although in practice His Majesty saw almost everybody who wished to speak with him. The King would first hold a small private *majlis* for those whose business was of some importance. Visitors were introduced to him one by one in order of their priority and prominence. After the most important callers had been dealt with and the visitors had begun to thin out, His Majesty would start to deal with the day's correspondence. It was quite common to see him talking to a bedouin chief and dictating two different letters at the same time. After this the King held his general *majlis*. Anybody could attend and there were usually between eighty and one hundred and thirty people present. His Majesty would first recite a verse from the Koran and present an interpretation of it. He would then choose some topic of national importance and speak about it for a time to the assembled company. Finally he would invite questions, whereupon the visitors were free to ask him about anything they liked. The proceedings were rather like a modern press conference, except that they were far less impersonal. The King had a remarkable ability to grasp instantly the important points of any question which was asked of him and was always able to give an immediate and full reply in a few well-chosen sentences. In this way, each man could leave satisfied that he had received the King's personal attention. The general *majlis* seldom lasted more than forty minutes but an astonishing amount of work was always done in the time.

After each general *majlis* the Chamberlain would bring the King a list of people who had been present and His Majesty wrote against each name whatever gift he thought the man should receive. Nobody who attended the *majlis* ever went away empty-handed. Indeed, the quantity of goods given away was so great that the distribution of them had to be organized from a central warehouse in the middle of Riyadh. There was often more to these gifts than simple generosity. By tradition, all the bedouin who fought for the King came to the general *majlis* once a year. If they needed accommodation overnight, it was provided free of charge. The gifts they received were, in effect, a retainer for their services. The average gift for a bedouin tribesman would be three gold pounds, a robe and a cloak. If he was a minor chief, he would receive six gold pounds and a robe of finer quality. All the bedouin could rely upon leaving the Court with sacks of rice, baskets of dates and small bags of tea, sugar and coffee. Anybody who had performed a particular service for the King or distinguished himself in battle could expect to receive further gifts as a token of His Majesty's gratitude. These gifts to the tribesmen made up a significant proportion of their annual income and for this reason were obviously a major factor in guaranteeing the loyalty of the royal army.

It is worth noting here that when the formidable army of

Ibn Saud went into battle, or indeed on any desert expedition, the provisions were usually provided by individual soldiers themselves. This was true even of those members of the army who were closest to the King. The King only carried extra provisions as a precaution in case of exceptional need. This was because, in addition to his gifts at the general *majlis*, the King supplied his bedouin troops regularly throughout the year with items such as dates, rice and flour (small quantities of which were used to bake bread in the hot sand). When necessary, the King could therefore gather a strong force almost immediately, at no extra cost to himself.

A few bedouin were tempted to return to the Court a second time during the year to receive another helping of the King's bounty. Pride and prudence usually deterred a third visit. Although the King was aware of this, he never allowed anyone to leave without a gift. He was by nature the most generous of men, even to the undeserving, and it would have affronted his sense of honour if anybody who visited his palace had left empty-handed. Although this arrangement might sound like a free meal-ticket for everybody in the kingdom, there was a clear unwritten understanding among the King's subjects that a man did not go to the palace unless he had particular business with the King, or the visit was a traditional right such as the annual visit of the bedouin. The townspeople of Riyadh, for instance, never came to the palace unless they had a special reason to do so.

The traffic in largess was not all one way. Visiting bedouin brought the King gifts of all kinds, depending upon their rank and wealth. The King received many horses, camels and cows in this way; and sometimes falcons or hawks, for his love of hunting was well known. Often the donations were more modest. I remember that one day a poor bedouin walked into the *majlis* carrying a club. He raised it above his head and cried out, 'O Protected, I have only this to offer!' His Majesty called him forward and with a few apt words praised his gift and graciously accepted it. Parcels occasionally arrived from foreign friends and admirers of the King or those seeking to find favour with him. Once a large consign-

ment of petrol arrived unexpectedly in Jeddah sent by the
government of Soviet Russia. The Russians had only a commercial Consul in Jeddah left over from the Sherif's time
and, somewhat naively, they hoped to persuade the King to
establish diplomatic relations with them. His Majesty was
happy to accept the petrol, but refused to have anything
whatever to do with the Soviet government. Other gifts were
more personal, such as a little package received from a German doctor who must have been seriously misinformed
about His Majesty's medical requirements. When
unwrapped, the package revealed a small tin of aphrodisiac
tablets!

By the time His Majesty had finished his general *majlis*,
the morning was usually over. He would take his midday
meal and sometimes retire to the harem (the women's quarters) for a while. After the midday prayers he would attend
the daily meeting of his political committee. The only func-
tion of this committee was to advise the King; it had no
executive power. Some of the members of the committee
were powerful and important men in their own right, and I
shall have more to say about them in a later chapter. As an
interpreter, it was often necessary for me to be present at the
meetings. I could thus observe at first hand the way in which
the committee worked. The King would raise a subject upon
which he wished to have advice. A general discussion then
followed, in which every member of the committee was quite
free to give his true opinion and make any suggestion he
wished. The King would end the discussion when he thought
that enough had been said and he would then make up his
own mind about what to do. No member of the committee
would ever have considered suggesting a topic for discussion
on his own initiative; this was entirely the prerogative of the
King.

After the audience with his advisers was over, the King,
accompanied by a few members of his retinue, would go for
a short car ride around the outskirts of the city until sun-
down. His Majesty loved driving, and it had the advantage
that he was able to show himself daily to his people. Some-

times he would travel for a short distance into the desert, where he would say his evening prayers before returning to the palace for dinner. One of his favourite places in the desert was a low hill, some distance outside Riyadh, which had a striking feature at its crest in the form of a huge natural archway formed in the rock. We called this 'the hill with the hole'. With the growth of Riyadh in recent years, the hill has now been absorbed into the outskirts of the city and is surrounded by roads and buildings. Because of its importance to His Majesty, it has been carefully preserved and made into a national monument.

An hour and a half after sunset the King prayed again. Afterwards he held another *majlis*, this time an informal one, which was an open house for all the dignitaries and high officials in the city and for any prominent visitors. The first half-hour of the *majlis* was taken up with the reading, usually by the King's *ulema*, Sheikh Abdul Rahman Al-Guwaize, of religious history or traditional stories about the Prophet Mohammed. The floor was then open for anybody who wished to raise a topic for general comment or discussion. The mood of this meeting was always more relaxed and light-hearted than at the business *majlis* in the morning. After the reading by the *ulema*, it was the custom for a large bowl of camel's milk to be brought to the King. He would drink from the bowl and then pass it to his guests, who would each drink from it in turn. As the night wore on, the guests departed one by one, and His Majesty finally left the *majlis* himself and made a tour of the Court. He usually ended up in the political section, where his advisers would often be waiting to discuss some matter of importance. Finally, before he retired to his harem, he would pay a last visit to the Court offices, where we were of course still working, to see if anything there required his personal attention. Even after a long day he was always ready to listen patiently to any of our problems, however small, and to offer a few words of advice. We had our fair share of peculiar correspondence which required his personal attention. Foreigners used to write to the King requesting his personal guidance in religious matters, and I can remember translating a letter from an American in Chicago who said he knew nothing about Islam and wanted the King to explain it to him. On His Majesty's advice, we wrote back suggesting that the American buy a translation of the Koran. There were any number of people with dubious commercial propositions who wanted the King's patronage. Many of these concerned the animals which were sacrificed during religious ceremonies which took place in Hejaz during the hajj. One man wanted to buy the meat of the beasts, another the bones, another the skin, and so on. Such requests were always refused, for His Majesty had no desire to turn the hajj into a commercial bazaar. There was no shortage of suggestions from people wishing to improve the communications in the kingdom. One of the more bizarre proposals came from a gentleman who wanted to buy up an entire narrow-gauge railway in India, including the track, and ship it to Hejaz to run between Jeddah and Mecca. These are only a few examples of the sort of problem we might discuss with the King late into the night.

The routine of the King's Court continued in much the same way whether His Majesty was in Mecca or Riyadh. Being in the King's service was by no means a sedentary occupation, for it was a unique feature of the Court that almost the whole Court staff followed His Majesty wherever he went. Not only did we accompany the King on his annual pilgrimage to Mecca and back, but also on all his military and political expeditions. It was somewhat reminiscent of the medieval kings of Europe, whose courts accompanied them on all their journeys. When the King travelled, he would take with him most of the staff in the Domestic and Foreign Courts, numbering in total about twelve clerks and six servants. We would take with us not just the usual supplies and weapons but also all the Court records, files and correspondence. They were stored in huge wooden chests and were carried first on camel-back but later by car over countless thousands of miles of desert, following the King's caravan wherever it went. Inevitably, each year the mass of paperwork became more and more unmanageable. Eventually it became just too great to handle. Subsequently, essential files only were carried with us and the remainder kept in store in Riyadh.

From the Chamberlain's section of the Court would come three Chamberlains and three servants. Three of the King's personal servants would also travel with him to take care of his clothing and personal requirements. Two or three cooks would accompany the King and they would usually have some soldiers to assist them. His Majesty also took his personal bodyguard, numbering fifty or sixty men, made up of members of the families of Riyadh who were noted for their long-standing loyalty. There would, in addition, be an armed group of thirty or forty of His Majesty's trusted black guards. Other soldiers came as well, and in total the King's personal entourage would include about two hundred armed men. On his military expeditions His Majesty took no women with him, but on the annual pilgrimage to Mecca he would take some of his wives and daughters and their servants. By the time I joined the King in 1926, he was beginning to use cars extensively. There would be fifteen or twenty cars carrying the King and the members of the Court and a few of the bodyguard. The rest of the party would follow on camels. His Majesty had a magnificent, custom-built Mercedes saloon for his own use. The other cars were a motley assortment of Fords, Chevrolets, Buicks and Hudsons. When I joined His Majesty there were two Fords allocated to the Foreign Staff. The Chief of the Court and two clerks travelled in one, and I travelled with three colleagues and a driver in the other. Every year the number of cars increased until by 1935, when I left the King's service, the camels had all been retired and the royal caravan consisted of over two hundred and fifty cars crossing the open desert together. There was no road between Riyadh and Mecca, or indeed anywhere else in the kingdom, and travelling was done with the assistance of local guides who knew the best routes through their part of the desert. Cars broke down frequently in these arduous conditions, and we took with us some ten or fifteen

Indian and Indonesian driver-mechanics who became expert at doing makeshift repairs.

Inevitably there were the occasional accidents. I remember one such incident when we were returning from Hufuf in Al-Hasa. The car in which I was travelling was crossing a series of undulating dunes. As we reached the top of one of the dunes we realized to our horror that, instead of a gentle gradient on the other side of the crest, there was a sheer drop instead. The car slithered over the edge and plummeted downwards. Luckily for us, it landed on a slope of soft sand and nobody was seriously hurt. But it was the end of the road for the car, which for all I know is still there today. It is about five hundred miles from Riyadh to Mecca. When I first joined the King the journey took about five or six days; later on, when everyone was in cars, it became about four days. In 1926 I remember that the womenfolk accompanying the party, usually about fifteen in all, travelled in a large lorry. It may sound uncomfortable but it was a considerable improvement on travelling by camel. By 1935 each of the women had a car to herself.

When we stopped in the desert for the night, a large tent was erected for the use of the King so that he could entertain those of his family and advisers who were travelling with him. There was a small tent nearby for his personal servants which was also used as a kitchen and food store. Everybody else slept on the ground in the open, in the manner of the bedouin. The cooks in the party catered for the King's needs. Everyone else carried his own food, which was supplemented by sheep and other supplies which we bought from local tribes along our route. At night the desert would twinkle with camp-fires in the best romantic, Hollywood tradition. Less romantic were the biting desert insects, which made life extremely uncomfortable for those not accustomed to sleeping in the open.

It is remarkable to think that our travelling Court, comprising barely thirty men, was only fifty years ago responsible for the central administration of the whole of Saudi Arabia. It is true that there were small subsidiary Courts to assist in

Hejaz. Nevertheless, the administrative machinery of our great country was tiny. That it was so successful is a tribute to the patience and skill of His Majesty King Ibn Saud.

11

Personalities

وَاحْلُلْ عُقْدَةً مِنْ لِسَانِي . يَفْقَهُوا قَوْلِي . واجْعَلْ لِي وَزِيراً مِنْ أَهْلِي ...

سورة طه (٢٧ - ٢٨ - ٢٩)

And loose a knot from my tongue,
That they may understand my saying.
Appoint for me an advocate from my folk . . .

(Koran, Tâ Hâ 27/28/29)

My days in the Court of Ibn Saud were the happiest of my life. I had the privilege and great good fortune to be able to serve my country at a time when it was rapidly emerging from centuries of obscurity and neglect to take its place among the great nations of the world. All my colleagues in the Court shared this sense of excitement in playing a part, however small, in the vital administration of the kingdom during a historic period of growth. All of us, too, were united in our unswerving devotion and loyalty to the King. Anybody who met His Majesty, however briefly, could not fail to realize that he was in the presence of an utterly exceptional man, a born leader and a great monarch. To work for him and converse with him daily was like basking in continual sunlight. Every one of us in the Court staff would have followed him unhesitatingly to the ends of the earth. Our shared allegiance to the King bonded us together and gave us a very high morale and *esprit de corps*. For him we cheerfully worked long hours and endured conditions (especially when on the move) which no employee working merely for money would ever have contemplated. Although everyone in the Court had a defined job and a particular degree of seniority, there was never any feeling of regimentation. We were like a family united under a kind and wise father, with everybody making an equal contribution towards the common good. Many of my friends in the Court became in later years men of great wealth and importance, and I feel that they deserve at least a small mention for their services to His Majesty while on his staff.

The Chief of the Court was Sheikh Ibrahim Ibn Muammar, whose forbears had been the Amirs of Uwainah at the time

of the great reformer, Mohammed Abdul Wahhab. Ibn
Muammar had been brought up by his father in Kuwait and
subsequently went to India, where he set up in business for
a while as a merchant trading with Kuwait. He travelled
extensively in Arabia and Europe and then for a time settled
in Egypt. There he contributed many articles and letters
about Ibn Saud and Najd to Egyptian newspapers. His knowledge of the affairs of Arabia was profound, and he was
frequently able to counter malicious or ignorant propaganda
against Najd which appeared from time to time in the Egyptian press. After the conquest of Hejaz, His Majesty was in
need of able administrators and Ibn Muammar was an
obvious choice. A message was sent to him asking if he
would come to Mecca to serve the King. Ibn Muammar
gladly agreed. He was immediately appointed Chief of the
Court, a role he was to perform with increasing distinction
for several years. Ibn Muammar was an energetic and con-
scientious man, who ran a happy and efficient Court. He
was devoted to the King, whom he served with utter sincerity.
Unfortunately, shortly before I myself left the Court, he fell
out with one of the Princes and resigned his post. The King
was most reluctant to lose him completely and appointed
him Ambassador to King Faisal of Iraq in Baghdad. Here his
crusading talents were put to good use on behalf of the many
Najdis who lived in Iraq and who often suffered from dis-
crimination and bureaucratic harassment. His efforts on their
behalf eventually made him such a thorn in the side of the
Iraqi administration that Ibn Saud was requested by King
Faisal to recall him. This he reluctantly did, but not before
Ibn Muammar had left his mark in the form of a lasting
betterment of the lot of his countrymen in Iraq.

As soon as wireless equipment and modern methods of
communication began to be used regularly in the Court, it
became necessary for somebody to be engaged to take charge
of them. The man chosen for this post was my old friend
Mohammed Dughaither. Mohammed was from a prominent
family in Riyadh, noted for their loyalty to the house of
Saud. Indeed, he could trace his family back to one of the

188

wives of the Amir Mohammed Ibn Saud, who was the founder of the Saudi dynasty. Mohammed had been well educated and had studied for a time in Zubair. His duties at Court required him to inform the King immediately of any important news, whether it be good or bad. Bad news required all Mohammed's reserves of tact, for the King's rage could be fearsome indeed. Good news, however, often inspired His Majesty to acts of generosity, and Mohammed was the recipient of many gifts made to him as the bringer of glad tidings. Once, after Mohammed had brought news of the successful crushing of a small rebellion, the King gave him some acres of land just outside the city walls. The land was then of small value but Mohammed shrewdly held on to it. Today it forms a large part of the commercial centre of Riyadh!

When I joined the Court, the Deputy Chief was Abdullah Othman, who was also from a well-known family in Riyadh. He had been brought up by his father in Kuwait, where he had received a first-class education. Both he and Mohammed Dughaither had been brought to Riyadh by the acting Consul in Kuwait, Sheikh Abdullah Al-Niffisi, only months before I arrived in Hejaz. Abdullah Othman took over as Chief of the Court after the departure of Ibn Muammar.

Like any monarch, Ibn Saud received a constant flow of written petitions from his subjects. Most of these seemed to have been composed on the principle that the greater the length and verbosity of the petition, the better would be its chances of success. To cope with this, a clerk was appointed. His task was to read through all the petitions and condense them to a manageable length, so that when they were put to the King, His Majesty could see immediately what was being asked of him. This job fell to Hamad Ibn Mudhaian, who dealt efficiently and uncomplainingly with ever-increasing mountains of paperwork throughout the time I was at the Court.

There were two clerks in the Court who had no specific duties but assisted wherever it was necessary. They were Mohammed Ash-Shubaily from Unayzah and Mohammed Ibn Dhawi from Harma. Both men were educated in Zubair, and both were to achieve great success in later life. Ash-Shubaily became Consul in Basra and was later appointed as Ambassador successively to Iraq, Pakistan, India and Afghanistan. Mohammed Ibn Dhawi impressed everybody as an extremely clever young man as soon as he had joined the Court, and after he had gained some experience, he was commissioned by the King to lead several state missions to the Yemen.

My own position was that of Chief Translator and Interpreter. I was responsible for translating into Arabic all letters and documents in English and Urdu. I also translated letters from the King into these languages for dispatch to foreign governments. I was often obliged to try my hand at other languages as well, for the Court was distinctly short of linguists. My workload steadily mounted and it was not long before I was joined by my brother, Abdul Aziz Almana, who acted as my assistant. Eventually my cousin, Abdul Aziz Zamil Jawasir, also came to work in the Court. He was later attached to the political committee, and subsequently became Prince Faisal's personal translator in Hejaz. My colleagues and I, together with a couple of typists and a few servants, comprised the entire Foreign Court of Ibn Saud. Naturally, we all came to know each other intimately, and the family atmosphere in the Court was something which a modern civil servant working in a vast, computerized administration would find hard to imagine.

While on the subject of the unsung heroes who helped His Majesty to build his kingdom, I feel I should give a mention to the many Najdis who represented their country abroad. Before the conquest of Hejaz, the King had no formal consular or diplomatic representation in foreign states. Instead, private businessmen from Najd who happened to be living in foreign countries would often act as the King's agents. The Najdis have a reputation throughout Arabia as a very religious group, who live by the highest moral principles. His Majesty chose men who had been a long time in a particular place and had acquired a reputation for honesty, sincerity and moral integrity. The men thus chosen received no remuneration for their services. However, they were amply rewarded by having the honour of being the King's representative, which gave considerable prestige and some advantages in trade. The fact that the system operated so well is a tribute to the close-knit nature of Najdi society, for all Najdis consider themselves to be part of a large family and remain loyal and faithful to each other, particularly when they are abroad. Prominent Najdis who acted as 'ambassadors' were Sheikh Fawzan As-Sabgh in Cairo, Abdul Latif Pasha Al-Mandil in Baghdad and Basra, Sheikh Abdullah Al-Niffisi in Kuwait, Sheikh Abdullah Al-Fawzan in Bombay, Sheikh Abu-Leila in Damascus and Sheikh Abdul Rahman Al-Gossaibi in Bahrain. These men spent considerable effort in promoting the interests of their country abroad, and it is sad that so many of them are now hardly ever remembered. As the King's domain expanded, he slowly began to establish a formal consular service. This involved the gradual replacement of his previous representatives. As in all such matters, His Majesty was most tactful and considerate, and any new ambassador was usually put under the nominal supervision of the King's previous agent until such time as the agent chose to retire.

Through my work, I came to know slightly most of the more prominent men surrounding the King, particularly those on his political committee. Some of these men, too, are almost forgotten today. The numbers of the political committee varied from time to time, but there were usually about eight members, drawn not just from Central Arabia but from all over the Middle East. Sheikh Hafiz Wahba, an Egyptian by birth, was an important senior adviser. He was present at the committee meetings only when not engaged on some important mission. He eventually became Minister Plenipotentiary, and later Ambassador to the Court of St James's in London. From Syria came Sheikh Khalid Al-Hakim, an elderly man of great wisdom, who had been an engineer associated with the Hejaz railway during the Turkish regime. Another Syrian was Sheikh Yusuf Yassin, who was in charge of the political department of the Court and was made responsible for organizing meetings of the political committee. From the Lebanon came Sheikh Fuad Hamza, the First Secretary to the King's son and Foreign Minister, the Amir Faisal. Sheikh Fuad spent much of his time in the Foreign Office in Mecca and Jeddah, where all the foreign ambassadors were to be found. Another of the King's advisers was Sheikh Khalid Al-Ghargini, a Libyan from Tripoli, who had been Governor of that town during the Italian occupation of his country. One must also number among the King's foreign advisers Sheikh Abdullah Philby, who was always welcome at the meetings but rarely attended them. He preferred to be with the King at his special and general *majlis*, where he had the occasional opportunity to be alone with His Majesty after the meetings had dispersed. Another prominent member of the committee was the King's brother, Prince Abdullah Ibn Abdul Rahman. He attended the council whenever possible, and his advice was highly valued by His Majesty.

Perhaps the most important of the King's advisers was a man who almost never attended the political committee because of his many engagements outside it, Sheikh Abdullah Suleiman, the Finance Minister. Suleiman was from Unayzah in Najd. As a youth he had left Arabia for Bombay, which was about the only avenue then open for young Arabs who sought adventure and fortune. He grew up without any formal education as a servant in the house of Sheikh Abdullah Al-Fawzan, who was one of the leading Najdi merchants in Bombay during its heyday as a trading metropolis. Suleiman never forgot his venerable old master, a man both religious and astute, who taught him much about the skills of a successful trader. Anxious to try his hand in commerce, Suleiman left Bombay for Bahrain, where he started up a small business of his own. It was not a great success and he soon found himself looking round for some more secure employment.

Suleiman's uncle occupied a minor position as a finance clerk in His Majesty's Domestic Court. He was somewhat overworked and, having obtained permission to take on an assistant, asked Suleiman to join him. Suleiman, lacking

Above: The main street at Mecca in the 1920s, with part of the outer wall of the Great Mosque on the right. *Popperfoto*

Left: The ceremony of the washing of the Kaaba, just before the start of the *hajj*. The black cloth which covers the Kaaba is the Kiswah. Until the incident of the Egyptian Guards of the Mahmal in 1925, the Kiswah was made in Egypt and sent to Mecca with the annual Egyptian caravan. *Keystone Press Agency*

Above: Harry St John Philby, at the end of his journey across Arabia in 1917. *Royal Geographical Society*

Left: St John Philby in 1960, shortly before his death in Beirut. *Popperfoto*

Court personalities

Above left: Sheikh Yusuf Yassin, Deputy Minister of Foreign Affairs and Minister of State, who was in charge of the political section of the Court. *Camera Press*

Above right: Sheikh Abdullah Suleiman, Minister of Finance. *Middle East Institute, Washington D.C.*

Below: Sheikh Hafiz Wahba, important senior adviser and later Saudi Ambassador to London, shown here with Prince Faisal at the UN General Assembly in 1946. *Keystone Press Agency*

Crown Prince Saud, second son of Ibn Saud. *Keystone Press Agency*

Prince Faisal, younger brother of Prince Saud, Viceroy of Hejaz and Foreign Secretary. *Camera Press*

The Sultan's palace at Shibam in the Hadramaut. *Popperfoto*

Home of the Zaidi Imam Yahya in Yemen in the 1930s.
Royal Geographical Society

Opposite: Imam Ahmad, Crown Prince of the Yemen, known as 'Abu
Jinnah'. *Sir Tom Hickinbotham*

Left: Major Frank Holmes, who, as representative of the Eastern and General Syndicate, was granted the Al-Hasa oil concession in 1923. *British Petroleum*

Below: A dinner given in May 1939 to celebrate the first tanker-load of oil. On Ibn Saud's right, L. N. Hamilton, on his left, F. W. Ohliger, both of Aramco. *Aramco World*

His Majesty King Ibn Saud joining in a war-dance during celebrations at Riyadh. *Popperfoto*

Ibn Saud and foreign heads of state

Left: Ibn Saud's state visit to Egypt in 1945. The picture shows King Ibn Saud and King Farouq leaving Cairo station to drive through the streets of the city. *Keystone Press Agency*

Below left: King Ibn Saud and President Roosevelt during their meeting in Egypt in 1945. *MEPhA*

Below right: King Amanullah of Afghanistan, deposed in a coup in 1928. Later, his warm welcome at Mecca by Ibn Saud helped scotch the rumour that he had become a Roman Catholic. *Popperfoto*

anything more promising to do, agreed to come. Thus, as a lowly assistant to a clerk, he began his career at Court. He showed an immediate flair for financial administration but, following the usual custom in such matters, he received no official credit for his work while his uncle continued to occupy a position senior to him. However, on his uncle's death, he immediately took over the post, and it was not long before Ibn Saud came to recognize the abilities of this hardworking, intelligent and enterprising young man. Gradually the King's admiration for Suleiman grew, and by the time I joined the Court, the former assistant clerk had been appointed Finance Minister wholly responsible for the state treasury.

Suleiman remained Finance Minister throughout the King's life. Seldom can any man have presided over such a dramatic improvement in his country's fortunes as took place in the latter part of those years. When Ibn Saud captured Riyadh in 1902, it was literally true that the royal treasury was contained in its entirety in his saddle-bags. Twenty years later the situation was often little better, and His Majesty was almost always drastically short of money. When the King conquered Hejaz in 1926, Suleiman travelled with him to organize the financial side of the take-over, and was immediately faced with an established bureaucracy of infinitely greater sophistication than the one he was used to in Najd. It is a tribute to his ability and hard work that the finances of Hejaz and Najd were linked together with so little trouble. From this date, Suleiman was based permanently in Hejaz, while the King's Court remained in Riyadh. Although the Finance Minister rarely interfered in foreign affairs, he was in sole charge of all domestic affairs in the kingdom.

Hejaz brought to the King a substantially increased revenue, and Suleiman now controlled the money from Customs and the Post Office, as well as the important taxes on pilgrims. These taxes were charged whenever a pilgrim travelled from one part of Hejaz to another, particularly between Jeddah, Mecca and Medina, and provided a high percentage of the country's revenue. But even with these increased revenues, the King remained in continual financial difficulty. Somehow, Suleiman always managed to keep some white coins for black days, and when funds were really short, he could always turn to the market-place and milk the merchants. If one was a wealthy trader, it was as well to be out of town when the King was in sudden need of cash. I remember one occasion when I was at the Court in Riyadh, shortly before the battle of Sibillah. His Majesty needed money to finance his military expedition, so he sent Suleiman's deputy in Riyadh to see what he could collect from the merchants of the town. The deputy was a man called Shalhowb, who had been with the King since the capture of Riyadh in 1902. Unfortunately for Shalhowb, the merchants heard he was coming and made themselves scarce. As a result, his quest proved less fruitful than the King had hoped. We all joked with Shalhowb about his failure to collect more money, but he took it in good heart and replied, 'Oh, these little troubles are nothing. When I came out of exile in Kuwait with the King, I had the whole royal treasury in my purse.'

Suleiman was the ultimate *éminence grise*, always self-effacing and keeping himself in the wings. Nevertheless, his power and influence became so monumental that I often thought of him as the uncrowned king of Arabia. Although he claimed never to have done anything without consulting the King, in fact he frequently implemented and enforced his own decisions entirely without royal permission. This is not to suggest that he was in any way disloyal. On the contrary, his devotion to the King was absolute and he worked tirelessly for the good of the kingdom.

As Suleiman grew in stature and importance, he naturally attracted enemies. When Hejaz was conquered, the King asked all the government employees of the former Hashemite kingdom to remain at their posts. However, there were still gaps in the bureaucratic structure, so His Majesty invited Najdis from all the more advanced areas of the Arab world, such as Egypt and the Fertile Crescent, to come to take positions in the administration of Hejaz. His Majesty hoped that such men would not only prove loyal, but would also have a more sophisticated, cosmopolitan education and outlook gained through working in foreign countries. Some of his recruits were hard-working and able men like Ibrahim Ibn Muammar, the Chief of the Court. Many others, however, turned out to lack the most rudimentary knowledge or ability. A number of such men were placed under Suleiman's control. It was not long before it became obvious that they were total novices, conducting their duties haphazardly, with no understanding of what they were supposed to be doing. Suleiman quickly saw their defects. He was not a man to suffer fools gladly and he criticized them mercilessly. In their turn the Najdis came to begrudge Suleiman his power, seeing him as no better than themselves. They conspired against him and probed into his personal life, which was not entirely above question. Then they wrote petitions to the King, making complaints against Suleiman and listing what they thought to be his personal shortcomings. This could have been a dangerous moment for Suleiman, but the King showed his faith in his Finance Minister by gathering all the letters together and sending them to Suleiman, authorizing him to take whatever action he thought best. Not surprisingly, Suleiman lost no time in dismissing the individuals concerned, all of whom were sent back to their native towns or wherever else they wished to go. Suleiman was then able to replace them with men of his own choosing. The resulting improvement in efficiency was so marked that the King henceforth gave Suleiman his complete support in any plans he wished to initiate and left entirely to him the choice of his own staff. From that moment, Suleiman's position and power became unassailable. By remaining strictly within the fields of administration and finance, he eventually controlled all the directorates. He appointed the staff, with the King's approval, and this gave him enormous power. In fact, Suleiman was the real founder of the newly emerging bureaucratic system; his work laid the corner-stone of the fully-fledged ministries which were to grow out of the old directorates.

Although Suleiman craved power, he had little time for its

trappings. He shunned publicity, for he knew this could be bad as well as good. He realized that the greater his public recognition the more bitter would be the jealousy of his enemies. Nor did popularity concern him. He was by nature reserved and aloof, and made little attempt to gain the love of his subordinates. Indeed, he often made himself unpopular with them. Although he was quick to criticize inefficiency or incompetence, he often refused to give advancement to men who displayed talent, for fear they might endanger his own position. He was always reluctant to delegate responsibility; as a result, his own work-load became quite astonishing. At the zenith of his career he was working eighteen or nineteen hours a day, stopping only for such sleep as was absolutely necessary before resuming his labours.

Suleiman was a man of boundless resource and was forever conceiving new ideas to assist the King with his financial problems. An example of this occurred towards the end of my period of service with the King in about 1935, when the state finances became so bad that our salaries could no longer be paid. Suleiman surmounted this problem by devising a scheme whereby the state officials and civil servants were paid only one-third of their salary in cash. Another third was paid in the form of provisions, and the remaining third was retained by the state as a compulsory loan. This situation lasted for about six or seven months until money became available. A simpler scheme used by Suleiman to conserve money was simply to refuse to pay it out. The King's son Prince Faisal was Governor of Hejaz, and frequently gave authority to tribal chiefs to collect money or provisions from Suleiman. The Finance Minister often infuriated the Prince by paying out less than the amount shown on these authorizations, or sometimes refusing to pay anything at all. However, the Prince never took any action against Suleiman, no doubt because of all the money he was saving. A more difficult problem for Suleiman arose when the Royal Princes came to him for money. Although the Princes had authorization from the King to draw money from the Treasury, Suleiman often refused to pay out these sums when funds were particularly low. Although the King did not openly condone Suleiman's behaviour in this respect, I am sure he was secretly in agreement with him. The Princes sometimes threatened Suleiman with physical violence if he did not pay. During one such incident, Prince Saud became so enraged with Suleiman that the unfortunate Finance Minister had to leap into his car and drive from Mecca to Jeddah to escape the Prince's wrath. Saud followed in another car, obliging Suleiman to borrow a launch and take refuge in one of the ships anchored in Jeddah harbour until the royal anger had subsided. I am sure that the King was very grateful for Suleiman's steadfast obstinacy in such matters. However, this kind of thrift could go too far. On another occasion, Suleiman's brother Hamad, who worked as his assistant, inadvisedly refused to pay out money to one of the King's wives who had been given authority by His Majesty to collect it. The King was furious, and sent two of his servants in a car with instructions to grab Hamad and take him to a far-off hill outside the city and leave him without food or water. He was there for two days before Suleiman was able to obtain permission to fetch him back.

At the height of his power, Suleiman was by far the most important man in the kingdom outside the royal family. I remember that on our annual visits to Hejaz, there were many impressive meetings and conferences between the King and the tribal chiefs and religious leaders of the region. But the real business of state was done in the cool of the early morning, when Suleiman used to come with his books, alone and unobserved, to His Majesty's private chamber immediately after the morning prayer.

Suleiman had never received any formal training in bookkeeping or accountancy. The book-keeping methods he used for administering the state finances worked efficiently enough while he was in charge, but they utterly confused foreign financial experts who came into contact with them. Suleiman was aware of this problem and made tentative efforts to modernize the system. Once he sent for an old retired Dutchman who was a noted financial expert and asked him for general advice. The Dutchman spent some weeks investigating the problem and started to prepare a lengthy report which would have recommended the introduction of orthodox Western methods of administration, including a sophisticated system of double-entry book-keeping. However, as he progressed, it became obvious that Suleiman did not understand his system any more than he could understand Suleiman's. So the Dutchman packed his bags and left. On the one occasion when (rather to my surprise) Suleiman requested my advice, it was to ask if I knew any Najdi who was well versed in modern techniques of banking. As it happened, I did, and was able to recommend my cousin Abdul Aziz Zamil Jawasir. Suleiman sent for my cousin but, rather to my embarrassment, Abdul Aziz politely declined to come. However, as I have already mentioned, he did later join the Court, where he enjoyed a distinguished career as a translator.

Towards the end of the King's reign, as the country expanded rapidly under the influx of oil revenues, Suleiman's accounting system began to break up under the strains imposed upon it. By that time he was an old man, but still as obstinate as ever. Prince Saud and Prince Faisal began gently to ease him out of his position of power, and appointed other men to take over some of the ministries and directorates which he had previously controlled. Eventually, a few years after the King's death and following an investigation into the affairs of a German construction company with which Suleiman had been involved, the Finance Minister was persuaded to resign and go into a well-earned retirement.

I personally knew Suleiman only slightly. I seldom met him because he spent most of his time in Hejaz, which we visited only once a year. Whenever I spoke to him, his manner was hostile and peremptory. (Perhaps this was a compliment, as he tended to behave like this towards anybody whom he thought might have influence with the King.) This does not prevent me from regarding him as one of the foremost characters in the recent history of our country, for it was he who laid the foundations of our modern administration and fully justified the King's affectionate nickname, 'my support'.

12
The Yemen

أَوَلَمْ يَرَوْا أَنَّا نَأْتِي الأَرْضَ نَنْقُصُهَا مِنْ أَطْرَافِهَا واللهُ يَحْكُمُ لا مُعَقِّبَ لَحُكْمِهِ وَهُوَ سَرِيعُ الحِسَابِ .

سورة الرعد (٤١)

See they not how We visit the land, reducing it of its outlying parts? (When) Allah doometh there is none that can postpone His doom, and He is swift at reckoning.

(Koran, The Thunder 41)

By 1930 Ibn Saud had been obliged to fight countless battles to the east and north of Najd in order to defend and extend his kingdom. Yet he had never fought a war in the south. This was not altogether surprising, since between Najd and the states on the Arabian Sea lay the vast and empty expanse of the Rub' Al-Khali, which few men would enter and none would consider worth fighting over. But one potential enemy existed in the south-west of the Arabian peninsula in the shape of the state of the Yemen, and the possibility of conflict with that enemy grew as the power of Ibn Saud expanded. The northern borders of the Yemen adjoined the kingdom of Ibn Saud to the south of Hejaz on the comparatively populous and fertile coast of the Red Sea. After the conquest of Hejaz and Asir, a covert antagonism simmered between the Saudis and the Yemenis. This was, I believe, due in part to the religious mistrust which stemmed from two differing ideologies in Islam: one was that of the puritan Wahhabis, who opposed all practices not sanctioned by the Koran; the other, equally extreme, was that of the Zaidis, whose members were of the Shiite sect prominent in the Yemen. Although the differences in dogma between this sect and the Wahhabis were not in truth very great, each group nevertheless considered the members of the other to be heretics. There were also good political reasons for the hostility. Imam Yahya of the Yemen considered the rising power of the Saudis a threat to his independence, and he feared that his small country might be swallowed up by Ibn Saud in the same way as Jabal Shammar and Hejaz. There were certainly many influential people, both inside and outside Najd, who thought that the Yemen would be a logical and desirable addition to Saudi territory. For some time, Philby had been writing articles hinting that His Majesty should annex the Yemen. In one such piece, Philby said openly that his desire was to see His Majesty wear the triple crown of Mecca, Riyadh and Sana (the capital of the Yemen). I remember on an occasion, shortly after the King had conquered Hejaz, he was visited in Jeddah by a prominent writer, Amin Al-Raihni. Al-Raihni was a Christian Arab from the Lebanon who had become a prominent historian in America. He had come to congratulate the King on his conquest, and expressed the fervent hope that his next visit to honour His Majesty would be to Aden.

The general opinion in the Court was that the Yemen was a hard and difficult country, inhabited by a ferocious people, and that the King had little to gain by adding it to his already substantial kingdom. I am sure that His Majesty shared this view. I remember telling him of Philby's suggestion about the triple crown. The King's immediate reaction was to dismiss the idea out of hand, saying that the Yemen was not for him. Nevertheless, Imam Yahya can hardly be blamed for his unease, particularly when one considers what had recently happened to the neighbouring Amirate of Jizan.

Until the late 1920s Jizan had been a tiny independent state adjoining the northern borders of the Yemen on the Red Sea. It was ruled by an amir from its capital town of Sabya. A disagreement had occurred between Jizan and the Yemen, as a result of which the Amir of Jizan had appealed to Ibn Saud for protection. His Majesty readily agreed to ally himself with the Amir, and generously suggested that a Saudi commissioner should be sent to Jizan to assist the Amir with the arduous business of government. The commissioner duly arrived and the Amir found him a great help. Later on the Amir found himself in financial difficulty and asked the King to lend him money. Again His Majesty agreed, and kindly provided a financial inspector to assist the Amir with the administration of the funds. Then the King quietly replaced the first commissioner, who was a mild and unassuming man, with another who was more forceful. Soon the

Amir found himself with very little say in his own government. Realizing too late what was going on, he gathered such forces as he could and besieged the commissioner's residence. Naturally, this left Ibn Saud with no alternative but to send in reinforcements and annex Jizan. This was done with great speed and little bloodshed, and with every justification in the eyes of the outside world. Somewhat ironically, the Amir fled to sanctuary in the Yemen.

Having witnessed with alarm this example of His Majesty's devastating statescraft, Imam Yahya was determined that his kingdom should not suffer a similar fate. He decided that a little belligerence was the best way to convince Ibn Saud that the Yemen had no intention of becoming part of his domain. The method he chose was to lay claim to the area of Najran, which lay on his north-eastern border, and the region of Southern Asir, which lay to the north-west. Both these areas had been on the edge of the Saudi kingdom since the annexation of Hejaz and Asir but had never been fully incorporated into it. They enjoyed a kind of uneasy and lawless independence and were ruled by local amirs. Their boundaries with Saudi Arabia and the Yemen were entirely undefined, although the Saudis maintained that the areas were part and parcel of Arabia. Ibn Saud had wisely never attempted to alter this state of affairs, since Southern Asir and Najran were, in effect, convenient buffer states between his kingdom and the Yemen. It was obvious that any attempt by Imam Yahya to alter the *status quo* would cause the King great concern.

The situation was complicated by the activities of the Amir of Najran, who had himself been trying, somewhat ineptly, to play the dangerous game of power politics. At different times he had sought to ally himself with, and seek assistance from, both Saudi Arabia and the Yemen. Possibly he hoped to play one off against the other to his own advantage. If this was the case, he made a grave miscalculation. The result was that each country came to regard Najran as its protectorate, and in the dispute which followed, neither side took any notice of the Amir's claim to independence.

Imam Yahya's claims to Najran were at first only made verbally. They were dealt with by means of missions from both countries which attempted to survey and map the precise boundaries of the Yemen. This proved to be a fruitless task, because it had never before been considered necessary to mark the exact position of the frontier and nobody could agree where it lay. Endless disputes arose over which country owned particular areas of land. A good example of His Majesty's magnanimity and diplomacy was shown during one such disagreement, which was over the nationality of a hill in the Najran area. The Yemeni and Saudi missions referred the matter first to Imam Yahya, who declared that the question should be put to the arbitration of 'my brother, Abdul Aziz'. A telegram was sent from the Yemen to this effect. I was with the King on a hunting expedition in the desert at the time. On His Majesty's orders, a recently acquired portable wireless set accompanied him wherever he went, and it was my duty to receive the messages from the wireless operator and present them to the King. When the message from the Yemen came through, His Majesty had left the main camp for a remote, secluded corner of the desert. I immediately went to give him the message. He read it with a smile, saying, 'I have been asked to judge the disputed mountain.' On His Majesty's instructions, I sent the following brief reply: 'I henceforth declare that the mountain belongs to the Yemen.' News of this decision spread rapidly throughout the Arab world. One Egyptian newspaper came out with the headline, 'God speaks' and, after narrating the full story behind the decision, declared, 'Let those Western powers take note who say that the Arabs have no statesmen or great politicians.'

But the ownership of a mountain by no means brought to an end the controversy over Najran. The negotiations became more protracted and bitter, and the tension between the two countries worsened when Imam Yahya decided to support his claims by sending detachments of troops into Najran territory, where the Yemeni camels encroached on the pasturage of Saudi forces stationed there. The Saudis sent notes of protest to the Imam about these infiltrations, but the Yemenis persisted and made no attempt to withdraw their forces. On the contrary, the Imam replied by sending the King numerous letters of protest of extravagant length, phrased in terms of exaggerated eloquence. There is an Arab saying, to the effect that within written expression lies wisdom. The Imam took this proverb to extremes. His letters exasperated the King, for they were couched in the highest classical Arab phraseology, which was clearly calculated to show the Imam to be learned and wise but which, when unravelled, usually proved quite meaningless. His Majesty was further infuriated by the fact that the Imam persisted in misusing theological points in support of his arguments, in a manner obviously intended to suggest that the King himself had no knowledge of the Koran. It was hardly surprising that His Majesty began to despair of finding a peaceful solution to the problem.

Finally in 1932 the Najran issue was settled temporarily when a force of Saudi tribesmen under Khalid Ibn Luway drove the Yemenis from Najran and formally annexed it in the name of Ibn Saud. Although this was a serious reverse for the Yemen, it did nothing to subdue Imam Yahya, who redoubled his efforts to claim the region of Southern Asir. Relations with the Yemenis deteriorated steadily until, one grey morning in the spring of 1934, His Majesty entered the Court and told his officials of a dream he had had the previous night. He related it as follows:

I was in a room in an old, abandoned house. The room was in pitch darkness and there was not the smallest glimmer of light to be seen. The darkness was so total that it was as if my eyelids had been sealed together. Suddenly, in a far corner of the room, an apparition materialized out of the darkness. It was in the form of an evil snake. Its scaly, elongated shape began to writhe and twist, and its forked tongue darted in and out as it slowly coiled itself up ready to strike. Then its jaws snapped open, revealing two dagger-like fangs dripping with venom. I was seized with terror, realizing that at any moment those fangs would sink into my flesh and deadly poison would be pumped into my blood. Like a bolt of lightning I pounced upon the snake, grasping it by the neck and pinning it to the wall. I pressed my fingers tighter and tighter about its throat until it was overpowered. At that instant I awoke, and as consciousness returned, I realized that my peril had only been imagined in a dream and I gave thanks to God for my safety.

Everyone who heard the King tell his story was deeply affected. We Arabs believe strongly that dreams can foretell what is to come. We were all aware of His Majesty's mental powers, and nobody doubted that the dream showed clairvoyant insight. At that time the dispute with the Yemen was the foremost issue of the day, and there could be little doubt that Imam Yahya was the threatening snake in the dream. As the King left the Court to muse over the implications of his nightmare, there was much eager speculation as to what his next move would be. The general consensus of opinion was that he would attack the Yemen.

The following day, the King did indeed decide he had no alternative but to resort to force. His first step was to call a small gathering of the chiefs of his loyal tribes. The recent purging of the Ikhwan, while absolutely necessary for the security of the kingdom, had left the King seriously short of experienced and reliable warriors. The principal sections of the Mutair and Utaiba tribes were in disgrace, and so were represented by their secondary sections. These had remained loyal to the King, but they were numerically smaller than the main sections and did not have the same military reputation. Despite their depleted numbers, the tribesmen were bursting with enthusiasm for the coming conflict. The Utaiba were now represented by the Rawaga section of the tribe. Its chief, Omar Ibn Rubaian, rose to his feet and cried out to the King, 'O Abdul Aziz, if you want the Yemen, then allow me to lead the invasion. You may remain in Mecca or in Riyadh and I shall bring it to you.' Ibn Saud declined Ibn Rubaian's offer to take over his army. No doubt he had in mind what had happened after the conquest of Hejaz, when Ad-Dawish and Ibn Bijad, having played a major part in the fighting, considered the governorship of the region to be their due.

His reply to Omar Ibn Rubaian was, as always, brief and to the point. He declared, 'Your tribe shall not move a foot without my orders. I hereby appoint my sons Saud and Faisal to lead our forces, and you shall go with them.' The King did, however, accept one part of Ibn Rubaian's advice, for he decided to remain at Mecca and direct his forces from there by wireless. This came as something of a surprise to us, as the King usually led his troops personally on major expeditions. In retrospect, I can see that His Majesty had very sound reasons for acting as he did. It is probable that he had no desire to annex the Yemen, and merely wished to subdue Imam Yahya and teach him a lesson. He realized that he would therefore have to stop short of total occupation and reach a compromise peace. It would be easier to be magnanimous from a distance than if he were personally involved in the fighting. In addition, he was probably worried about Hejaz, which had been part of his kingdom for barely eight years. Not all of its people were reconciled to his reign, and the region might well have taken the opportunity to revolt if he had departed with his army. The conference was dissolved, and the tribesmen were ordered to proceed to their designated positions near the frontier of the Yemen and await further orders before moving onwards. His Majesty's departing words to his men were in the form of a simple prayer to God which he always used when he was about to go to war: 'We worship you and ask for your aid.'

In a last effort for peace, the King delivered an ultimatum to Imam Yahya, stipulating reasonable terms for the settlement of the outstanding boundary disputes and threatening war if the terms were not accepted. The ultimatum was ignored, and on 5 April 1934 the Saudi forces marched over the borders of the Yemen. The strategy of the assault was that Prince Saud should attack from Najran into the mountainous regions of north-east Yemen, while Prince Faisal simultaneously attacked from the west down the Tihamah, the coastal strip along the shores of the Red Sea. From the start, Prince Saud's advance was slow. He would never have claimed to be a brilliant general and the task he was given was hard. A huge problem was the difficult nature of the country, which often necessitated raising and lowering the transport by rope over sheer cliffs. Prince Ahmad, the Crown Prince of the Yemen, was in command of the Yemeni forces in this region. He made his headquarters in the town of Sa'ada, which was situated on top of an impregnable mountain and was never in serious danger of being taken by the Saudis. The Crown Prince was known with good reason as 'Abu Jinnah', which means 'the frenzied one'. He was given to bouts of uncontrollable rage and was greatly feared by his troops and servants. One story told about him was that he used to keep a venomous snake in a basket by his side. The snake was harmless, for its poison sacs had been cut out, but only the Prince knew that. Any unwary visitor who annoyed the Prince (and that was not difficult) was likely to find the snake suddenly thrown about his neck.

Despite such sadistic eccentricities, or possibly because of them, the Prince was an excellent general. He had a large part of the Yemeni army under his command and he directed it with skill. For the most part, his forces remained in fortified positions in the mountains; whenever the Saudi troops mounted an attack up the slopes, they were met with determined resistance. When the Saudis tired, the inevitable counter-attack would be launched against them, forcing them back to the plains. On more than one occasion, the Yemenis reached the camp of Prince Saud and ransacked it, plundering all his provisions and stores and burning his tents before retiring back to their mountain fortress. Stung by these defeats, Prince Saud tried new tactics; he divided his troops into several sections, under the leadership of his cousins Prince Faisal Ibn Sa'ad and Prince Fahd Ibn Sa'ad. He ordered them to move further south and attack the mountains from a number of different points on the eastern slopes. These attacks, too, all met with disaster. Wherever the Saudis went, they were forced to scale mountain ridges which were often more rugged and difficult than those on the northern slopes, and the Yemenis beat back the attacks with little difficulty.

The whole expedition in the north-eastern region can only be described as a spectacular failure. There was, however, one very real consolation, for it kept a large part of the Yemeni army pinned down in the mountains, thus giving Prince Faisal a comparatively free hand in the west. In contrast to the campaign of his unfortunate brother, Faisal's mission was a resounding success. Setting off from Jizan on the Red Sea, and sweeping down the Tihamah coastal plain, he crossed the Yemeni frontier and was immediately confronted by a large enemy force based in the town of Harad. The Yemenis were able to hold Prince Faisal for a time, but eventually a full-scale battle took place. The Yemeni forces were routed and withdrew in complete disorder, losing much of their equipment. Unfortunately, the Saudi general, Hamad Al Shuair, was killed during the battle. Nonetheless, the victory gave a much-needed boost to Saudi morale. After the battle of Harad, Faisal met with practically no resistance and was able to advance with great speed down the western seaboard of the Yemen towards Al-Hudaidah, the principal Yemeni port on the Red Sea. He encountered only a few pockets of enemy troops on the way, and they were immediately liquidated. Some Yemeni forces were positioned in the hills to the east of the Saudi line of advance, but Faisal made no attempt to attack them and none dared to come down and face him in the plains.

As the Saudi troops moved irresistibly southwards, news reached Prince Faisal that Imam Yahya had, in desperation, called on various foreign powers for assistance. The Italians had decided to help him, and an Italian sea-borne force was steaming up the Red Sea towards Al-Hudaidah, apparently with the object of occupying the town and preventing the Saudis from entering. Prince Faisal had no intention of allowing this to happen, and reacted with a rapidity which paid tribute to the training he had received at the hands of his father. Scouts were immediately sent ahead to Al-Hudaidah and the Prince ordered his army to advance towards the city with the utmost speed. Outpacing the rest of his forces and accompanied by barely one hundred men, Prince Faisal reached the outskirts of Al-Hudaidah, where he met his returning scouts. They reported that the Yemeni forces had withdrawn from the city, but that a number of Italian warships were already in the harbour, on the point of landing a force of occupation. Faisal's companions urged him to hold back, for his small body of men were no match for the Italian army. But the Prince had not yet lost his race against time and he was determined not to be beaten at the last moment. He ordered his men to proceed immediately to the harbour and open fire on the Italians before they had a chance to land. This they did, and the Italians, believing that the Saudis were already firmly in possession of the port, withdrew in haste to a safe distance. The Prince was delighted with the outcome and, pointing to the retreating ships, said to his followers, 'Look! Perhaps I was not as mad as you thought when I sent my men to fire at them.'

The fall of Al-Hudaidah, despite the attempted foreign intervention, was a crushing blow for Imam Yahya, and matters were made worse for him by a communications error on the part of the Saudis. When the Italian fleet withdrew from Al-Hudaidah, they sent a wireless message in morse code back to Italy. The message, which for some reason was worded in French, was to the effect that the port was in the hands of the Saudis and that Imam Yahya had decided to withdraw his forces to his capital of Sana. This was quite correct, but a Saudi wireless operator in Jeddah who intercepted the message misread the French word '*décidé*' as '*décédé*', an easy mistake when reading morse, and concluded that the Imam had died while withdrawing with his forces. This was the message which was passed to the press, and subsequently appeared in headlines all over the Arab world.

The spreading of the false story about his death seemed to be the final straw for the Imam, who sued for peace. Ibn Saud agreed to a truce, and his armies remained in possession of the territory they had conquered while negotiations took place at Ta'if between the representatives of both countries. The League of Arab Nations urged the King to be magnanimous and allow the Yemen to retain its independence within the existing boundaries. His Majesty was happy to agree to a settlement along these lines, and the Saudi forces withdrew after the Imam had agreed to pay reparations of £100,000 in gold to the King to compensate him for the expenses of the campaign. The peace treaty was finally signed at Mecca. A joint boundary commission was then set up and was able to agree the line of the frontier without further difficulties. Although Ibn Saud could easily have deposed Imam Yahya and taken the Yemen by force, he did not do so, but contented himself with subduing the country and ensuring that it could no longer be a threat to him. Thus the prophecy in his dream was fulfilled, for the King had not dreamt that he killed the snake but merely that he held an iron grip upon it until it had been overpowered.

The war in the Yemen gave rise to a dramatic incident one year later, when His Majesty was in Mecca for the hajj. The King was performing the *Tawaf*, the ritual circumambulation of the Kaaba in the centre of the Holy Mosque in Mecca. As always, he was surrounded by thousands of other devout pilgrims. Suddenly two youthful Yemeni fanatics, who had managed to push their way through the throng, leapt forward to attack the King with knives. His Majesty was saved by the quick reactions and gallantry of Crown Prince Saud, who threw himself in front of his father to ward off the blows. Saud was fortunate to receive only a slight wound in the shoulder. One of the Yemenis was immediately shot by the King's bodyguard, but the other managed to escape through the crowd. Thus were fired the last shots of the war of the Yemen. Through the grace of God the King was unhurt, and the incident even had its positive side, for it marked the beginning of a period of reconciliation between the Yemen and Saudi Arabia. It has never been clearly established who was behind the assassination attempt. Imam Yahya immediately disclaimed any involvement, and indeed was one of the first to send a message to His Majesty deploring the assassination attempt and expressing his thanks and relief that the King was safe.

13
The oil story

وإذا قربت نهاية العالم فسوف تلفظ الجزيرة خزائنها وتخرج ثرواتها .

حديث عربي قديم

As the end of the world draws nigh, the peninsula
will disgorge its treasures and spill out its wealth.

(Arabic saying)

With the unification of Central Arabia and the emergence of a stable government there, it was inevitable that the commercial moguls of the outside world would begin to wonder what treasures might lie under Arabia's desert sands, and set about obtaining permission to search for them. The possibility that oil might be found in the country had been known for some years, since by 1920 it was already being exploited in Iraq and Persia, which had similar geological features.

In 1923, three years before I joined the Court, the first oil concession had actually been signed. An adventurer from New Zealand by the name of Major Holmes, acting on behalf of an English group calling itself the 'Eastern & General Syndicate', managed to obtain an introduction to Ibn Saud. After some months of sporadic discussion, Holmes was granted an exclusive concession to explore for oil and other minerals in the Al-Hasa area. Although nobody knew it at the time, the territory covered by the concession contained almost all the vast oil deposits in the Eastern Region, upon which the world now finds itself so dependent. The Al-Hasa concession was to last for seventy years, at the astonishing bargain price of £2,000 in gold per annum, payable in advance. Everybody seemed content with the agreement. Holmes had obtained most favourable terms for his syndicate and Ibn Saud, who believed that God had endowed his kingdom with plenty of sand but precious little else, was more than happy to allow foreigners to pay him £2,000 a year for the privilege of discovering that his country contained no oil. Strangely enough, almost no serious exploration was done by the Eastern & General Syndicate, and after paying two years' rent totalling £4,000, they seemed to lose interest altogether. No further rent was forthcoming from them and in 1928, after three years had passed without payment, the King terminated the concession. At that stage he regarded himself as being owed £6,000 by Holmes and this fact, as will be seen, was to assume some importance later on in the story of Arabian oil.

No further approaches for concessions were made until 1930. In that year His Majesty was in very serious financial trouble, for the world-wide slump had drastically reduced the number of pilgrims coming to Mecca, and the King's revenues from Hejaz had dropped dramatically. Despite all the ingenuity of Suleiman, the situation had become very grave. The King was having difficulty in paying his foreign debts and even his staff. Even so, I do not think that further attempts to exploit the country's mineral wealth had even occurred to him as a way of resolving his problems until he was approached by an American by the name of Charles Crane. Crane was a Quaker millionaire, a former American minister to China, and a very influential figure in American business circles. He had been one of the two American appointees to the King–Crane Commission on Syria and Palestine which reported in 1919, and had also visited the Yemen, so he was not unfamiliar with the Middle East. Crane had developed a genuine, if sometimes rather eccentric, desire to hasten the progress of the emerging states in the Middle East. He was not, in fact, completely unknown to the King. During my first December in Riyadh in 1926, one of the weekly mail-bags from the Foreign Office in Mecca contained a cable sent from Geneva. It read: 'To His Majesty King Ibn Saud. I am interested in Arabia and desire to meet Your Majesty if permitted. Charles Crane, friend of the Arabs.' Friend or not, His Majesty had no idea at that time who Crane was or what he wanted, and he certainly did not have the time to meet every foreign well-wisher who desired to see him. The Foreign Office was therefore instructed to cable a polite refusal, which read: 'The time is not propitious as His Majesty is busy with the approaching hajj season and internal affairs.'

Not to be put off, Crane cabled again in 1927, this time from Cairo, saying that he would like to see the King. Again, no details were given as to why Crane wanted to come. The cable arrived just after the hajj, and the King was in Mecca about to return to Najd. A telegram was sent in reply, explaining that the King was about to return to Riyadh and unfortunately there was no time for a meeting. Crane was nothing if not persistent. He went to Basra and made arrangements to drive into Najd by car via Kuwait. In this project he enlisted the help of John Vaness, an American missionary in Basra, who lent Crane one of his young assistants to guide him as far as the Kuwait border. The pair set off in two separate cars, accompanied by Arab guides and servants. Most unfortunately, while they were driving through Kuwait, they encountered an Ikhwan raiding party, made up of members of the Ajman tribe under Dhaidan Ibn Huthlain. The raiders immediately opened fire on the cars. Both vehicles managed to escape, but not before the young American missionary had been hit and killed. When news of the incident reached Riyadh, the King was furious. Of course, nothing could be done, and Crane had already been forced to return the way he had come. By now, His Majesty was impressed by Crane's perseverance and was happy to agree to a meeting with him. The American was in Cairo at the time, having recently completed a programme of road- and bridge-building in the Yemen. It was therefore an easy matter to arrange with him that he would visit Jeddah early the following year.

Crane arrived in Jeddah in February 1931. His Majesty travelled to the city especially to meet him, and the American was treated to a magnificent reception. The guards and retinue of the King put on a grand display of ceremonial war-dances; this was followed by a similar performance by the inhabitants of Jeddah, among whom the Hadramis were particularly impressive in their dancing. Crane was invited to a number of state banquets and was given the honour of being accommodated in Sheikh Mohammed Nassif's house, which until then had always been used by the King himself when he was in the city.

The American remained in Jeddah until the beginning of March, and had several lengthy discussions with the King and Suleiman. Crane's vision of Arabia was one of splendid factories, massive dams, great highways and gleaming bridges, all of which could be built by his engineers once the riches of the country had begun to be exploited. The King and his Finance Minister listened politely, but what was immediately required was cash, not concrete, so that His Majesty could pay his staff and his foreign debts. At all events, before anybody's dream could be realized, it was necessary to discover whether Arabia did indeed have any underground minerals, and Crane promised to supply an expert surveyor to look for them. The agreement reached was that Crane would pay the surveyor's salary and the King would provide him with all the necessary food, accommodation and transportation, together with a personal guard. After this had been arranged, Crane left Jeddah with as much ceremony as when he had arrived, having received from His Majesty a kingly gift of two fine Arabian horses.

Two months later, Karl Twitchell arrived in Jeddah. Twitchell was a civil and mining engineer, who had already worked for Crane in the Yemen and had been commissioned by him to carry out the necessary surveys. He was put to work immediately. His first task was to visit the neighbourhood of Jeddah and the spring of Aziziyah in the adjoining hills, to see what could be done to improve the city's notoriously inadequate water supply. Then he went on a journey down the Red Sea coast to Jizan and Yanbu, taking with him a translator I knew, called Ahmad Fakhry. Subsequently he travelled to Najd, where he paid particular attention to the area around Ar-Rass and Niffi. In this region he found a hillock with veins of gold, and the ruined remains of an old mining village. Some of the derelict dwellings still contained the remnants of grinding stones which had been used to crush the rock dug from the hill. Despite the fact that there still seemed to be gold present in encouraging quantities, Twitchell did not think it worth trying to extract it, as modern methods required greater quantities of water than were available in the area.

After returning to Jeddah for a time, Twitchell travelled back through Najd to Al-Hasa, this time accompanied by Najeeb Salha as translator. There he spent several months compiling a detailed report on everything he saw. He paid particular attention to the oases of the region, and became enthusiastic about the possibility of making the desert flower by irrigation. Among other minerals in the area, he noticed outcrops of gypsum near Dhahran. Finally, after spending about eighteen months in Arabia, he found geological formations in the Dhahran area which pointed strongly to possible reserves of oil.

Twitchell took his reports to the King and explained what would be needed to search for the oil and what would happen if it were found. Like Crane, he spoke in lyrical terms of cities, roads, railways, airports, schools, hospitals and the other paraphernalia of a modern industrial state, all of which could be created by oil wealth. Despite Twitchell's enthusiasm, His Majesty was sceptical, still believing in his heart that there was nothing but valueless rock under his barren desert. However, he agreed that if there was any oil in his kingdom, something should be done to get it out and sell it. At about this time, Prince Faisal was due to go on a visit to England. On His Majesty's instructions, I personally gave the Prince a copy of Twitchell's report. While in England, Faisal handed the report to the British government and, as his father had asked him, offered to give the British the Al-Hasa oil concession. Shortly afterwards, the King received a telegram from the British Embassy in Jeddah to the effect that the British government was obliged for the offer but was not interested.

It is perhaps surprising that Ibn Saud should have offered his oil to the British after its possible location had been found by the Americans, and even more surprising that the British should have turned it down. I think that the reason for the King's gesture was probably that he felt in debt to the British for the help they had given him in the past, and thought that this gesture of goodwill might go some way towards repaying it. The refusal of the offer by the British could, of course, have been due simply to stupidity, but I suspect that there were other influences at work. I have always thought it likely that there was an unwritten agreement between the international oil companies and the British and American governments to the effect that the British would control oil reserves to the east of a line drawn from the north of Iraq down to Qatar, while the Americans had everything to the west of the line. The British, after all, already dominated oil production in Kuwait, Iraq, Qatar and the Trucial States, and to a large extent in Bahrain, and at that time this was ample for their needs. There was much to gain by bringing the Americans into the area, for it would give them a powerful economic interest in Arabia. This, in turn, would encourage them to make a military alliance with the British to defend the region against the potential enemies of both countries.

At all events, whatever the reason, the British did not want the oil concession. Ibn Saud's next move was to try to reach an agreement with Twitchell himself, whom he had come to admire and trust. Sheikh Yusuf Yassin and Fuad Hamza, on behalf of the King, asked Twitchell to form a national oil company for the Saudi government. As General Manager of the company, Twitchell was to receive ten per cent of the profits. He declined, however, on the grounds that he did not consider the venture to be practical. With increasing admiration for Twitchell's bargaining skill, Yassin raised the proposed percentage to fifteen per cent and finally to a staggering twenty per cent. When Twitchell still refused, it finally dawned upon the King's negotiators that Twitchell actually meant what he said; he quite genuinely did not believe the venture to be feasible. I think another reason he refused was that he was perfectly happy as a surveyor and had no particular ambition to become an oil tycoon. He was, however, more than willing to help the King, and promised to take a copy of his report to America to see if he could find a company there which would be interested in the oil concession. Everybody in the Court was glad that the Americans seemed likely to get the concession, for we all felt that the British were still tainted by colonialism. If they came for our oil, we could never be sure to what extent they would come to influence our government as well. The Americans on the other hand would simply be after the money, a motive which the Arabs as born traders could readily appreciate and approve.

Before Twitchell left, he came to me and said that he did not know to whom he should write in the Court. If he found a company interested in the concession he would therefore write to me; he asked me to translate any letter he sent and present it to the King. About a month after he left I received the promised letter. I translated it and gave it to His Majesty, who in turn passed it to Suleiman. The letter informed the King that Twitchell had found a company interested in exploring the oil prospects, and that he was prepared to come and negotiate an agreement on behalf of the company. I wrote to Twitchell acknowledging his letter. All further correspondence took place between Twitchell and Suleiman and I did not see any of it personally.

Suleiman must have invited Twitchell to Jeddah, for in due course he appeared, accompanied by a Mr Lloyd Hamilton of the Standard Oil Company of California. His Majesty instructed Suleiman to form a committee to negotiate with the Americans, and Suleiman decided to do this himself, together with Sheikh Abdullah Mohammed Al-Fazal and Sheikh Hassan Al-Gossaibi. The King asked me to accompany the committee as translator. The committee took rooms in the Baghdadi Building in Jeddah and talks with the Americans started immediately. As the long and tricky negotiations proceeded, it became obvious that the principal obstacle was the question of the initial payment to be made for the concession. Since the King still doubted that any oil existed at all, he was much more interested in obtaining a sizeable down payment for exploration rights than he was in possible future royalties. Suleiman was therefore demanding a 'loan' of £100,000 as a condition of granting the concession. The sum was to be repaid, if at all, from royalty payments as and when oil became available in commercial quantities. The company had in mind a much lower figure in the order of £25,000.

Shortly after Hamilton and Twitchell arrived in Jeddah, they found themselves with some rather unexpected competition. A deputation from the British-owned Iraq Petroleum Company arrived in Jeddah, led by a man named Longrigg. They were followed by the appearance of none other than Major Frank Holmes, accompanied by an Armenian translator. Major Holmes's stay in Jeddah was extremely short. He was met by Sheikh Abdullah Suleiman and myself and the conversation which followed was, from Holmes's point of view, distressingly brief. Holmes assured us that he represented 'Mellon interests' and 'The Gulf Group', which he said was a very big company. He assured us that a magnificent, but unspecified, deal could be made with his company if he was given the concession. Suleiman was not impressed. He reminded Holmes that he still owed the government £6,000 in respect of the previous concession which had been allowed to lapse. He added that, since Holmes's reliability was obviously open to question, he required the Major to make a payment of 'earnest money' before any negotiations could take place. A figure of 200,000 riyals was mentioned. Holmes was not prepared to pay this and was probably afraid that, even if he did, it would simply be confiscated on account of the unpaid rent owed by the Eastern & General Syndicate. I think that he probably arrived in the expectation of being able to pull the wool over the eyes of the Saudi government a second time, and securing the Al-Hasa concession for a nominal sum. Once he realized that this was out of the question, he caught the next ship out of Jeddah and was never seen again.

The IPC delegation, which was met by Philby and Suleiman, lingered in Jeddah rather longer than Holmes had done. They were somewhat like figures from *Alice in Wonderland* while they wandered about the city in a distracted state, moving from place to place as if they had lost their way. IPC were never seriously in the running for the concession because, as it turned out, they were never prepared to offer anything like as much as the Americans in the matter of the all-important initial loan. However, the Americans did not know this at the time, and the very presence of IPC made life much more difficult for Hamilton and Twitchell, who were no longer the only runners in the field and were worried that at any time their rivals might be able to outbid them.

At first I was asked to translate for Twitchell and Hamilton as well as for Suleiman. Then all of a sudden, Philby became involved in the negotiations and took over as translator for the Americans. He had apparently been appointed by Standard Oil to represent them in the discussions. This was a shrewd move on their part, because nobody knew better than Philby what sort of offer was likely to be acceptable to the King. I never quite understood how Philby managed to reconcile his position as self-appointed and impartial adviser to the King with that of paid agent for one of the two international companies who were competing for His Majesty's oil. In fact, at the same time as he was negotiating on behalf of the Standard Oil Company with Suleiman, he was also having meetings with IPC in which he represented the Saudi government! But whatever his motives, I think that Philby must still have had the interests of the King at heart because the eventual result, as will be seen, was most beneficial for our country.

The discussions with the Americans continued much as before, with Twitchell and Hamilton trying to dissuade Suleiman from pressing for a lump sum by painting rosy pictures of the benefits and prosperity which would accrue to the nation once oil was discovered. Suleiman, on the other hand, came back again and again to the simple point that, however much jam there might or might not be tomorrow, His Majesty needed jam today. Philby helped to break the impasse. I remember him saying to Twitchell, 'These Arabs do not understand your theoretical and abstract explanations of what will happen in the future. They want to know something concrete – what they will get now. You will have to offer them a lump sum or risk losing the concession altogether.'

Eventually the Americans were convinced that a large down payment really was necessary, and after much additional talking, a provisional agreement was reached. Briefly, it gave the Al-Hasa concession to Standard Oil for sixty years in exchange for an initial interest-free loan of £30,000 in gold and a second loan of £20,000 in gold within eighteen months. There was to be an annual rental of £5,000 in gold, and a further loan of £15,000 in gold to be made as soon as oil was discovered in commercial quantities. Thereafter, the government would receive royalty payments at the rate of four shillings per ton of crude oil extracted. These terms were discussed between Suleiman and the King and, on Philby's advice, His Majesty decided to accept them. His instructions to Suleiman were as always simple and direct: 'Put your trust in God and sign!' The concession was signed by Suleiman and Hamilton in Jeddah on 29 May 1933. The Saudi Arabian oil age had finally begun.

The sequel is well known. The search for oil was initially fruitless and everybody's hopes sank (except those of the King, who never expected oil to be found anyway). Then in 1935 a trial well drilled in Dhahran proved the existence of oil in commercial quantities. As time passed, the true and staggering size of the oilfields was established. Production began in 1938, but fell almost to nothing during the Second World War. After that, it rocketed to the huge volumes produced today. The Standard Oil Company became first the California Arabian Standard Oil Company and finally Arabian American Oil Company, or Aramco as it is now universally known. The King found himself richer than he had ever imagined possible, and was able to use his new wealth to initiate public works of all kinds to the benefit of his people. Thus was set in motion, under the wise leadership of Ibn Saud, the process of rapid growth and modernization by which all of us in Saudi Arabia have been so enriched.

14
Ibn Saud

إِنَّمَـا الأُمَـمُ الأَخْـلاقُ مَا بقيتْ   فَإِنْ هُمُ ذَهَبَـت أخلاقُهــم ذَهِبَوا

(أحمد شوقي)

Nations are their ethics. They endure only as long as their ethics do.

(Ahmad Shauqi)

The towering achievements of His Majesty King Abdul Aziz
Ibn Saud were those of a truly remarkable man. To have
united almost the entire Arabian peninsula in a permanent
and harmonious union was an accomplishment which would
have been beyond even the dreams of any ordinary monarch.
It was the Arabs' good fortune that God in his wisdom sent
such a man to us, at a time when he was most needed to
unify Arabia and prepare it for the dominant role it now
plays in world affairs – a role which no amount of oil could
have enabled it to play, had its territory remained fragmented
and its people divided. In this chapter I hope to give an
analysis of what it was that made Ibn Saud so uniquely
successful, both as a monarch and as a man.

In 1935 Colonel T. E. Lawrence wrote his famous book
about his experiences in Arabia entitled *Seven Pillars of Wisdom*. The title of the book seems to me a most apt way of
describing the character of the King, which in my view was
based on seven pillars upon which he raised his kingdom
from nothing. The first pillar was that of religion. From the
earliest days of his life until its very end he remained a
staunch and devout Moslem, following scrupulously the dictates of the Koran in its every detail. His education in exile
in Kuwait was necessarily limited, but this did not prevent
him from mastering the Koran and other religious works to
a degree which often astounded the *ulemas* of his own country. One of the injunctions of the Koran is that the faithful
should read it as often as possible, and His Majesty always
managed to set aside half an hour a day in his crowded
schedule to read the Koran and other religious works, particularly those which listed all the many hundreds of names

by which God is known. His Majesty seldom had a conversation without quoting a verse from the Koran, upon which he drew as a bottomless source of wisdom and inspiration. He was adept at interpreting and explaining the verses in a manner which kept his audience spellbound and enthralled with his insight.

Religion gave a purpose to the King's life in that the more he expanded and consolidated his kingdom, the greater was his service to Islam, which was thus strengthened by his actions. His religious conviction gave him strength in many different ways, yet, however powerful he grew, there was never any danger of his becoming complacent or conceited. The Wahhabi Moslems did not believe in glorifying individuals, and the King knew that as a man he was merely doing his best; everything he achieved was through the will of God alone.

Religion gave Ibn Saud a rigid routine and order to his life which was essential for success in his harsh desert land. Islam requires its adherents to pray facing Mecca five times every day at specified hours, wherever they may be. To do this day in and day out for a lifetime imposes a discipline and dedication to the faith which makes a disciplined and dedicated approach to one's other duties all the easier. The King's daily routine, which has already been described in some detail, began at 4.30 a.m. before the morning prayer. The activities of the day revolved around the other prayer times, culminating in the evening prayer before His Majesty went to his bed. In fact, the King made it a rule never to sleep more than six hours out of every twenty-four, and his sleep was taken in three short periods. He slept for only four hours after midnight, for another hour after morning prayer, and again for about forty-five minutes after lunch. This discipline coupled with his natural physical strength enabled His Majesty to maintain a punishing schedule, both in the Court and in the desert, which would have been beyond men who lacked his faith. His obvious devotion to Islam also inspired his followers and enabled us (though not always without considerable effort) to keep up with the amazing pace which he set.

Even when travelling in the desert, life with the King was extremely ordered. His Majesty would set off exactly one and a half hours after sunrise, with stops during the day based around the times for prayer, and we would continue travelling until just before sunset. Similarly, there was an established routine in the way we travelled each year to and from the Holy Land. Perhaps the greatest personal satisfaction which the King gained from the conquest of Hejaz was that it enabled him every year to perform the hajj, whose ritual was itself established by the Prophet.

For non-Moslems, it is worth recording briefly the ritual of the hajj. On the eighth day of the hajj month, the pilgrims leave Mecca for Mona. The following day is spent at Arafat, and at sunset the pilgrims move to Muzdalifa, where they spend the night. Having collected handfuls of pebbles from here, they move at dawn to Mona and immediately afterwards proceed to Mecca for the seven ritual circumambulations of the Kaaba. The pilgrim robes are then discarded for festive robes and finally the pilgrims return again to Mona for the ritual stoning of the devils which takes place over the next three days. On the evening of the sixth day, the King used to hold a great feast for all the leaders of the Islamic world who were attending the pilgrimage. Before the banquet, His Majesty would deliver the hajj speech, which was always full of good advice and sound religious instruction. The meeting, which also served as an international Moslem conference, was open to all pilgrims of importance, and large crowds would always come to hear the King's words. After the speech, the meeting was open for any leader to air his views on current events. The tradition continues to this day, under King Khalid.

The capture of the Holy Land by the King was the greatest possible good fortune for Islam as a whole, although this was not immediately appreciated by all Arab countries. Shortly after the conquest of Hejaz, the leaders of the principal Arab and Moslem states called a conference to decide the fate of the Holy Cities. While His Majesty doubted the value of this enterprise, he nevertheless generously accommodated the conference at his own expense. After a period of discussion, certain Islamic leaders put forward a proposal that the Holy Land should be recognized as a common country for all Moslems of the world. They suggested that it should be an Islamic Republic, governed democratically by representatives of all the Moslem states. The King had grave doubts about the practicality of this arrangement and his terse reply to the suggestion was, 'Almost all of you are leaders from countries subject to colonial powers. You should free your own countries from foreign domination before you presume to tell me who should rule the Holy Land.' As ever, His Majesty's shaft struck home and the foreign leaders were humbled and speechless. They went away satisfied that the Holy Places were in strong, capable hands which would defend and protect them.

The new confidence of the Moslem leaders in Ibn Saud was more than justified. From the time the King took over Hejaz, he took pains to ensure that the funds donated by the pilgrims for the upkeep of the Holy Places were diligently and honestly administered – which had not always been the case under Hashemite rule. He also took steps to ensure that pilgrims were not swindled by unscrupulous guides at the Holy Places. One of the King's advisers, Hafiz Wahba, was given the task of creating both a system of licensing the guides and a scale of fixed charges by which they should be paid. Unfortunately, the funds which His Majesty was able to set aside for the upkeep of the Holy Places were not always sufficient. In 1949 the Great Mosque of Mecca was showing signs of disrepair and a group of Egyptian Moslems raised £30,000 to put towards its renovation. They came to see His Majesty and asked him for a personal contribution. By that time the King was just beginning to receive substantial oil revenues. He was able to tell the Egyptians that he would personally ensure the restoration of the mosque to its full glory, and that their money could be donated to their own poor. From that time onwards, the Saudi government has assumed full responsibility for the care of all Holy Places, and donations from the faithful are made available for other worthy causes. Over the years, the government has spent countless billions of riyals upon the repair, upkeep and maintenance of the Holy Places.

Such was His Majesty's mastery of religious knowledge and his extreme devotion to Islam that many compare him to the first four Caliphs who succeeded the Prophet Mohammed as leaders of the Moslem faith. These Caliphs are considered to be the wisest men in the history of Islam and were particularly renowned for their interpretation of Holy Writings. It has been said with truth that the King was as great as these Caliphs, for one could only marvel at his ability to make penetrating analyses of the Koran; he could explain and interpret that great book in a manner which was most profound, and yet readily comprehensible to the simplest bedouin. For my part, I believe that His Majesty did more for the faith than any other man this century.

The second of His Majesty's pillars was that of his generosity and mercy. His benevolence was natural and unselfconscious, and he would give unstintingly even when his own cupboards were empty, much to the despair of his Finance Minister, Suleiman, who had to balance the books afterwards. Indeed, I once heard the King say jokingly that he often felt like a *jazur*, or slaughtered camel, because anybody with a deft hand could cut from him as much as he wished.

It is true that his open-handedness could often be a matter of calculated policy, in particular in his dealings with the bedouin, but he also derived a simple joy from giving, which had nothing to do with politics. A story is told that one day the King was travelling in his car with his retinue when several of the vehicles in his convoy became stuck in the sand. As was his custom, he refused to go any further himself until he was quite sure that the cars of all his followers had been dug out. While this was being done, he left his car and sat under the shade of a tree. All of a sudden, a bedouin appeared from nowhere. He did not recognize the King, who was wearing a simple robe and head-cloth. The tribesman sat down beside His Majesty and asked where the Sheikh might be. Ibn Saud replied with a smile that the Sheikh must be somewhere amongst the people he saw. Patiently, the bedouin waited for an opportunity to see the King. When the cars had all been dug out His Majesty prepared to leave and, taking a handful of riyals, gave them spontaneously to the bedouin. At this, the tribesman immediately put out his hand and said, 'I salute you, O Abdul Aziz.' The King asked him, 'How do you know I am Abdul Aziz?', to which the bedouin replied, 'Nobody gives as generously as you.'

However parlous the royal finances might be, His Majesty made it a point never to let a foreign visitor leave the Court without a sumptuous gift. A supply of pearls and other jewellery, and the most beautiful swords and daggers inlaid with precious stones, was kept in the palace for presentation to distinguished guests. It was not uncommon either for the King to give away cars and fine Arabian horses. In 1928 General Clayton was visiting the King in Jeddah. He became ill and had to leave hastily. It was customary for the King to give a farewell party when a guest departed and also customary that, if the guest was in a hurry, he would be given the provisions uncooked so that he could eat them later. When offered the usual party, Clayton politely declined and asked to be excused, saying that he did not feel like eating anything. Thereupon, he was told of the custom that guests in a hurry were given the feast uncooked, and the General accepted this. The King immediately made arrangements for the Royal Navy sloop which had brought General Clayton to be given sufficient provisions to feed the entire crew throughout the whole journey back to England.

On another occasion, shortly after the battle of Sibillah, a deputation of the Sheikhs of Kuwait arrived in Riyadh, headed by Sheikh Ahmad Al-Jaber Al Subah. They had come on a courtesy visit to the King, to congratulate him on finally subduing the Ikhwan. I remember that the members of the Court waited with bated breath to see how His Majesty would deal with this delicate situation, for the treasury was exhausted after the long campaign. Our surprise knew no bounds when we saw the Sheikhs leaving, armed with the most generous gifts. His Majesty had somehow managed to provide them all with cars, gold and silver swords, slaves and sums of money.

Perhaps the most outstanding example of His Majesty's boundless liberality occurred in 1952. In that year, he ordered the construction of a complete palace in Hejaz for King Farouq of Egypt, who was planning a state visit to Arabia. The palace was called Qasr Az-Zafran, and was an exact replica of one of Farouq's palaces in Egypt of the same name. It was built in a very secluded place outside Mecca. At that time, the Egyptian uprising was at its height and it had perhaps been agreed between both monarchs that it might be unsafe for Farouq to be accommodated in a busy city. In fact the palace was never used, for Farouq was deposed by Nasser before the visit took place; even if Farouq had come, he would have occupied the building for only a few days.

To his own family Ibn Saud was endlessly bountiful. There are numerous stories told about this, but perhaps one of the most notable took place towards the end of the King's life, when money from oil was beginning to flow in quantity. A favourite wife asked him if she could have a villa of her own in the garden of his palace. His Majesty at once agreed and gave instructions to his contractor, Ibn Laden, to build a villa. When it was finished, the wife went to inspect it and decided that it was not to her liking. The King immediately ordered Ibn Laden to tear it down and build another in its place. On another occasion, the same wife asked for a gift of a sum equivalent to £100,000. His Majesty calmly enquired why she should request so little and gave her £500,000.

The King's natural generosity was allied to a natural compassion and mercy. In contrast to the long-established custom of cutting off the heads of one's opponents at the earliest opportunity, Ibn Saud displayed the utmost clemency towards defeated enemies. Once a foe was overcome, the King greatly preferred a policy of merciful rehabilitation to one of vengeful retribution. The numerous reprieves given to Ad-Dawish are an excellent example. The King's forbearance could extend even to those who plotted personal violence against him. Once in about 1930, when he was staying in Ta'if, news reached him that a group of youths from a nearby football club were planning to assassinate him in the local mosque. The youths were arrested, but instead of ordering their execution, His Majesty merely imprisoned them. They were released only six months later, after a deputation from Jeddah had petitioned on their behalf.

The King's compassion for the vanquished extended not only to those whom he had defeated personally. One example was that of King Amanullah of Afghanistan. When King Amanullah ascended the throne, many heads of state invited him to visit their countries. Ibn Saud's envoy in Bombay, Sheikh Abdul Rahman Al-Gossaibi, wrote to Ibn Saud suggesting that he should invite Amanullah to visit Mecca while he was on his tour of other states. The King replied that he would not invite him but that Amanullah, as a fellow Moslem, was welcome to visit Mecca. Amanullah was later overthrown by a coup led by Bacha Sag'a, and went into exile in Italy. Although Amanullah was a devout Moslem, after a year or so rumours began to spread that he had become a Roman Catholic. In order to disprove this suggestion and clear his name, he took the earliest opportunity of performing the hajj. Although Ibn Saud had nothing whatever to gain by helping Amanullah, he felt sympathy for a fellow Moslem down on his luck and, while at Mecca, went to greet him personally. I was translating for His Majesty at the time and I can remember him greeting Amanullah with the words, 'I am glad to see you in Mecca.' Having given Amanullah a royal reception, Ibn Saud then personally accommodated him as a guest and instructed his servants to give him all the services befitting a monarch. His Majesty's attention helped to vindicate Amanullah, and he left full of gratitude for the King's kindness.

Another incident concerns the Sheikhs of Kuwait once again. It occurred in 1920, shortly after Faisal Ad-Dawish had attacked Al-Jahara, a small village just outside Kuwait. Many lives were lost during the assault, and there were few families in Kuwait who did not suffer in one way or another. To this day, there are blood stains on the city walls of Al-Jahara. The King had not ordered the attack, however; Ad-Dawish had acted entirely on his own initiative. After the battle, the Sheikhs of Kuwait came in a deputation to His Majesty, assuring him that they realized he had been in no way involved, and protesting their friendship. After the preliminary courtesies, Sheikh Salim Al Subah, who was leading the deputation, told the King that the boundaries of Saudi Arabia extended up to the city walls of Kuwait. His Majesty immediately replied that the borders of Kuwait ran up to the city walls of Riyadh!

Ibn Saud's third pillar was his power of discretion and secrecy. The Prophet once said, 'Take advantage of secrecy to gain your ends and say nothing of your objectives until you achieve them.' His Majesty followed this wise advice to the letter and even those nearest to him, including his own family and closest advisers, would often not know his plans. Because of this, no amount of careless talk would ever reveal those plans to his enemies. I have no doubt that His Majesty's camp was often full of spies, anxious to glean any information they could about the King's intentions. This they failed to do, although His Majesty was able to make full use of information gained by spies of his own from men less able to keep silent. In a country where any rumour travelled like wildfire, His Majesty's reticence was a most powerful weapon against his opponents.

Courage was His Majesty's fourth pillar. There has been no shortage of valiant men in the history of Arabia, but none could have been more valiant than King Abdul Aziz Ibn Saud. He often needed all his courage, for no man could have begun to undertake the task he had set himself, were he not a warrior of unflinching valour. There are countless stories about his bravery. Many tell of his steadfast courage in bearing wounds suffered in battle. Once he bore a serious stomach-wound throughout an arduous campaign for some six months before receiving proper medical attention. The King's surgeon, Rashad Faraon, told me of another occasion when two spent machine-gun bullets had entered His Majesty's abdomen and were lodged just beneath the surface of the skin. Faraon was starting to prepare an anaesthetic when the King asked him what he was doing. When Faraon explained, His Majesty burst out laughing and told him to throw the anaesthetic away. Then, taking a scalpel in his own hand, he cut away the flesh above the bullets and told Faraon to get on with his job.

الــرَأْيُ قَبْـلَ شَجَاعَـةِ الشُّجْعَــانِ   هُوَ أولاً وهــيَ المحــلُّ الثاني

(المتنبي)

Thought ranks above physical courage.

(Al-Mouttanabi)

Although Ibn Saud was renowned for his acts of daring and audacity, his courage was not just that reckless fearlessness which overcomes a man in the heat of battle like a madness and makes him blind to all hazards. He also possessed the calm fortitude of one who sees clearly the danger to himself of a course of action, but takes it all the same because he knows it to be right. He never once bragged about his heroism, nor indeed do I believe that he even thought of himself as a hero. He once said to me, 'What God has given to me has not been given because of my strength, but because of my weakness and his strength.' I remember Yusuf Yassin reporting a conversation he had with the King, when His Majesty said that he felt himself to be a weak person at heart, but that this very feeling spurred him on to feats of gallantry and adventure. He felt that he was really no braver than other men, but God had given him a special gift: in emergencies, his reactions became so fast and keen that he could act more swiftly and decisively than others. He also thought he had been blessed with outstanding luck – the best illustration of which was his own scarred body, where each of a score of wounds told a story of death missed by the merest inches. There was an occasion when Saud Al-Urafa, a cousin of the King (and a man who always considered himself to be a more direct descendant of the Saudi line than Ibn Saud himself), declared in a moment of angry bravado that he was much more courageous than the King. Ibn Saud came to hear of this and, far from being annoyed, smiled broadly and remarked, 'Saud is quite right. He is indeed braver than I, but I am luckier than he!' He also once said, 'If God sends my children the same luck as he has sent me, they will be able to rule the whole Arab world.'

I believe the King's fifth pillar to have been his exceptional powers of perseverance. Once he had set himself a goal he strived tirelessly to achieve it, and no amount of setbacks or reverses could deflect him from his ultimate objective. Those near to him could feel this tenacity of purpose almost as a psychic power, which overwhelmed men of lesser will who dared oppose him. One aspect of this characteristic which affected all of us at the Court was his unflagging appetite for the latest news from all corners of the kingdom, for he knew that in order to be the most powerful man in the country it was necessary first to be the best informed.

His Majesty could, if he wished, apply his indefatigable resolution not only to great affairs of state but also to the most trivial problems of his subjects. Once an old man came to see the King at Mecca in his general *majlis* and handed him a petition concerning some property. His Majesty passed the petition to his son Faisal, who was asked to deal with it. The following year, when the King was again in Mecca, the old man stood outside the Court near His Majesty's chamber and started shouting that nothing had been done about his petition. Ibn Saud immediately ordered that the man be admitted to the palace and, after speaking privately to him, promised that the matter would be cleared up within two days. Faisal was immediately sent for; he explained that he had entrusted the petition to two of his officials. No trace of it could be found, so upon the King's order the entire government office concerned was turned upside down and ransacked until the petition was eventually discovered in an attic. The two officials who had neglected it were instantly dismissed, and the old man at last received satisfaction. This had a salutary effect on all the government staff, who realized that no dereliction of duty, however slight, could be certain of escaping the attention of the King himself.

The King's sixth pillar was that of honesty and justice. In his dealings with everybody from simple bedouin to foreign monarchs, His Majesty's policy was always one of utter integrity and straightforward candour. This could be disconcerting for foreign guests used to hypocritical 'glad-handing' from those they visited. When the great American president Franklin D. Roosevelt was visited by Ibn Saud in Egypt in 1945, Roosevelt's reception could hardly have been what he expected. Roosevelt thrust out his hand in greeting but His Majesty refused to take it, saying, 'How can I shake hands with you when you are assisting the Zionists against us?' Roosevelt was greatly taken aback, but he managed to carry on a conversation with the King during which he promised never to do anything which would prejudice Arab interests.

One thing which I noted particularly about His Majesty was that, however great the provocation, he would never contribute to malicious rumour or gossip. He might become totally cold towards somebody who had incurred his displeasure, and would have no hesitation in condemning him in the strongest terms to his face. But I never knew him to denigrate a man behind his back. An illustration of this was the case of the Al-Mandil family in Iraq, who had been His Majesty's agents there and had become rich and influential under his patronage. After they had acquired wealth and position from their association with the King, they turned their back on Najd and elected to become Iraqi citizens. His Majesty was most hurt by their action and in future became very frosty if their name was mentioned but, despite the fact that there were many stories about their activities in Iraq, he was never heard to speak a word against them.

Being a religious, upright and honourable man himself, His Majesty took a serious view of crime and lawlessness.

240

The Koran supplied Ibn Saud with a ready-made system of law, which he imposed upon all his people with scrupulous impartiality. One of his mottoes was that no government could last without justice. He made no attempt to exempt himself from the rule of law, and if any subject had a claim against the Crown, the King himself would appoint an agent to represent that subject in the Sharia'h court and would make sure that the court was entirely impartial. Needless to say, he invariably abided by the court's decisions.

When His Majesty annexed Hejaz he found that he had inherited a serious crime problem. During the last years of Hashemite rule, villainy of all kinds had flourished, and in the principal towns of the province there were isolated cases of theft, adultery, homosexuality, rape and murder. Outside the towns, some of the more unscrupulous bedouin were making a rich living by highway robbery, particularly of unprotected pilgrims. The King refused to tolerate such conduct in the Holy Land of Islam, and he took note of the saying of the Prophet that harsh punishments are often necessary for the protection of the innocent. In Mecca, examples were made of criminals who had been guilty of premeditated acts of serious theft; their right hands were cut off in strict accordance with Sharia'h law. A notorious bedouin highwayman who had robbed and murdered many pilgrims was caught by the King's Amir in Medina, Mishari Ibn Jelawi. He was handcuffed and his legs were tied together, and he was then thrown into a thorn-tree and left to die in the sun. His remains were deposited on the side of the road as a warning to others. A particularly horrible crime was committed in Mecca when a group of five or six young men kidnapped a teenage boy for homosexual purposes. They held him for several days, then killed him and buried his body in a cellar. All were apprehended, and later executed in the main square of Mecca in front of Government House.

As well as the drastic measures taken against hardened criminals, lesser offenders were also dealt with firmly. Prostitution, for example, was stamped out by gathering up and deporting all known prostitutes. The harsh steps taken by the King to suppress crime were, I believe, in no way inconsistent with his usual clemency. Mercy must never be seen as weakness, and it was essential for the protection of the King's subjects that forceful remedies should be adopted to counter the problems of lawlessness. It should also be remembered that it took only a few stern examples to deter potential criminals and impress upon the citizens of Hejaz that the law was there to be kept. The suppression of crime in Saudi Arabia is very much a success story. It is significant that, although there are large numbers of foreigners living and working in our country, the strict and just nature of our laws is such that they very rarely find criminal acts committed against them, or for that matter cause any trouble themselves. I am aware that researchers have been sent to Saudi Arabia by European countries to find out how it is that the government manages to keep such good order. For myself, I attribute this phenomenon simply to the religion of Islam, the absence of alcoholism and the wise policies laid down by Abdul Aziz Ibn Saud himself.

The King's seventh and final pillar I would describe under the general heading of 'mind-power'. The saying 'Time given to thought is the greatest time-saver of all' neatly sums up His Majesty's attitude. His Majesty was gifted with powers of memory, perception, observation and wit which were utterly out of the ordinary. Additionally, there was about him an almost psychic aura of nobility and wisdom which, coupled with his sheer physical height (he was over six feet two inches tall) and his manly bearing, had an amazingly sobering effect on even the most foolish braggart who came into his presence. There was a grandeur and a magnetism about him which captivated everyone he met, and made him a natural and effortless leader of men. The strength of his will was like a physical force, shaping and bending the minds of lesser men so that they obeyed him eagerly and without question. There were instances too numerous to count when I saw proud chiefs come to his *majlis* in a mood of open hostility; I watched them first being overawed by the King's personality, then won over by his smile and radiant charm.

His Majesty's memory was more impressive than that of any man I have known. He carried in his head sufficient information to fill a library, and had a talent for instant recall which would put a computer to shame. He was, for example, familiar with all the tribes and tribal sections in his kingdom and their history and traditions. Within a few seconds of starting a conversation with a bedouin, the King could tell by the tribesman's manner of speech precisely where he came from and to which section of what tribe he belonged.

The King was a superb conversationalist and debater, and most eloquent in all his speeches. His self-control was such that I cannot remember him ever speaking a word out of place or a word too many, and I never knew him to say anything which he might later regret or wish to withdraw. His ordinary speech was full of cunning metaphors, proverbs and wise sayings which were always to the point, and were such a delight to listen to that one wished he would never stop. He could always find exactly the right remark or proverb to cover any situation. To give just one example, I remember once in Hejaz hearing the King talking to one of Sherif Hussein's former ministers, Abdul Wahhab Naib Al-Haram. On shaking His Majesty's hands, Al-Haram imprudently commented on their softness and expressed surprise that they were the hands of a warrior. Far from being annoyed or embarrassed, the King merely smiled and quoted an old proverb: 'A viper is soft to the touch, but if it turns upon you its fangs are deadly.'

The King's charisma affected not only his subjects; as he became more widely known outside his kingdom and stories about him began to circulate in the Islamic world and in the foreign press, we started to receive some quite peculiar 'fan mail' in the Court. A constant stream of letters arrived, frequently accompanied by photographs of beautiful girls in Europe and America, asking for jobs as maids or governesses in the palace. One letter from Australia enclosed a photograph of an extremely well-dressed and attractive girl who begged for a post, however menial, in His Majesty's household. The King passed the picture to the bedouin chief of the Qahtan tribe, Faisal Ibn Hashar, and asked what he thought. Faisal replied (probably with more truth than he realized), 'Your Majesty, she has obviously fallen in love with you!' If that was the effect which Ibn Saud had on an unknown girl on the other side of the world, imagine his influence on those of us who lived and worked in his presence every day!

His Majesty rarely left the Arabian peninsula. He only made three trips abroad during his lifetime: once to Basra in 1916, at the invitation of the British when they had landed there; secondly, to Kuwait and Bahrain on his return to Arabia after the meeting with King Faisal of Iraq in the Arabian Gulf in 1930; and finally, to Egypt in 1945, to meet President Roosevelt, Winston Churchill and King Farouq. He had friendly diplomatic relations with all the neighbouring Arab leaders except the Hashemite dynasty, represented by Prince, later King, Abdullah of Jordan and King Faisal of Iraq. (It was understandable that relations were strained between the Saudis and the Hashemites, since Ibn Saud had conquered their territory, Hejaz.) The King also enjoyed friendly relations with many other foreign powers. Since most of the neighbouring Asiatic and African states were under colonial rule, the King's diplomatic relations in these areas were, of course, restricted to England, France, Holland and Italy.

No account of Ibn Saud's life would be complete without some mention of His Majesty's sympathy towards the nationalist aspirations of those Arab states under colonial domination, and his particular concern for the people of Palestine. The story of Palestine really merits a chapter all of its own. It has been inextricably linked with the history of the Arab world in general for the greater part of this century, and in particular since the Balfour Declaration of 2 November 1917, which pledged British support for a 'national home' for the Jews in Palestine. However, the 'Palestine problem', as it is still called to this day, has been discussed and written about at length elsewhere. I shall restrict myself here to Ibn

Saud's role in the matter, since his longstanding involvement and untiring concern is perhaps not widely recognized.

From the very beginning of his reign, the King was in the habit of giving help and advice to prominent Arab nationalists in their fight for independence from the colonial Mandatory powers. Hajj Amin Al-Husseini and Shakeeb Arslan, the editor of a magazine published in Switzerland and entitled *The Arab*, were only two of the many prominent political figures in the Arab world to whom Ibn Saud gave his support and assistance. Many of these men received financial help in the form of regular payments which were made through the Saudi Consulates in such countries as Egypt, Syria, Lebanon and Iraq.

As the leading Arab head of state of his time, Ibn Saud was naturally deeply involved in the issue of Palestine. It would be difficult to over-emphasize his concern for the rights of the Palestinian people. Although he preferred to remain out of the limelight, behind the scenes he was in constant communication with the Western powers concerned, and with other Arab leaders. He was always ready to offer his advice, and constantly appealed to the West on behalf of the Palestinians. He frequently issued strongly worded statements expressing his views, and warned of the consequences of ignoring a just solution to the question.

Throughout the general strike which took place in Palestine in 1936, the King was constantly in touch with the British government and the Arab rulers of Iraq, Transjordan and the Yemen. The strike dragged on for six months, and the British eventually appealed to the Arab leaders to intervene. Ibn Saud was instrumental in persuading the Palestinian leaders to bring the strike to an end. It is worth mentioning that, during the strike, the King had arranged for his regular contributions to the Palestinians to be diverted specifically to the orphans and other victims of the strike.

As the issue of Palestine grew in importance, and the implications became ever more serious, so the King's concern increased. I have already mentioned Philby's visit to Saudi Arabia in 1940 to try to persuade the King to accept the

245

suggested plan for Palestine. It is clear that both Britain and the United States considered Ibn Saud's agreement essential if any such plan was to be implemented.

In 1938 a British envoy was sent to Riyadh to request the King's presence at a conference to be held in London the following year on the subject of Palestine. Fully realizing the importance of such a conference, the King accepted the invitation on behalf of his son, Prince Faisal, then Viceroy of Hejaz and Foreign Secretary. When Faisal left for London as head of the Saudi Arabian delegation in January 1939, he took with him a letter from Ibn Saud to the British Prime Minister, Neville Chamberlain. In it, the King reminded Britain of the support the Arabs had given to the British during the war, and appealed to the British government to state clearly, and in a spirit of friendship to the Arabs, their policy on Palestine. Despite all the King's efforts, the so-called London conferences, or Round Table Conference, of February–March 1939 contributed nothing towards the hoped-for settlement. Ibn Saud's correspondence with various Western heads of state makes interesting reading, and a selection of these letters is included in this book. (See Appendix 7.) In his letters, the King made constant appeals to the sense of justice and fair play of Britain and the United States, and was just as constantly reassured that these two powers would do nothing which would be detrimental to the interests of the Arabs. Subsequent events are only too well known.

I have so far said very little about His Majesty's private life, and I do not intend to say very much now, as I feel that great men are entitled to their privacy even after they are dead. There are, however, some facts I can give without disrespect, particularly details concerning His Majesty's family. During the course of his life the King had many wives, although of course never at one time more than the four permitted by religious law. Marriage was for him an important political tool and a powerful instrument in the unification of Saudi Arabia, for when the King married into a particular family, that family and their tribe were greatly honoured and more likely to remain loyal to His Majesty. Even if the wife was eventually divorced, the family remained honoured by the marriage, particularly if the woman had borne children to the King.

Some marriages lasted longer than others; a few endured only a day or so. There were perhaps two wives of whom the King was particularly fond. One was Hassa As-Sudairi, mother of Crown Prince Fahd and his six brothers. She was the daughter of Ahmad As-Sudairi, His Majesty's uncle on his mother's side. The other was Shaheeda, a Syrian from Latakia, who was brought to Arabia when she was only ten or twelve years of age and became a member of the harem in the palace before becoming a wife. His Majesty had at least sixty children. Towards the end of his life he had thirty-six sons still living and numerous daughters (though he never mentioned the exact figure). He lived to see many grand-children on the male side and great-grandchildren on the female side. If a family photograph had ever been taken of His Majesty with all his children and grandchildren, the photographer would have had to fit at least three hundred people into the picture!

Many of the King's sons each deserve a book to them-selves, but there were three who stood out as being his particular favourites. The first was his eldest son Turki, who was born in 1901. During his short life, Turki proved a brave and resourceful warrior and a most skilful hunter. He had already shown a considerable talent for administration and was beginning to develop a personality almost equal to that of his father. Tragically, and to the lasting grief of all who knew him, he died at the age of eighteen in the influenza epidemic which swept Najd in 1919. That year is still known in Arabia as 'the year of mercy' because of the number of people whose souls found peace during its terrible passage.

After the death of Turki, Prince Saud was the King's eldest surviving son. He had been born on the very day that Riyadh fell to his father in 1902. The King placed such confidence in him that he appointed him Viceroy of Riyadh, and nom-inated him as his successor in the early 1930s. Saud was tall and charming like his father and possessed many of his father's qualities, in particular his generosity. He did not, however, have quite the same military prowess or force of will with which his father was endowed.

The third son, Prince Faisal, was also born at an auspicious moment, on the day of the battle of Rowdhat Muhanna in 1906. As a child he showed an early maturity; at the astonishing age of twelve he was sent by his father on a state visit to England, at the invitation of the British government. He impressed everybody he met there with his wisdom and kingly bearing. As he grew up Faisal became adroit, intelligent and an astute politician. After the conquest of the Holy Land, when Faisal was still only twenty years old, Ibn Saud made him Viceroy of Hejaz and subsequently Foreign Secretary. In 1932, when the kingdom was formally given the name of Saudi Arabia, many of the important nations of the world asked Ibn Saud to make a state visit. His Majesty disliked the idea of leaving the country himself, but allowed Faisal to go in his place. The young Prince came through this important grand tour brilliantly, and afterwards became the obvious person to represent the Saudi state whenever a foreign visit became necessary. Once or twice, when I met Faisal myself, he spoke with great enthusiasm and eloquence about his journeys to Europe, and particularly about the city of London, which had impressed him more than any other capital. On top of all his other abilities, Faisal also inherited his father's flair as a general, as was demonstrated by his lightning campaign in the Yemen. I believe that Ibn Saud placed more reliance upon him than on any other of his sons, and I once heard the King say that his only regret about Faisal was that there was only one of him.

His Majesty's greatest private pleasure was his contact with his family. He liked to have as many of his relatives as possible around him at Court, and on most days held a special *majlis* at 7 a.m., when any of the family elders, his sons or other relatives could come to see him and discuss any problems they had, or simply pay their respects. Once a week he would hold an audience with all the men in his family. He held a separate audience with all the women about once a fortnight. The women came veiled or unveiled, according to the closeness of their family connection with him. The King often ordered fine materials from his agents in Bombay and Damascus to distribute as gifts among his entire family. Similar presents were made to all Court officials and the members of the King's retinue. The King adored his younger children, who had the run of the palace and were welcome to visit him at any audience without special permission.

Despite the massive wealth which His Majesty accumulated in the latter part of his reign, he led a frugal and austere life in accordance with the moral dictates of the Koran. His appetites were simple and his personal living accommodation modest. It need hardly be said that he never smoked tobacco or touched any liquor or intoxicating drug. The only indulgence he permitted himself in the way of drink was cardamom coffee, which he consumed in huge quantities and of which he became something of a connoisseur. (Cardamom is a small, fragrant Indian bean.) There was a small group of servants in the Court, all of the same family, who made all the coffee for the King; they travelled with him wherever he went, especially for that purpose. The ritual for producing the coffee was elaborate in the extreme. It was first roasted and boiled in a huge pot. The residue was then poured into a medium-sized pot and reboiled with fresh coffee. The resulting mixture was sifted into a small pot and cardamom added. From this pot the servants poured the coffee into small cups, an endless succession of which were taken to the King wherever he might be. The servants' special technique, the secret of which was jealously guarded, of boiling the dregs of the coffee and adding them to the next brew was a process which added an indefinable 'extra' to the taste. Certainly, I never drank better coffee anywhere in the kingdom.

His Majesty had a well-developed sense of humour, which could sometimes take an impish turn. I remember one occasion when the Manager of Aramco, a Mr Ohliger, came to see him. As soon as Ohliger walked through the door, the

King pretended to mistake him for an enemy and, putting on a face like thunder, ordered his immediate arrest. The order was of course immediately withdrawn, amongst general amusement, but poor Ohliger was still trembling hours later. However, the King would never countenance any frivolity in public, particularly if it seemed to him in any way irreligious. At one time early in his reign when he visited Kuwait, the people were so overjoyed to see him that they organized a grand reception at which a young teenage boy was called upon to sing. Music and dancing are anathema to a strict Wahhabi. As the youth launched into his high-pitched song, the King became so enraged that he leapt to his feet and drew his sword. Calling himself 'son of Faisal' (always a sign of extreme displeasure), he expressed outrage at the indecent performance. The boy went white and withdrew in haste, whereupon His Majesty's composure returned and he sat down as if nothing had happened. Most of history's great leaders are seen to have their frivolous moods and moments in a lighter vein from time to time, but not Ibn Saud. Perhaps he reserved these for his small children in the seclusion of the harem. They certainly never happened in public.

In the very brief intervals which were available to His Majesty for recreation, he loved to indulge his passion for hunting. Sometimes in the winter, he would leave for the desert with a small party and hunt game of all kinds, particularly wild deer. At that time of the year, bustard would fly over Najd in long columns, heading for their winter quarters in the Yemen. As spring approached they would return the same way, probably travelling to Siberia or Manchuria. Many of them fell victim to the King's gun. Once His Majesty shot a bird which had a brass ring on it with a Chinese or Japanese inscription. I was asked to decipher it, but unfortunately the language was unknown to me.

If His Majesty had only a brief time available to him, he sometimes went a short distance outside Riyadh to a place called Al-Khafs. This was a depression in which water would collect if there had been recent rain. The area was much fresher and more fertile than the surrounding desert and was full of colourful vegetation. Sometimes the King would take his favourite counsellors and chiefs there for a picnic; on these rare occasions, talk of state business was forbidden and there would be relaxation and good food. His Majesty was known to unbend very slightly at these picnics, and would sometimes take along a servant with a particularly ready wit to act as jester. One of the jester's tasks was to ask foolish questions of the King's guests. Unless a suitable foolish answer was immediately forthcoming, the guest would be given an appropriate mock punishment or forfeit. Such antics were of course played out far from the public view, for His Majesty had the wisdom always to keep a certain distance between himself and his subjects, however great or important they might be. In this way, the reverence of his people for him was constantly maintained and the dignity of his position upheld. The jester episodes happened only over the last decade of the King's life, and they never occurred more than once a year.

Abdul Aziz Ibn Saud died peacefully in Ta'if on 11 November 1953. His body was wrapped in a simple shroud and buried in the manner of a true Moslem, in an unmarked grave in his capital of Riyadh, there to lie at rest forever after a life of unsurpassed service to the nation he had created and to Islam. His reward from God can be seen on earth as well as in heaven, for the kingdom which he united under him has been given a legacy of unimaginable wealth, administered by an enlightened monarchy. Saudi Arabia sits at the crossroads of the world, and has a strategic and economic significance which is more relevant today than ever before. The unification of the kingdom and the restoration of the pride and dignity of its people through the inspired leadership of Ibn Saud at this crucial moment in our history illustrates the workings of the benign and all-powerful hand of God.

Appendices and Index

APPENDIX 1

The Saudi dynasty

A.D.	A.H.*	
1726–65	1139–79	Mohammed Ibn Saud (39 years)
1765–1803	1179–1218	Abdul Aziz Ibn Mohammed (38 years)
1803–13	1218–29	Saud Ibn Abdul Aziz (10 years)
1813–17	1229–33	Abdullah Ibn Saud (4 years)
1817–19	1233–5	Period of occupation by the forces of Mohammed Ali and Ibn Muammar (2 years)
1819	1235	Mishari Ibn Saud (1 year)
1819–33	1235–49	Turki Ibn Abdullah Ibn Mohammed (14 years)
1834	1250	Mishari Ibn Abdul Rahman Ibn Mishari Ibn Saud (40 days)
1834–8	1250–4	Faisal Ibn Turki (first time; 4 years)
1838–41	1254–7	Khalid Ibn Saud (3 years)
1841–3	1257–9	Abdullah Ibn Thunaian Ibn Saud (2 years)
1843–65	1259–82	Faisal Ibn Turki (second time; 22 years)
1865–9	1282–6	Abdullah Ibn Faisal (first time; 4 years)
1869–74	1286–91	Saud Ibn Faisal (5 years)
1874–84	1291–1302	Abdullah Ibn Faisal (second time; 10 years)
1884–9	1302–07	Period of Al Rashid (5 years)

*Anno Hegirae, the Mohammedan era.

1889–91	1307–09	Abdul Rahman Al-Faisal (2 years)
1891–2	1309–10	Mohammed Ibn Faisal (1 year)
1892–1902	1310–19	Period of regime of Al Rashid (10 years)
1902–53	1319–73	King Abdul Aziz Ibn Saud (51 years)
1953–64	1373–84	King Saud (11 years)
1964–75	1384–95	King Faisal (11 years)
1975–	1395–	King Khalid

The Saudi dynasty: a brief résumé to 1865

The Saudi dynasty takes its name from Saud Ibn Mohammed Ibn Mugrin Ibn Markhan Ibn Ibrahim Ibn Musa Ibn Rabia Ibn Mana Ibn Assad Ibn Rabia Ibn Nizar Ibn Maad Ibn Adnan, from the tribe of Al-Masalikh, a section of the Aneyza. Saud Ibn Mohammed Ibn Saud was the chief of the tribe, which lived in the Eastern Region of Arabia, across the Dahna. He was related by marriage to Durra, the Amir of Hajar Al-Yamamah (Riyadh), and the two men had a long-standing friendship. In 1446 (A.H. 850) the Amir of Hajar asked Mohammed Ibn Saud to come and settle near him and gave him some lands near Dara'iyah. These areas, known as Al-Mulabid and Ghassibeh, are where Mohammed Ibn Saud settled with his people and relatives; they and their descendants developed and built on these lands. When Mohammed Ibn Saud assumed the Amirate, it became known as the Amirate of Al Saud (Dara'iyah). He died in 1724 (A.H. 1137).

The reign of the Saudi dynasty is divided into three major periods. The first period dates from the middle of the reign of Imam Mohammed Ibn Saud (1726–65, A.H. 1139–79), after the death of his father. The Imam was a man of charitable disposition, just and fair towards all his subjects. Sheikh Mohammed Ibn Abdul Wahhab's period as a religious leader lasted from 1745 (A.H. 1158) to the end of the reign of

*The information for this Appendix is derived from *Islamic History in Brief* by Mutlaq Ibn Ba'adi Al Utaiba (Al-Mouttawa', Dammam, 1974).

Abdullah Ibn Saud. Shortly after this came the reigns of Ibn Muammar and Mishari Ibn Saud.

The second period began with the rise of Imam Turki Ibn Abdullah Ibn Mohammed Ibn Saud. The succession shifted from the sons of Abdul Aziz Ibn Mohammed (a section of the Saudi dynasty) to the sons of his brother, Abdullah Ibn Mohammed Ibn Saud, from 1819 (A.H. 1235) up to the end of the reign of Faisal Ibn Turki in 1865 (A.H. 1282). Afterwards followed a period of great confusion, under the rule of the Al Rashid family, which lasted until 1902 (A.H. 1319).

The third period opened in 1902 (A.H. 1319) with the rule of His Majesty King Abdul Aziz. This marked the beginning of the present modern period.

During the first period, it is important to mention the Moslem reformer, Sheikh Mohammed Ibn Abdul Wahhab Ibn Suleiman Ibn Mohammed Ibn Rashid Al-Tamimi, who arose as the leader of a reformist movement in Najd during a period of great social upheaval, when religious ignorance and social degradation were prevalent in the Islamic world. This reformist movement in the heart of the Arabian peninsula – the cradle of Islam – awakened the faithful by calling them to the right path of the true religion. Sheikh Abdul Wahhab was born in 1703 (A.H. 1115) in the town of Uwainah, and obtained his religious instruction from his father, the Qadhi of Huraimleh, who died in 1740 (A.H. 1153). Abdul Wahhab suffered at the hands of religious unbelievers, but was helped by the dedicated faithful. They supported him in the spreading of his movement, whose aim was to enforce the Islamic Sharia'h religious law. The reformer died in 1793 (A.H. 1206) at the ripe old age of ninety-two.

During the reign of Imam Mohammed Ibn Saud from 1726 to 1765 (A.H. 1139–79), the Imam assumed control of the Amirate of Dara'iyah. This was after he had made an agreement in 1747 (A.H. 1160) with Sheikh Mohammed Ibn Abdul Wahhab to spread the message of the Prophet Mohammed, to fight idolatry and superstition, and to wage Holy War in the name of God. At the time, Amir Othman Ibn Muammar was ruling the town of Al-Aienah, and was on good terms with the Amir and the Sheikh. Daham Ibn Dawas had been the ruler of Riyadh since 1682 (A.H. 1093). He was a tyrannical despot, who refused to accept the new doctrine. He became the enemy of Imam Mohammed Ibn Saud and Sheikh Abdul Wahhab. Fighting continued between Dara'iyah and Riyadh from 1746 (A.H. 1159) up to the reign of Imam Abdul Aziz, who swept away the rule of Daham Ibn Dawas and occupied Riyadh. During these battles several people were killed, including Faisal and Saud, the sons of Imam Mohammed. The Imam died in 1765 (A.H. 1179) at Dara'iyah and was succeeded by his son Abdul Aziz.

Imam Abdul Aziz Ibn Mohammed Ibn Saud ruled from 1765 to 1803 (A.H. 1179–1218). He was a brave, courageous and liberal leader, and was much loved by his subjects. He encouraged the spread of learning and knowledge in the towns as well as amongst the tribes. He co-operated with Sheikh Mohammed Ibn Abdul Wahhab in spreading the reformist movement, and countered and fought all opposition to it. He continued the attacks on Daham Ibn Dawas (then Amir of Riyadh) until he forced him to flee the town with his family and followers, most of whom died of thirst on reaching the Sahaba.*

Abdul Aziz entered Riyadh without any opposition in 1764 (A.H. 1178), and remained as ruler of the districts of Najd such as Al-Washim, Sudair and parts of Al-Qasim. Sherif Ghalib in Hejaz prevented the Najdis from performing the pilgrimage to Mecca. Ghalib attacked Al-Qasim in 1790 (A.H. 1205) and later attacked Raniah, Turabah and Khurma. After this, he was forced to make peace with Ibn Saud and subsequently allowed the pilgrims of Najd to perform the hajj unmolested. There was peace until 1803 (A.H. 1217),

---

*The Sahaba is the end of Wadi Hanifah, across the Dahna. It eventually flows across the Summan and into the Gulf of Qatar (also known as the Gulf of Salwa).

when hostilities began again. Abdul Aziz captured Ta'if in 1803 (A.H. 1218) and Ghalib retired to Jeddah.

In 1799 (A.H. 1214) the armies of Abdul Aziz, under the command of his son Saud, reached Karbala in the middle of Iraq. Iraq was highly vulnerable on its left desert flank to the armies from the Arabian peninsula. Saud's forces destroyed all the domes on the graves, since it was believed that they distracted people from the worship of God. The dome and tomb of Al-Hussein (which were very sacred to the Shia'h sect) were also destroyed. This campaign resulted in Imam Abdul Aziz extending his dominion from the shores of the Arabian Gulf in the east to the shores of the Red Sea in the west, and from the southern reaches of Iraq to Bishah and Asir. Islam was firmly established throughout these regions; peace and unity prevailed. But before this, these lands had been wild and uncharted, known only to the tribes who lives there.

In 1803 (A.H. 1218) Imam Abdul Aziz was assassinated by a Shia'h calling himself Othman (a Sunni name), who had come to Dara'iyah from the town of Al-Amarah in Iraq, in the guise of an ascetic. Othman stabbed the Imam with a poisoned scimitar while he was at evening prayer at the Tariff Mosque in Dara'iyah. Behind the Imam was his son, Saud, the grandson of Mohammed Ibn Saud, the founder of the dynasty. Imam Saud Ibn Abdul Aziz Ibn Mohammed Ibn Saud the Great became Imam on the death of his father and ruled from 1803 to 1813 (A.H. 1218–29). Saud was a learned and wise man, both liberal and generous. He performed the hajj nine times, taking with him every year the drapery of red velvet to be placed over the Kaaba. One of Saud's particular concerns was the spread of education in Oman; in 1808 (A.H. 1223) he sent some learned men there as teachers.

The expansion of the Saudi kingdom had provoked the Ottoman Empire into sending their armies from Iraq to Al-Hasa to fight the Saudis in 1798 (A.H. 1213). Sherif Ghalib also moved against the Saudis from the west. At the same time, Mohammed Ali of Egypt started his great expedition against the Najdis in response to the request of the Sublime

Porte. (This was because the Sultan's mother had been denied permission to perform the hajj.) A punitive expedition set out from Egypt for Najd in 1811 (A.H. 1226). The forces travelled by sea and land, under the command of Prince Toussoun, son of Mohammed Ali. They captured Yanbu on the Red Sea, and were then attacked near Badar by the Najdi forces under the command of Prince Abdullah Ibn Saud. The Egyptians were defeated, and the remnants of the army returned to Egypt. In 1812 (A.H. 1227) the expedition returned and occupied Medina after fierce fighting. They went on to occupy Jeddah and Mecca in 1813 (A.H. 1228). Imam Saud died in 1813 (A.H. 1229).

Imam Abdullah Ibn Saud Ibn Mohammed assumed power on his father's death and ruled from 1813 to 1817 (A.H. 1229–33). He was a brave man, but his manner with the bedouin was not that of his father, who had managed to unite the tribes under him. During the rule of Abdullah, many of the bedouin deserted him, and even thought of rebelling against his authority. The thought of independence appealed to them. This gave Mohammed Ali of Egypt the opportunity to invade Najd once again. (When Imam Saud died, Abdullah had been leading the forces both in Hejaz and in Asir, where fighting was continuing. The Saudi-appointed Amir of Hejaz and Asir, Tami Ibn Shuaib, was second-in-command.)

When Abdullah heard of his father's death, he was at a place called Al-Khanigia. He immediately made Ghassab Al-Utaibi Commander of his forces, and ordered him to proceed to Hejaz to lead the battles there. Abdullah himself returned to Dara'iyah in 1813 (A.H. 1229) and sent his brother Faisal to be Supreme Commander in Hejaz. At the time, fierce battles were raging in Hejaz, in Asir, and in the Tihamah, among other places.

The onslaught of the Egyptians continued. Mohammed Ali performed the hajj in 1814 (A.H. 1230) with his armies, and sent Sherif Ghalib and his sons to Egypt. Ghalib was replaced by Sherif Soroor. The battle of Bassil took place near Ta'if; the Saudi army, under the command of Amir Faisal with

Tami Ibn Shuaib, Fahd Ibn Salim and Muslid Ibn Gatnan, was defeated. The Egyptians occupied Bishah and Turabah and captured the Saudi Commander, Tami Ibn Shuaib. Ibn Shuaib was sent first to Egypt and then to Constantinople, where he was paraded through the streets and finally beheaded. Thereafter, the battles shifted to Al-Qasim and all the townships of Najd, ruled over by Imam Abdullah. Shortly afterwards, the two parties made peace and Prince Toussoun returned to Egypt.

In 1815 (A.H. 1231) Mohammed Ali equipped another expedition under the leadership of his son Ibrahim Pasha, and the battles started again. Imam Abdullah first met the Egyptian armies in 1816 (A.H. 1232) in the Hanakieh, and then at the town of Ar-Rass. The inhabitants of Ar-Rass fought like heroes before surrendering. Abdullah then returned to Dara'iyah and fortified the town.

The attacks on Dara'iyah started next, and the town was constantly besieged for the next six months. The Egyptians were receiving reinforcements from Egypt, and from Basra and Zubair in Iraq. Ibrahim Pasha finally attacked Abdullah's headquarters and burnt it down. The Imam then surrendered, after about twenty-one Saudi princes had been killed. The inhabitants of Dara'iyah sued for peace, but Abdullah at first refused to do so. Eventually he was forced to surrender, and was taken to Egypt as a prisoner. When the ruler of Egypt asked Abdullah why the conflict had gone on so long, Abdullah replied that this was in the nature of war. He was then asked his opinion of Ibrahim Pasha. He replied that Ibrahim Pasha had done his best, just as the Saudis had; it was God who ordained the final outcome. Abdullah was sent to Constantinople and killed in 1818 (A.H. 1234) at the gate of Humayun, after being paraded through the streets of Constantinople. His followers were killed in various parts of the city.

In 1818 (A.H. 1234) Ibrahim Pasha killed and tortured many men of great learning and wisdom in Najd; he destroyed the cities as well as committing other atrocities. Many poems were inspired by these tragic events. One such was composed in Bahrain by Abdul Aziz Ibn Ahmad Ibn Muammar, and laments the deaths of so many of the inhabitants of Dara'iyah.

After Ibrahim Pasha had returned to Egypt and Najd was free of members of the Saudi dynasty, Mohammed Ibn Mishari Ibn Muammar of Najd availed himself of the opportunity to return Najd to the old state of affairs. He determined to become the ruler of the area and moved from his town of Uwainah to the capital, Dara'iyah, at the end of 1818 (A.H. 1234). In rebuilding the ruined town of Dara'iyah, he was helped by the people of Al-Mahmal, Sudair and Al-Washim. In 1819 (A.H. 1235) Mohammed Ibn Uraiar Al-Khalidi occupied the Eastern Province, and trade relations were opened up between Najd and the Eastern Province.

Turki Ibn Abdullah Al Saud then returned from his refuge in the south and joined Ibn Muammar (who had taken refuge after the battle of Dara'iyah). Mishari Ibn Saud also returned to the north, after escaping imprisonment by the Egyptians. Mishari then attacked Ibn Muammar and wrested power from him in 1819 (A.H. 1235). One year later, Mishari was attacked by Ibn Muammar, who captured him by stealth and handed him over to the Turkish Commander of Al-Qasim, Abbush Agha.

Mishari was imprisoned until his death; Turki fled Dara'iyah and was joined by several bedouin tribes. Once again, Dara'iyah was attacked and occupied by Turki. Ibn Muammar was captured, together with his son, the Amir of Riyadh. Turki asked the Turkish regime to release Mishari from prison, but the Turks refused. Annoyed at this refusal, Turki killed Ibn Muammar and his son.

Mishari Ibn Saud, brother of Abdullah Ibn Saud Ibn Mishari, was one of the Sauds who had been deported to Egypt by Ibrahim Pasha. He was able to escape from the prison where he was being held in the town of Yanbu, in Hejaz. On his return to Najd in 1819 (A.H. 1235), he was joined by his followers from Al-Qasim, Zilfi and Thurmada. He was chosen as Amir of Sudair, and advanced on Dara'iyah with a large cavalcade. Ibn Muammar was overthrown; he surrendered and relinquished power to Mishari. All those members of the Saud family who had fled Dara'iyah then returned to it. Turki became Amir of Riyadh.

At this point, Ibn Muammar asked for permission to go to Sadoos. After this had been granted, he rebelled and incited other townships to revolt; he was joined by Faisal Ad-Dawish, who sent him an army from the Mutair tribe. He entered Dara'iyah, captured Mishari and imprisoned him. He also tried to capture Turki, but without success; Turki fled with his family to Al-Hair, near Al-Kharj in the south. This marked the end of Mishari's reign, which had lasted only one year (1819, A.H. 1235).

The second Saudi period started in 1819 (A.H. 1235) with the reign of Imam Turki Ibn Abdullah Ibn Mohammed Ibn Saud. Turki had taken refuge first in Al-Hair and then in Dhurma. In 1819 (A.H. 1235), however, he killed Mohammed Ibn Muammar and his son Mishari. Turki then controlled Dara'iyah and other towns in Najd.

In 1819 (A.H. 1236) Hussein Beg and his army reached Al-Qasim from Egypt; they advanced towards Riyadh and conquered it. Turki fled the town, but returned in 1822 (A.H. 1238) with the people of Sudair. He attacked Riyadh repeatedly until he finally breached and entered it in 1824 (A.H. 1240). With him was his cousin, Mishari Ibn Nassir, who had expelled the Turks from Najd. Mishari Ibn Abdul Rahman Ibn Saud arrived in Riyadh after having escaped from Egypt. He was given a warm welcome and treated with great honour and respect; he was made Amir of Manfuha. Sheikh Abdul Rahman Ibn Hassan Ibn Mohammed Ibn Abdul Wahhab also arrived and started a new reform movement.

In 1827 (A.H. 1243) Amir Faisal Ibn Turki returned from Egypt for the first time and came to assist his father. Again in 1829 (A.H. 1245) there were battles between the Saudi armies and the army of Ibn Uraiar Al-Khalidi of Al-Hasa, under the command of Mohammed and Majid Al-Uraiar. These ended in a victory for the Saudis, who annexed the province of Al-Hasa.

One Friday in 1833 (A.H. 1249) Imam Turki was assassinated at the mosque by one of the servants of his nephew (his sister's son), Mishari Ibn Abdul Rahman. Mishari had given the order for the assassination because he thought he had a better right to be ruler. Mishari then assumed power in place of his uncle. At the time, Amir Faisal, Turki's son, was in Al-Hasa. When he heard the news of his father's death, he immediately proceeded to Riyadh and besieged the city in January 1834 (A.H. 19 Muharram 1250). Mishari was killed; his rule had lasted only forty days.

Imam Faisal Ibn Turki Ibn Abdullah Ibn Mohammed Ibn Saud then assumed power and reigned from 1834 to 1838 (A.H. 1250–4). He appointed one of his followers, Abdullah Ibn Ali Ibn Rashid, as Amir of Jabal Shammar. At this point, Amir Faisal reigned supreme from north to south, including Al-Hasa. In 1836 (A.H. 1252) Ismail Agha arrived from Egypt; with him came Amir Khalid Ibn Saud, who had been taken to Egypt by Ibrahim Pasha along with some other Saudi amirs. Imam Faisal felt that the people of Najd had little inclination to fight or go to war, so he took whatever valuables he could carry from his house and retired with his family to Al-Hasa. He remained there until 1837 (A.H. 1253).

Ismail Agha and Khalid occupied Riyadh and started making attacks into the hinterland of Najd until they were defeated by the people of Al-Hair, Al-Hautta and As-Salwa. Faisal then quickly joined forces with the men who had defeated Ismail Agha and Khalid. With their help, Faisal attacked Riyadh, and surrounded and defeated Khalid and his companion at Al-Masana, now a suburb of Riyadh. Faisal then spent a day in talks with Khalid, in an attempt to bring about a truce. This was in 1837 (A.H. 1253). The meeting proved a failure. Meanwhile, Khurshid Pasha entered Najd and asked the Imam to desist from waging war against the Turks; in return, the Turks would appoint the Imam as Amir of Najd. Shortly afterwards, Faisal left Riyadh and went to stay in the town of Dilam, south of Riyadh, having ordered his army to withdraw. He sent Omar Ibn Yahya Ibn Ghaibab to Oman, and appointed Zuhairi as Amir of Wadi Dawasir, and Mohammed Ibn Abdullah Ibn Jalajil as Amir of Al-Aflaj. He allowed his brother, Jelawi, to remain with Khurshid Pasha in Unayzah. But when differences arose between them, Jelawi rejoined his brother.

Khurshid then returned to Riyadh and a great battle took place at Al-Kharab in December 1838 (A.H. 23 Ramadan 1254). After peace terms were agreed, Imam Faisal, his brother Jelawi, Faisal's two sons Abdullah and Ahmad, and Faisal's nephew Abdullah Ibn Ibrahim were sent to Egypt.

Amir Khalid Ibn Abdul Aziz Ibn Mohammed Ibn Saud, who ruled from 1838 to 1841 (A.H. 1254–7), was the brother of Abdullah Ibn Saud. His mother was from Ethiopia. He had a keen brain, and was a sensitive, pleasure-loving man. He was brought up under the aegis of Mohammed Ali and became Egyptianized in his ways. Amir Khalid was brought by the Turks to rule Najd on their behalf; he was to be ruler in name only. He was able to gain control of Najd with the Turks' help after Imam Faisal had left for Egypt in 1838 (A.H. 1254). But in 1841 (A.H. 1257) differences arose between Khalid and Abdullah Ibn Thunaian, who was in league with the people of Al-Hawta and Al-Hariq; they occupied Najd and forced Khalid to escape to Al-Hasa, later to Kuwait and from there to Al-Qasim. He then proceeded to Mecca, where he died.

Amir Abdullah Ibn Thunaian Ibn Ibrahim Ibn Saud, who ruled from 1841 to 1843 (A.H. 1257–9), first rose to prominence when he had a dispute with Khalid Ibn Saud in which he was joined by the people of Al-Hawta and Al-Hariq. Khalid was driven from Najd, while Ibn Thunaian assumed power. He appointed Abdul Aziz Ibn Qaif as Amir of Sudair, and Abdullah Ibn Aubaikan as Amir of Wadi Dawasir. Next he appointed Omar Ibn Affaisan as Amir of Al-Hasa, and Ahmad As-Sudairi as Amir of Al-Qatif. After Ibn Thunaian had ruled for two years in Najd, Imam Faisal emerged from exile in Egypt.

Imam Faisal had been in exile in Egypt until 1843 (A.H. 1259). Thereafter, with God's help, he returned as the ruler of Najd. He ruled from 1843 to 1865 (A.H. 1259–82). When

Imam Faisal reached Jabal Shammar with his followers, he was well received by Abdullah Al-Ali Al Rashid. Al Rashid and his men accompanied Faisal's troops until they reached Riyadh. During this time, they were joined by the people of Al-Qasim. On entering Riyadh, they imprisoned Ibn Thunaian (who died in prison the same year) and Faisal assumed power for the second time.

In 1844 (A.H. 1260) Faisal entered Al-Hasa and appointed Ahmad Mohammed As-Sudairi as Amir. In 1845 (A.H. 1261) the chief of the Ajman tribe, Fallah Ibn Huthlain, carried out several attacks on pilgrims' caravans travelling from Bahrain and Persia. These attacks displeased the Imam, who ordered the capture and arrest of Fallah. Fallah was finally executed in Al-Hasa in 1846 (A.H. 1262).

The following year, Faisal sent an expedition to Oman under the leadership of Abdul Rahman Ibn Ibrahim, who occupied it and established himself at the castle of Burraimi. In 1848 (A.H. 1265) differences again arose between Faisal and the people of Al-Qasim, and a fierce battle ensued. The Saudi Commander was Abdullah Al-Faisal. The battle was called the *Yattimah*, which means 'the orphan', because so many of the people of Al-Qasim were killed. Faisal then appointed his brother, Jelawi, as Governor of Al-Qasim.

In 1850 (A.H. 1267) the people of Qatar came under the rule of Faisal. When Qatar joined the government of Arabia, it became a naval state with three hundred ships in the Gulf. The same year, differences arose between Faisal and the people of Bahrain. The Bahrainis asked for help from the Amir of Abu Dhabi, Sa'id Ibn Dahnoon, who provided as many men and ships as he could. Later on, however, he took fright and sued for peace, asking to negotiate with Imam Faisal personally. A meeting was arranged and peace established. Under the treaty, the people of Bahrain were to continue paying their previous tributes, and in addition a new tax was introduced.

The same year the Khedive of Egypt sent a military expedition to Asir, but it was met by the Saudi Amir, Aiad Ibn Mar'ai of Asir. There were several battles and skirmishes during 1852 (A.H. 1269), in all of which the Saudis were victorious. In 1853 (A.H. 1270) the people of Al-Qasim rebelled again against Faisal, and there were constant outbreaks of rebellion until 1862 (A.H. 1279), when Faisal appointed Ahmad Ibn Mohammed As-Sudairi as Governor instead of Jelawi. Imam Faisal died in 1865 (A.H. 1282).

According to a traveller at the time, A. Cornell Billy, the states and leaders of the principalities of Bahrain, Abu Dhabi, Umm Al-Qaiwain, Ajman, Sharja and Ras Al-Khaima, and the Sultanate of Muscat all paid regular taxes and tributes to the Saudi Amirate of Bahrain.

The Al Rashid dynasty

A.D.	A.H.	
1834–48	1250–65	Abdullah Ibn Ali Ibn Rashid (14 years; died from natural causes)
1848–56	1265–73	Talal Ibn Abdullah (8 years; committed suicide after a mental breakdown)
1856–68	1273–85	Mutaib Ibn Abdullah (12 years; killed by his nephews, Bandar and Badr)
1868–71	1285–8	Bandar Ibn Talal Ibn Abdullah (3 years; killed by his uncle, Mohammed)
1872–97	1289–1315	Mohammed Ibn Abdullah the Great (25 years; died from natural causes)
1897–1906	1315–24	Abdul Aziz Ibn Mutaib Ibn Abdul Aziz (9 years; killed at Rowdhat Muhanna)
1906–07	1324	Mutaib Ibn Abdul Aziz (1 year; killed by Misha'al and Mohammed, sons of Homud)
1907–09	1324–6	Sultan Ibn Homud Ibn Obaid (2 years; killed by his brother, Saud)
1909–10	1326–7	Saud Ibn Homud (1 year; killed by Saud Ibn Abdul Aziz)
1910–19	1327–38	Saud Ibn Abdul Aziz Al-Mutaib (9 years; killed by Abdullah Ibn Talal)

1919	1338	Abdullah Ibn Talal (killed by one of the slaves of Saud Ibn Abdul Aziz Al-Mutaib)
1919–20	1338–9	Abdullah Ibn Mutaib Ibn Abdul Aziz (1 year; surrendered to Ibn Saud)
1920–1	1339–41	Mohammed Ibn Talal Ibn Naif (1 year; surrendered to Ibn Saud on the fall of Ha'il)

Important battles and events during the life of His Majesty King Ibn Saud

1900 (A.H. 1318)	Battle of Sarif between Sheikh Mubarak Al Subah, the Amir of Kuwait, and Abdul Aziz Ibn Mutaib Al Rashid, the Amir and ruler of Ha'il and Jabal Shammar.
1902 (A.H. 1319)	Capture of Riyadh, the capital of the kingdom.
1902 (A.H. 1319)	Battle of Dilam.
1904 (A.H. 1322)	Conquest of Unayzah in Al-Qasim.
1904 (A.H. 1322)	Conquest of Buraida, the capital of Al-Qasim, and the defeat of Aba Al-Kheil.
1904 (A.H. 1322)	Battle of Bukairiya.
15 November 1904 (A.H. 18 Rajab 1322)	Battle of Shinanah.
1906 (A.H. 1324)	Battle of Rowdhat Muhanna in which Abdul Aziz Al Rashid was killed.
22 September 1907 (A.H. 5 Sha'ban 1325)	Battle of At-Truffiah.
1910 (A.H. 1328)	Battle of Haddiah.

1910 (A.H. 1328)	Conquest of Al-Harriq and the defeat and liquidation of Al-Hazazinah, ruler of the Southern Province.
1913 (A.H. 1331)	Surrender of Hufuf and conquest of Al-Hasa province.
1915 (A.H. 1333)	Battle of Jurrab.
1915 (A.H. 1333)	Battle of Kanzam with the Ajman tribe.
1919 (A.H. 1337)	Battle of Turabah.
13 October 1920 (A.H. 26 Muharram 1339)	Battle of Jahare.
1921 (A.H. 1340)	Battle of Wadi Hajlah, surrender of Abha and conquest of Asir.
1921 (A.H. 1341	Capture of Ha'il.
1923 (A.H. 1343)	First oil concession granted to Eastern & General Syndicate.
1924 (A.H. 1343)	Fall of Ta'if.
1924 (A.H. 1343)	Entry into Mecca.
1925 (A.H. 1344)	Incident of the Egyptian Guards of the Mahmal.
1925 (A.H. 1344)	Surrender of Medina.
1925 (A.H. 1344)	Surrender of Jeddah.
1926 (A.H. 1344)	Proclamation of King Ibn Saud as King of Hejaz.
1928 (A.H. 1346)	The 'Big Gathering' at Riyadh.
1929 (A.H. 1347)	Battle of Sibillah.

27 February 1930 (A.H. 21 Ramadan 1348)	Meeting of King Ibn Saud with King Faisal of Iraq in Arabian Gulf.
1932 (A.H. 1351)	Revolt of Hamad Ibn Rifdh.
27 September 1932 (A.H. 21 Jumada I. 1351)	Changing of the name of H.M. King of Hejaz and Sultan of Najd to H.M. King of Saudi Arabia.
13 November 1932 (A.H. 5 Rajab 1351)	Revolt of the Al Adrisah.
11 May 1933 (A.H. 16 Muharram 1352)	Proclamation of Prince Saud Ibn Abdul Aziz as Crown Prince of Saudi Arabia.
1933 (A.H. 1352)	Oil concession granted to Standard Oil.
1934 (A.H. 1352)	First War of the Yemen.
1935 (A.H. 1353)	Attempted assassination of King Ibn Saud by Yemenis in the Great Mosque at Mecca.
1945 (A.H. 1365)	Meeting with President Roosevelt, Winston Churchill and King Farouq in Egypt.
11 November 1953 (A.H. 1 Rabia I. 1373)	Death of H.M. King Abdul Aziz Ibn Saud.

The men who took part in the capture of Riyadh in 1902 (A.H. 1319)

Prince Abdul Aziz Ibn Saud
Abdullah Ibn Jelawi*
Abdul Aziz Ibn Mussaud
Ibn Jelawi*
Nassir Ibn Farhan Al Saud*
Mohammed Saleh
Shalhowb*
Ibrahim Al-Niffisi*
Fahd Al-Mashook*
Sa'ad Ibn Bakhit*
Abdul Aziz Ar-Rubai*
Mohammed Ibn Abdul
Rahman (the Prince's
brother)
Fahd Ibn Jelawi
Abdul Aziz Ibn Abdullah
Ibn Turki Al Saud
Abdullah Ibn Snitan Al
Saud
Fahd Ibn Ibrahim Mashari
Al Saud
Haizam Al-Ajalin Ad-
Dossari
Abdullah Ibn Shater Ad-
Dossari

Thalab Al-Ajalin Ad-
Dossari
Mansour Ibn Hamza Al-
Mansour
Saleh Ibn Saban
Yusuf Ibn Mashkas
Said Ibn Bishan Ad-Dossari
Massaud Al-Mabrook
Mohammed Al-Mashook
Nassir Ibn Shaman
Mohammed Ibn Wabir Ash-
Shammari
Sattam Aba Al-Khail Al-
Muargab Ad-Dossari
Mohammed Ibn Hazza
Zaid Ibn Zaid (cousin of
Mohammed Ibn Zaid)
Fahd Ibn Shair Ad-Dossari
Feyrooz (the Prince's body-
guard)
Abdul Latif Al-Mashook
Farhan Al Saud
Mutlaq Al Ujaian
Abdullah Ibn Asker

* The men who scaled the city walls with Prince Abdul Aziz.

Majid Ibn Murraid As-Subai

Abdullah Ibn Othman Al-Hazani

Sa'ad Ibn Obaid

Abdullah Ibn Graiss

Muadhad Ibn Khuraisan Ash-Shammari

Talla Ibn Ajrash

Saud Ibn Jaifan

Aubaid Ibn Saleh Awaibil

Hashash Al-Arjani

Abdullah Abu Dhaib As-Subai

Shuia Ibn Shadad Ibn Al Mohammed As-Suhul

Mohammed Ibn Gamma'a

Abdullah Al-Jutaily

Ibrahim Ibn Muhaidhif

Abdullah Ibn Khanaizan

Mansour Ibn Fraij

Salim Al-Afijah

Aubaid (brother of Shawi Ad-Dossari)

Sultan (servant of the Prince)

Hatrash Al-Arjani

Sa'ad Ibn Hudaibi

Mutlaq Ibn Jaffal

Zaid Alifshi As-Subai

Munawar Al-Azzi

Nafea Aliawbi

Abdullah Ibn Muraid As-Subai

The men who accompanied His Majesty from Kuwait were picked from different tribes, as this was the practice of the bedouin when traversing hostile territory; a member of each tribe served as a protective shield, saving the group from members of his tribe who might be hostile, for they never harmed one of their own men. Although they had only forty camels, the bedouin traditionally double-mounted their camels when on a forced march.

Ikhwan settlements

This is a list of all the most important Ikhwan settlements. Under the name of each tribe are listed the settlements which they formed, and against each settlement are shown the names of the chiefs who governed it.

UTAIBA

Niffi	Omar Ibn Rubaian, Naif and Khalid Al-Hlag, Majid Al-Barak, Badr Ibn Al-Wash, Ash-Shokeree Ibn Az-Zhaf
Al-Hafera	Manahi Al-Hydle, Sultan Ibn Hashr, Salal Ibn Manas Al-Hydle
Al-Labeeb	Abdul Mohsin Ibn Badr Al-Hydle, Salal Ibn Badr, Omar Abu Rakaba
Masdah	Khalid Ibn Gama, Mutrik Ibn Gama
Sanam	Sultan Abu Al-Ula, Hazaa Ibn Mofirek
Ar-Rowedah	Gamal Al-Mohree
Aseela	Ghazi At-Toom, Daif Allah At-Toom, Dakhil Allah Ibn Wasmi
Sager	Zuaar Ibn Rabeaan, Naif Ibn Turki, Daif Allah Ibn Turki, Turki Ibn Fayhan
Orwi	Hashr Ibn Mogaad Ibn Hameed
Ar-Rodah	Majid Ibn Henawi, Fayhan Ibn Faheed
Himiyan	Badr Ibn Okel, Manas Ibn Okel
Kabshan	Sultan Abu Khashim, Gaed Ibn Bagad Abu Khashim
Al-Maklat	Majid Abu Khashim
As-Soh	Sultan Al-Gharbi
Arga	Kateem Al-Hobil, Talg Ibn Gazih, Abdullah Al-Wateer

276

QAHTAN

Ar-Reen Al-Ulya	Huzal Ibn Saeedan, Hezam Ibn Sagr, Eshk Ibn Musfer, Koblan Ibn Haweri, Abdul Aziz Ibn Libda, Faisal Ibn Libda
Ar-Reen As-Sofla	Sultan Ibn Safran, Khalil Ibn Omer, Sa'ad Ibn Gleeghm, Turki Ibn Saleem, Waydah Al-Agah
Al-Hayathim	Faisal Ibn Hashr, Khalid Ibn Faisal, Fahd Ibn Moriha, Faisal Ibn Magdal
Al-Hasah As-Sofla	Fanis Ibn Howeel
Al-Hasah Al-Ulya	Sa'ad Ibn Galban
Al-Gofair	Naser Ibn Sadhan
Al-Monaisef	Helal Ibn Aboud
Laban	Ruga Ibn Nasir

SUBAI

Al-Hessy	Fadghoshe Ibn Shewaya, Waleed Ibn Shewaya, Ghaythum Ibn Fahd, Mutlag As-Sayghee
As-Sobeaa	Ali Ibn Hudehid, Thanyan Ibn Hudehid, Faleh Ibn Gheda
Al-Khedr	Ad-Doury Ibn Gafran, Sobea Kharman Abu Thanin, Hanidan Abu Thanin

AS-SUHUL

Al-Mashash	Manahi Ibn Galoud
Ar-Rowedah	Abdullah Ibn Fatehoor
Al-Badaa	Sawar Ibn Meadel

HARB

Kebah	Abdul Mohsin Al-Ghorn, Nafea Ibn Fadela
Dakhta	Abdul Bahima, Zuar Ibn Betla, Badr Al-Moshdig, Eid Ibn Afra
Al-Kawara	Ali Ibn Hudib, Faleh Ibn Hudib, Eid Ibn Mukhlif

Al-Khashibee	Obaid Az-Zoghaiby, Abdullah Az-Zoghaiby, Ghanim Az-Zoghaiby
Deedah	Hathool Ibn Hudib
Khasiba	Zuaar Ibn Hammad, Sultan Ibn Hammad
Kahila	Naif Ibn Nahil, Shakir Ibn Halaf
Abu Mughir	Sa'ad Ibn Rabig
Al-Nahita	Debian Ibn Ghadin
Sadig	Bagad Ibn Ghamid, Mutib Ibn Ghamid, Bagad Ibn Hoban
Al-Kareen	Abdul Maneh Ibn Nafi, Abdullah Ibn Nafi, Saleh Ibn Nafi
Al-Brood	Naif Ibn Mudian, Fegan Ibn Mudian, Thallab Ibn Sumear
Al-Ba'ayeth	Rabah Ibn Mutlag, Mukhimer Ibn Mutlag
Al-Mahallani	Rashid Ibn Rashid
Al-Fawara	Hegab Ibn Nahet, Daif Allah Ibn Nahet, Zaid Ibn Nahet, Hamood Abu Aloon, Sameh Al-Beshri
Koton	Shadeed Ad-Dairy
Ad-Dolaimah	Zaban Ibn Godea, Doeg Ibn Godea, Dahwee Ibn Godea
Bakee-ah	Meshaan Al-Beshri
As-Sabikia	Hendi Az-Zowaiby, Faihan Az-Zowaiby, Mohammed Ibn Nahis Az-Zowaiby, Naif Ibn Nahis Az-Zowaiby
Al-Gheda	Okeal Az-Zuhairy, Nasir Ibn Merikhan
Al-Bada'a	Galwan Al-Balhy

UNAYZAH

Khaiber	Mohammed Ibn Farhan Al-Ayda, Hazaa Ibn Hayes Al-Ayda, Hazaa Ibn Mohammed Al-Ayda
Al-Gheda	Grebea Ibn Sewelem, Naser Ibn Sewelem
Bedenthil	Khalaf Al-Awagi

Ash-Shoeba	Sharea Ibn Mehlad, Farhan Ibn Mash'hur
Ash-Shemly	Abdul Mohsin Ibn Sha'aman
Al-Blazia	Abdul Rahman Ibn Moetag

SHAMMAR

Al-Agfar	Ayaa Ibn Nahber, Hamdan Ibn Geddy, Sultan Ibn Ayesh
Alsafra	Mugheleth Ibn Gar Allah
Om Al-Kalban	Ghadban Ibn Ramal
Gebesh	Udwan Ibn Ramal, Mareed Ibn Ramal
Al-Hafeer	Kateb An-Nammas
At-Teem	Fareeh Al-Hamazi
Al-Khebba	Fareeh Al-Harbeed
As-Saneena	Saadoon Ibn Abbas
An-Naabi	Abdul Kareem Az-Zobed
Al-Faseem	Godeel Ibn Alfa, Adeeb Ibn Alfaseem, Sabeeb Ibn Alfaseem
Al-Makhool	Marzooq Al-Adeem
As-Sahwa	Manzel Ibn Ha'il
Ash-Shakeek	Muwafee Ibn Mouref
Al-Kaseer	Hawas Ibn Khamsan, Mugbel Ibn Khamsan
Al-Gheda	Gadi Ibn Qandeel, Khatlan Qandeel, Sultan Ibn Qandeel
Al-Akla	Hawas Ibn Twala, Mohammed Ibn Dary Ibn Twala, Mashl Ibn Salem Ibn Twala

MUTAIR

Artawiya	Abdul Aziz Ad-Dawish, Naif Ibn Mussaud, Faisal Ibn Shiblan, Mohammed Ibn Badr, Hazaa Ibn Badr, Museer Ibn Muzyed
Karyet As-Sofla	Hayef Af-Fagham, Sa'ad Ibn Kredy Af-Fagham, Bandar Ibn Dedan Af-Fagham

279

Karyet Al-Ulya	Treheen Ibn Shogeer, Fallah Ibn Shogeer, Faisal Ibn Naif Ibn Shogeer, Hezam Ibn Zereeban, Majid Al-Askah, Gassab Ibn Mandeel
Al-Gharothee	Yagoob Al-Hameedani, Kaed Ibn Bases, Majid Ibn Khashman, Turki Ibn Bases, Khalid Ibn Bases
At-Tamereya	Yagoob Al-Hameedani, Mohammed Ibn Muleh Al-Hameedani, Baghdad Ibn Kanan Al-Hameedani, Zoar Ibn Yagoob Al-Hameedani
Al-Hasow	Gamean Ibn Dawi
Boda	Mutlag Al-Hafta
Om Hazm	Awad Al-Maghawi
Al-Lisafa	Gaser Ibn Lami
Maleeh	Alwash Ibn Shakyan, Ghazi Ibn Shakyan
Al-Atla	Howel Ibn Samhan, Muzker Ibn Samhan
Waddakh	Munaif Ibn Fateem
Mubayed	Tamim Al-Koreefa

AZ-ZUFAIR

Ash-Shoebi	Agami Ibn Sowet, Hazaa Ibn Ekab Ibn Sowet, Abdullah Ibn Yagoob Ibn Sowet, Hamdan Ibn Dowehi Az-Zufair

AJMAN

As-Serar	Hezam Ibn Hathleen
Al-Kahfa	Fahd Ibn Hathleen
Alwana	Salem Ibn Wazeen
Haneen	Mansour Ibn Shafi
Naga	Mohammed Ibn Hessa
Az-Zoghain	Khalid Al-Motalkem
Orairah	Mana Ibn Gomaa
Al-Ayyena	Naif Ibn Hathleen
Ghenwa	Mohammed Ibn Aseedan

Al-Karadi	Khalid Ibn Hathleen
As-Sahaf	Fahd Ibn Bagash
Om Rabea	Malha Ibn Kadaan
Al-Barah	Mutlag Ibn Zeniker
Katnana	Mohammed Ibn Tebia

BANI KHALID

Ad-Doffi	Fares Al-Hasan, Shabeeb Al-Hasan
Halmooda	Karan Ibn Agran, Khalid Ibn Harbi Ibn Akl, Hezam Ibn Thanian, Faleh Ibn Kolaib

BANI HAJER

Ein Dar	Mohammed Ibn Naser Ibn Khalifa, Abdullah Ibn Mohammed Ibn Khalifa, Mohammed Ibn Mubarak Ibn Khalifa
Yakreb	Shafi Ibn Shafi, Hamood Ibn Shafi
Fooda	Mohammed Ibn Teaza, Shayeh Ibn Soda
Salasel	Ali Ibn Abed, Hamad Ibn Abed

AL MURRAH

Yabreen	Hamad Al-Mordef, Saleh Al-Mordef
As-Sekak	Hamad Ibn Hatrab, Fadel Ibn Fadel
Nebak	Sa'ad Ibn Nakawan
Al-Yaduo	Rashid Ibn Nedela, Naam Ibn Shareem, Saleh Abu Leila, Muteb As-Saffak

AL DAWASIR

Al-Homer	Huzal Ibn Wakyan
Musherfa	Manhi Ibn Hafeez
Al-Waseeta	Mohammed Ibn Wakyan, Sheban Ibn Waked, Sagr Ibn Deraan, Mehmas Ibn Sewelma
Al-Hazm	Abdullah Ibn Naser, Naif Ibn Hamlan, Haged Ibn Garwa, Salal Ibn Hamlan

HATEM
Nabwan	Daleem Ibn Yarak, Doar Ibn Amir
Ar-Roud	Ghazi Ibn Hadi
Al-Amayer	Shaker Ibn Kaaboob

AL-AWAZEM
Aneek	Fallah Ibn Gamea
Tag	Modaed Al-Molaby

The Palestine question

STATEMENTS AND CORRESPONDENCE BETWEEN KING IBN SAUD
AND WESTERN HEADS OF STATE ON THE QUESTION OF
PALESTINE.

Press Release Issued by the Department of State, October 14, 1938

Within the past few days this Government has received a
large number of telegrams and letters from individuals and
organizations in the United States concerning the Palestine
situation, with particular reference to the reported possibility
of the application by the British Government of a new policy
with respect to that country. It is obviously impracticable to
reply separately to the many communications which have
been received and this statement is therefore being issued in
lieu of individual answers.

As is well known the American people have for many
years taken a close interest in the development of the Jewish
National Home in Palestine. Beginning with President Wilson
each succeeding President has on one or more occasions
expressed his own interest in the idea of a National Home
and his pleasure at the progress made in its establishment.
American sympathy in a Jewish Homeland in Palestine was
further manifested by the Joint Resolution of Congress signed
by the President on September 21, 1922, recording the favorable attitude of the United States towards such a Homeland.

In submitting the resolution the House Committee on Foreign Affairs reported that it:

expresses our moral interest in and our favorable attitude toward the establishment in Palestine of a National Home for the Jewish people. It commits us to no foreign obligation or entanglement.

It is in the light of this interest that the American Government and people have watched with the keenest sympathy the development in Palestine of the National Home, a project in which American intellect and capital have played a leading role.

On several occasions this Government has brought its views regarding the rights of the United States and its nationals in Palestine to the attention of the British Government. As recently as 1937 a formal exchange of correspondence took place and the following self-explanatory paragraph is quoted from the concluding note dated August 4, 1937, communicated by the American Ambassador in London to the British Foreign Office:

In expressing satisfaction and appreciation for the assurances furnished that His Majesty's Government intends to keep the United States Government fully informed of any proposals which may be made to the Council of the League of Nations for the modification of the Palestine Mandate, I am instructed to request that these proposals may be communicated to my Government in ample time to enable it to determine what, if any, observations it may desire to make with a view to the preservation of American rights in Palestine.

It is expected, therefore, that this Government will have an opportunity to submit its views to the British Government with respect to any changes affecting American rights which may be proposed in the Palestine Mandate. These rights, which are defined by the American-British Mandate Convention or Treaty of December 3, 1924, comprise non-discriminatory treatment in matters of commerce, non-impairment of vested American property rights, permission for American nationals to establish and maintain educational, philanthropic and religious institutions in Palestine, safeguards with respect to the judiciary, and, in general, equality of treatment with all other foreign nationals.

The rights of the United States in connection with any changes in the terms of the Palestine Mandate are set forth in Article 7 of the above-mentioned Treaty, which reads as follows:

Nothing contained in the present Convention shall be affected by any modification which may be made in the terms of the mandate, as recited above, unless such modification shall have been assented to by the United States.

This article is substantially identical with corresponding articles included in eight other existing agreements concluded by this Government with respect to the mandated territories of Syria and the Lebanon, former German islands in the North Pacific, French Cameroons, French Togoland, Belgian East Africa and British Togoland. None of these articles empower the Government of the United States to prevent the modification of the terms of any of the mandates. Under their provisions, however, this Government can decline to recognize the validity of the application to American interests of any modification of the mandates unless such modification has been assented to by the Government of the United States.

It is the Department's understanding that the Palestine Partition Commission, which was appointed some months ago to make recommendations with respect to partition, will make its report to the British Government at the end of this month and that no decision will be reached by that Government on the subject until after an opportunity has been had to give consideration to that report. In reply to a question in the House of Commons on October 5, 1938, Mr. MacDonald, British Colonial Secretary, is reported to have stated that the House of Commons would not be in the position of having to confirm or reject a decision already taken and put into operation but would have an opportunity of considering the policy before it was adopted and put into operation by the British Government.

The Department will, of course, continue to follow the situation closely and will take all necessary measures for the protection of American rights and interests in Palestine.

The Chargé in Egypt (Merriam) to the Secretary of State

CAIRO, December 15, 1938

SIR: With reference to the Legation's telegram No. 94 of December 8, 10 a.m., 1938,[1] I have the honor to enclose herewith the original of a note in Arabic from the King of Saudi Arabia to the President, together with a careful suggested translation thereof which has been made in the Legation.

The note was handed to me on December 6, 1938 by Sheikh Fawzan Es Sabek, Saudi Arabian Chargé d'Affaires in Cairo, who called at the Legation for the purpose accompanied by Mohamed Reda, his First Secretary. The Sheikh did not allude to the contents of the note in any way in the course of the conversation that took place during his call, but merely asked me to transmit it. I agreed to do this and said that it would be accompanied by an English translation made by my staff.

The Legation has made a longhand copy of the Arabic original for its files.

Respectively yours,　　　　　　　GORDON P. MERRIAM

[Enclosure – Translation]

The King of Saudi Arabia (Abdul Es Saud) to President Roosevelt

MR. PRESIDENT: We have been informed of what has been published regarding the position of the Government of the United States of America concerning support of the Jews in Palestine. In view of our confidence in your love of right and justice, and the attachment of the free American People

[1] Not printed.

286

to the fundamental democratic traditions based upon the maintenance of right and justice and succor for defeated peoples, and in view of the friendly relations existing between our Kingdom and the Government of the United States, we wish to draw your attention, Mr. President, to the cause of the Arabs in Palestine and their legitimate rights, and we have full confidence that our statement will make clear to you and the American People the just cause of the Arabs in those Holy Lands.

It has appeared to us from the account which has been published of the American position that the case of Palestine has been considered from a single point of view: the point of view of the Zionist Jews; and the Arab points of view have been neglected. We have observed as one of the effects of the widespread Jewish propaganda that the democratic American People has been grossly misled, and it has resulted in considering support for the Jews in crushing the Arabs in Palestine as an act of humanity. Although such an action is a wrong directed against a peaceful people dwelling in their country, they have not ceased to have confidence in the fairness of general democratic opinion in the world at large and in America particularly. I am confident that if the rights of the Arabs in Palestine were clear to you, Mr. President, and to the American People, you would give them full support.

The argument on which the Jews depend in their claims regarding Palestine is that they settled there for a time in the olden days and that they have wandered in various countries of the world, and that they wish to create a gathering-place for themselves in Palestine where they may live freely. And for their action they rely upon a promise they received from the British Government, namely: the Balfour Declaration.

As for the historical claim of the Jews, there is nothing to justify it, because Palestine was and has not ceased to be occupied by the Arabs through all the periods and progression of history, and its sovereign was their sovereign. If we except the interval when the Jews were established there, and a second period when the Roman Empire ruled there, the ruler of the Arabs has been the ruler of Palestine from the oldest times to our own day. The Arabs, through the entire course of their existence have been the keepers of the Holy Places, the magnifiers of their situation, the respecters of their sanctity, maintaining their affairs with all faithfulness and devotion. When the Ottoman Government extended over Palestine, Arab influence was dominant, and the Arabs never felt that the Turks were a colonizing power in their country, owing to:

1. The oneness of the religious bond;
2. The feeling of the Arabs that they were partners of the Turks in government;
3. The local administration of government being in the hands of the sons of the land itself.

From the foregoing it is seen that the Jewish claim of rights in Palestine in so far as it rests upon history has no reality, for if the Jews dwelt in Palestine for a certain period as possessors, surely the Arabs have dwelt there a far longer time, and it is impossible to consider the annexation of a country by a people as a natural right justifying their claim thereto. If this principle be now held in esteem, then it is the right of every people to reclaim the country it formerly occupied by force for a certain time. This would bring about astonishing changes in the map of the world, and would be irreconcilable with right, with justice, or with equity.

Now regarding the other claim of the Jews, they take unto themselves the sympathy of the world because they are scattered and persecuted in various countries, and they would like to find a place in which to take shelter in order to be safe from the injustice they encounter in many countries.

The important thing in this matter is to discriminate between the cause of Judaism and Islam [anti-Semitism] in the world, as contrasted with the cause of political Zionism. The intention was sympathy for scattered Jews. But Palestine is a small country. It has already received such a great number of them as to exceed comparison with any country in the world, taking account of the limited area of Palestine as

288

compared with the lands of the earth where the Jews dwell. There is no power to remedy the straitness of Palestine in order to make room for all the Jews of the world, even supposing it were empty of its inhabitants, the Arabs (as Mr. Malcolm MacDonald said in a speech which he delivered recently in the British House of Commons). If the principle be accepted that the Jews now in Palestine are to remain there, then that little country has already performed a greater human justice than any other. You will see, Mr. President, that it is not just that the governments of the world – including the United States – have closed their doors against the immigration of the Jews and impose on Palestine, a small Arab country, the task of sustaining them.

But if we look at the matter from the standpoint of political Zionism this point of view resembles [*represents*] a wrong and unjust way. Its aim is to ruin a peaceable and tranquil people and to drive them from their country by various means, and to feed the political greed and personal ambition of a few Zionists. As to the reliance of the Jews upon the Balfour Declaration, surely that Declaration has brought the limit of oppression and iniquity to a peaceful and tranquil country. It was given by a government which at the time of the gift did not possess the right to impose it upon Palestine. Similarly, the opinion of the Arabs of Palestine was not taken in this regard nor with regard to the arrangement of the Mandate which was imposed upon them, as has been made clear also by Malcolm MacDonald, British Minister of Colonies, and this in spite of promises given by the Allies, including America, that they would have the right of self-determination. It is important for us to mention that Balfour's promise was preceded by another promise from the British Government with the knowledge of the Allies regarding the rights of the Arabs in Palestine and in other Arab countries.

From this it will be clear to you, Mr. President, that the historical pretext of the Jews is unjust and it is impossible to consider it. Their plea from the standpoint of humanity has been fulfilled more by Palestine than by any other country, and Balfour's promise on which they depend is contrary to right and justice and inconsistent with the principle of self-determination. The ambition of the Zionists renders the Arabs in all countries apprehensive, and causes them to resist it.

The rights of the Arabs in Palestine do not admit of discussion because Palestine has been their country since the oldest times, and they did not leave it nor did others drive them out. Places flourished there, Arab in civilization, to an extent calling for admiration, for the reason that they were Arab in origin, in language, in situation, in culture; and of this there is no uncertainty or doubt. The history of the Arabs is full of just laws and useful works.

When the World War broke out, the Arabs sided with the Allies hoping to obtain their independence, and they were wholly confident that they would achieve it after the World War for the following reasons:

1. Because they participated in the War by action, and sacrificed their lives and property;

2. Because it was promised them by the British Government through notes exchanged between its representative at the time, Sir Henry McMahon, and the Sherif Hussein;

3. Because of your predecessor, the Great President Wilson who decided upon the participation of the United States of America in the War on the side of the Allies in support of high human principles, of which the most important was the right of self-determination;

4. Because the Allies declared in November 1919 [1918], following their occupation of the countries, that they entered them in order to free them and to give the people their liberty and independence.

Mr. President, if you will refer to the report[2] submitted by the Commission of Investigation which your predecessor, President Wilson, sent to the Near East in 1919, you will find the demands which the Arabs in Palestine and Syria

[2] Report of the King-Crane Commission.

made when they were questioned as to what future they asked for themselves.

But unfortunately the Arabs found after the War that they were abandoned, and the assurances given did not materialize. Their lands have been divided and distributed unjustly. Artificial frontiers resulted from these divisions which are not justified by the facts of geography, nationality, or religion. In addition to this, they found themselves facing a very great danger: the incursion upon them of the Zionists, who became the possessors of their best lands.

The Arabs protested strongly when they learned of the Balfour Declaration, and they protested against the organization of the Mandate. They announced their rejection and their non-acceptance from the first day. The stream of Jewish immigration from various countries to Palestine has caused the Arabs to fear for their lives and their destiny; consequently numerous outbreaks and disturbances in Palestine took place in 1920, 1921, and 1929, but the most important outbreak was that of 1936, and its fire has not ceased to blaze to this hour.

Mr. President, the Arabs of Palestine and behind them the rest of the Arabs – or rather, the rest of the Islamic World – demand their rights, and they defend their lands against those who intrude upon them and their territories. It is impossible to establish peace in Palestine unless the Arabs obtain their rights, and unless they are sure that their countries will not be given to an alien people whose principles, aims and customs differ from theirs in every way. Therefore we beseech and adjure you Mr. President, in the name of Justice and Freedom and help for weak peoples for which the noble American People is celebrated, to have the goodness to consider the cause of the Arabs of Palestine, and to support those who live in peace and quiet despite attack from these homeless groups from all parts of the world. For it is not just that the Jews be sent away from all the various countries of the world and that weak, conquered Palestine should, against its will, suffer this whole people. We do not doubt that the high principles to which the American People adhere, will cause them to yield to right and grant support for justice and fair play.

Written in our Palace at Ar Riad on the seventh day of the month of Shawal, in the year 1357 of the Hejira, corresponding to November 29, 1938, A.D.

ABDUL AZIZ ES SAUD

The Under Secretary of State (Welles) to President Roosevelt

WASHINGTON, January 9, 1939

MY DEAR MR. PRESIDENT: I transmit the original of a communication addressed to you by His Majesty Abdul Aziz ibn Saud, King of Saudi Arabia, regarding the Palestine situation and the attitude of this Government with respect thereto. The original letter, of which a translation prepared by the American Legation in Cairo is also enclosed, was handed to the American Chargé d'Affaires in that city by the Saudi Arabian Chargé d'Affaires there, and transmitted by the former to the Department.

With regard to King ibn Saud's remarks concerning the position of President Wilson in respect of self-determination and the sending of a 'Commission of Investigation' to the Near East in 1919, it may be helpful, for convenient reference, to set forth briefly the chronology of events. It will be recalled that President Wilson, in the twelfth of his Fourteen Points, urged that 'the other nationalities which are now under Turkish rule should be assured an undoubted security of life and an absolutely unmolested opportunity of autonomous development'. In line with the foregoing principle Article XXII of the Covenant of the League of Nations accorded provisional recognition as independent nations to certain communities in the former Ottoman Empire, and stipulated that in selecting mandatories for such nations the 'wishes of these communities must be a principal consideration'.

With a view to carrying out that stipulation it was agreed

at Paris that commissions should be sent to the Near East to inquire into the situation and to submit a report thereon. It will be recalled that the other governments concerned refrained from sending such commissions but an American section, headed by Mr. Charles R. Crane and Dr. Henry Churchill King, did visit the Near East during the summer of 1919 and submitted a report, dated August 28, 1919. It is to this report that King ibn Saud refers in the fourth from the last paragraph of his letter. For convenience of reference I quote those of the Commission's recommendations regarding Palestine which King ibn Saud apparently had in mind:

If that principle (self-determination) is to rule, and so the wishes of Palestine's population are to be decisive as to what is to be done with Palestine, then it is to be remembered that the non-Jewish population of Palestine – nearly nine-tenths of the whole – are emphatically against the entire Zionist program. The tables show that there was no one thing upon which the population of Palestine were more agreed than upon this. To subject a people so minded to unlimited Jewish immigration, and to steady financial and social pressure to surrender the land, would be a gross violation of the principle just quoted, and of the people's rights, though it kept within the form of law.

The conclusions of the Commission on the question of Palestine read as follows:

In view of all these considerations, and with a deep sense of sympathy for the Jewish cause, the Commissioners feel bound to recommend that only a greatly reduced Zionist program be attempted by the Peace Conference, and even that, only very gradually initiated. This would have to mean that Jewish immigration should be definitely limited, and that the project for making Palestine distinctly a Jewish Commonwealth should be given up.

Although we have had numerous communications from Arab notables and organizations protesting that the attitude of this Government favored the Zionist cause and was consequently anti-Arab, this is the first letter which we have had from an Arab Chief of State. As you are aware, the special position of the Arab States neighboring Palestine with reference to that country has been recognized by the British Government on several occasions, the most recent of which was in connection with the forthcoming London Conference called by the British Government to effect a settlement of the Palestine question, to which the Governments of Saudi Arabia, Iraq, Transjordan, Egypt and Yemen have been invited to send official delegates. In view of the special position of the Arab States in respect of the Palestine question, and in view of the position of King ibn Saud as the outstanding Arab ruler and as the person most qualified to speak on behalf of the Arab people, it would seem that something more than a perfunctory acknowledgment should be made of his present communication.

I enclose for your consideration and your signature, if you approve, a reply to His Majesty which has been drafted with the foregoing considerations in mind. If you have some particular views which you desire to have incorporated in this communication, I shall be grateful if you will indicate their nature.

Faithfully yours,   SUMNER WELLES

[Enclosure]

Draft Letter From President Roosevelt to the King of Saudi Arabia (Abdul Aziz ibn Saud)[3]

YOUR MAJESTY: I have been greatly pleased to receive Your Majesty's letter of November 29, 1938, which was delivered by the Saudi Arabian Chargé d'Affaires in Cairo on December 6 to the American Chargé d'Affaires there, with regard to the Arab cause in Palestine.

As Your Majesty is no doubt aware, the Palestine situation is one which has engaged for long the attention of the American people. It is therefore with particular interest that I have read Your letter devoted to that subject.

---

[3] Apparently the President approved this reply, for a copy was transmitted to the Chargé in Egypt as an enclosure to instruction No. 357, January 17, 1939 (not printed). It was presented to the Saudi Arabian Chargé d'Affaires in Egypt on February 15.

The interest which the American people have in Palestine is based on a number of considerations. They include those of a spiritual character as well as those flowing from the rights derived by the United States in Palestine through the American-British Mandate Convention of December 3, 1924.

The position of the United States with respect to Palestine has been set forth in a public statement issued by the Department of State on October 14, 1938,[4] of which it gives me pleasure to transmit to Your Majesty a copy. I may add that this Government has never taken any position different from that which it has maintained from the beginning toward this question.

Your Good Friend,

THE TIMES, *Tuesday January 10, 1939*

Arab case in Palestine
Wahabi King's Note to U.S.A.

In a Note to President Roosevelt on the Arab case in Palestine the Wahabi King says:-

It seems to us that the Palestine question has been viewed in the United States of America solely from the point of view of the Zionist Jews and that the freedom-loving people of America have been so much misled on this question by extensive Zionist propaganda that they have come to look upon the Jewish attempt to crush the Arabs of Palestine as a humane act, when as a matter of fact it is nothing but a horrible crime on a peaceful people in their own homeland.

A distinction must be made between political Zionism and the world problem of the persecuted Jews, to which Palestine cannot possibly be the solution, although she has already done more than any other country in the world by accommodating the greatest possible number of Jews for her size.

The Arabs strongly protested against the Balfour Declaration as soon as they heard of it, as they also protested

---

[4] See pages 283–6.

against the Mandate and refused to acknowledge it. The influx of Jews into Palestine alarmed the Arabs and made them most anxious about their future and their very life, and as the flow of Jewish immigrants into Palestine continued to increase their worst fears became realized.

Interview of His Majesty the King with LIFE Magazine's Representative, Mr. Busch

RIAD, March 21, 1943

Ibn Saud's first pronouncement on the Palestine problem – Translation

Q. What is your Majesty's opinion concerning the Palestine problem?
A. I have withheld my opinion concerning the Palestine problem from the Arabs in order to avoid placing them in an embarrassing position with the Allies. But because you are one of our friends, I wish to acquaint you with my opinion so that it can be made known to the friendly American people, so that they may understand the truth of the matter.

First, I know of nothing that justifies the Jewish claims in Palestine. Centuries before the advent of Mohammed, Palestine belonged to the Jews. But the Romans prevailed over them, killed some and dispersed the rest. No trace of their rule remained. Then the Arabs seized Palestine from the Romans, more than thirteen hundred years ago, and it has remained ever since in the possession of the Moslems. This shows that the Jews have no right to their claim, since all the countries of the world saw the succession of different peoples who conquered them. Those countries became their undisputed homelands. Were we to follow the Jewish theory, it would become necessary for many peoples of the world, including those of Palestine, to move out of the lands wherein they settled.

Secondly, I am not afraid of the Jews or of the possibility

296

of their ever having a state or power, either in the land of the Arabs or elsewhere. This is in accordance with what God has revealed unto us through the mouth of His Prophet in His Holy Book. Thus I hold the demands of the Jews upon this land an error; first because it constitutes an injustice against the Arabs, and the Moslems in general; and secondly because it causes dissensions and disturbances between the Moslems and their friends the Allies; and in this I fail to see anything good. Furthermore, if the Jews are impelled to seek a place to live, Europe and America as well as other lands are larger and more fertile than Palestine, and more suitable to their welfare and interests. This would constitute justice, and there is no need to involve the Allies and the Moslems in a problem void of good.

As to the native Jewish population in Palestine, I suggest that the Arabs agree with their friends the Allies to safeguard the interests of those Jews, provided the Jews commit no action that might lead to strife and dissension, which would not be in the general interest, and provided the Jews give a guarantee, endorsed by the Allies, that they would not strive to buy Arab property, and would refrain from using their great financial power for that purpose. Such efforts would only bring to the people of Palestine loss and injury, and poverty and decay to their doors. Such efforts would inevitably lead to more trouble.

On the other hand the Arabs would recognize the rights of the Jews and would guarantee to safeguard them.

Q. *What does your Majesty think of Arab unity?*
A. There are no differences among the Arabs, and I believe that, with Allied aid, they will be united after the war.
                    (Signed) Head of The Royal Cabinet.

Life commented underneath:

In his royal interview at Riad, Mr. Busch asked, and Ibn Saud answered, a question on the No. 1 Arab problem – i.e. the future of the Jewish Homeland in Palestine as promised in the Balfour Declaration of 1917.... A newsworthy pronouncement by a No. 1 Arab on a world problem, Ibn Saud's pronouncement sets him in direct and personal conflict with world Zionism at a time when the whole Palestine question has been fervently reopened in the American press. Such a drastic statement will naturally dismay all those who have struggled through the years for some compromise of this most difficult problem. That Ibn Saud's position is disputable historically, economically and religiously will be demonstrated by competent Zionists in the pages of *Life* in a later issue.

King Abdul Aziz Ibn Saud to President Roosevelt[5]

[April 30, 1943]

EXCELLENCY: In this great world war in which nations are shedding their blood and expending their wealth in the defence of freedom and liberty, in this war in which the high principles for which the Allies are fighting have been proclaimed in the Atlantic Charter, in this struggle in which the leaders of every country are appealing to their countrymen, allies and friends to stand with them in their struggle for life, I have been alarmed, as have other Moslems and Arabs, because a group of Zionists are seizing the opportunity of this terrible crisis to make extensive propaganda by which they seek on the one hand to mislead American public opinion and, on the other hand, to bring pressure upon the Allied Governments in these critical times in order to force them to go against the principles of right, justice and equity which they have proclaimed and for which they are fighting, the principles of the freedom and liberty of peoples. By so doing the Jews seek to compel the Allies to help them exterminate the peaceful Arabs settled in Palestine for thousands of years. They hope to evict this noble nation from its home

[5] Copy transmitted to the Department by the Minister in Egypt in his despatch No. 1034, May 11; received May 25.

and to install Jews from every horizon in this sacred Moslem Arab country. What a calamitous and infamous miscarriage of justice would, God forbid, result from this world struggle if the Allies should, at the end of their struggle, crown their victory by evicting the Arabs from their home in Palestine, substituting in their place vagrant Jews who have no ties with this country except an imaginary claim which, from the point of view of right and justice, has no grounds except what they invent through fraud and deceit. They avail themselves of the Allies' critical situation and of the fact that the American nation is unaware of the truth about the Arabs in general and the Palestine question in particular.

On November 19 [29], 1938 (Shawal 7, 1357 H.) I wrote to Your Excellency a letter in which I set forth the true situation of the Arabs and Jews in Palestine. If Your Excellency would refer to that letter, you will find that the Jews have no right to Palestine and that their claim is an act of injustice unprecedented in the history of the human race. Palestine has from the earliest history belonged to the Arabs and is situated in the midst of Arab countries. The Jews only occupied it for a short period and the greater part of that period was full of massacres and tragedies. Subsequently they were driven out of the country and today it is proposed to re-install them in it. By so doing the Jews will do wrong to the quiet and peaceful Arabs. The Heavens will split, the earth will be rent asunder, and the mountains will tremble at what the Jews claim in Palestine, both materially and spiritually.

Having sent to Your Excellency my above-mentioned letter, I believed, and I still believe, that the Arab claim to Palestine had become clear to you, for in your kind letter to me dated January 9, 1939 you made no remark about any of the facts which I had mentioned in my previous letter. I would not have wasted Your Excellency's time over this case nor the time of the men at the head of your government at this critical moment but the persistent news that these Zionists do not refrain from bringing forth their wrong and unjust claim induces me to remind Your Excellency of the rights of

Moslems and Arabs in the Holy Land so that you may prevent this act of injustice and that my explanation to Your Excellency may convince the Americans of the Arabs' rights in Palestine, and that Americans whom Jewish Zionism intends to mislead by propaganda may know the real facts, help the oppressed Arabs, and crown their present efforts by setting up right and justice in all parts of the world.

If we leave aside the religious animosity between Moslems and Jews which dates back to the time when Islam appeared and which is due to the treacherous behavior of the Jews towards Moslems and their Prophet, if we leave aside all this and consider the case of the Jews from a purely humanitarian point of view, we would find, as I mentioned in my previous letter, that Palestine, as every human creature who knows that country admits, cannot solve the Jewish problem. Supposing that the country were subjected to injustice in all its forms, that all the Arabs of Palestine, men, women and children, were killed and their lands wrested from them and given to the Jews, the Jewish problem would not be solved and no sufficient lands would be available for the Jews. Why, therefore, should such an act of injustice, which is unique in the history of the human race, be tolerated, seeing that it would not satisfy the would-be murderers, i.e., the Jews?

In my previous letter to Your Excellency I stated that if we consider this matter from a humanitarian point of view, we would find that the small country we call Palestine was crammed at the beginning of the present war with nearly 400,000 Jews. At the end of the last Great War they only constituted 7% of the whole population but this proportion rose before the beginning of the present war to 29% and is still rising. We do not know where it will stop, but we know that a little before the present war the Jews possessed 1,000,332 donams out of 7,000,000 donams which is the sum total of all the cultivable land in Palestine.

We do not intend, nor demand, the destruction of the Jews but we demand that the Arabs should not be exterminated for the sake of the Jews. The world should not be too small to receive them. In fact, if each of the Allied countries would bear one tenth of what Palestine has borne, it would be possible to solve the Jewish problem and the problem of giving them a home to live in. All that we request at present is that you should help to stop the flow of migration by finding a place for the Jews to live in other than Palestine, and by preventing completely the sale of lands to them. Later on the Allies and Arabs can look into the matter of assuring the accommodation of those of the Jews residing in Palestine whom that country can support provided that they reside quietly and do not foment trouble between Arabs and the Allies.

In writing this to Your Excellency I am sure that you will respond to the appeal of a friend who feels that you appreciate friendship as you appreciate right, justice, and equity, and who is aware that the greatest hope of the American people is to come out of this world struggle, rejoicing in the triumph of the principles for which it is fighting, i.e., to ensure to every people its freedom and to grant it its rights. For if – God forbid! – the Jews were to be granted their desire, Palestine would forever remain a hotbed of troubles and disturbances as in the past. This will create difficulties for the Allies in general and for our friend Great Britain in particular. In view of their financial power and learning the Jews can stir up enmity between the Arabs and the Allies at any moment. They have been the cause of many troubles in the past.

All that we are now anxious for is that right and justice should prevail in the solution of the various problems which will come to light after the war and that the relations between the Arabs and the Allies should always be of the best and strongest.

In closing, I beg you to accept my most cordial greetings.

Written at Our Camp at Roda Khareem on this the 25th day of Rabi'Tani, of the year 1362 Hegira corresponding to April 30, 1943.

President Roosevelt to King Abdul Aziz Ibn Saud[6]

GREAT AND GOOD FRIEND: I have received Your Majesty's communication of April 30, 1943, relating to matters affecting Palestine, and I appreciate the spirit of friendship you have manifested in expressing these views to me.

I have noted carefully the statements made in this communication, as well as those contained in Your Majesty's letter of November 19 [29], 1938, and the oral message conveyed to Mr. Kirk, the American Minister, at the conclusion of his recent visit to Riyadh.

Your Majesty, no doubt, has received my message delivered by Mr. Moose to His Highness the Amir Faisal. As I stated therein, it appears to me highly desirable that the Arabs and Jews interested in the question should come to a friendly understanding with respect to matters affecting Palestine through their own efforts prior to the termination of the war. I am glad of this opportunity, however, to reiterate my assurance that it is the view of the Government of the United States that, in any case, no decision altering the basic situation of Palestine should be reached without full consultation with both Arabs and Jews.

I renew my expressions of best wishes for Your Majesty's good health and for the well-being of your people.

Your Good Friend,

FRANKLIN D. ROOSEVELT

---

[6] Copy transmitted to the Appointed Minister Resident in Saudi Arabia by the Secretary of State in his instruction No. 51, June 19; copy in Department's files undated.

The Acting Secretary of State to the Secretary of State, at Paris[7]

WASHINGTON, April 30, 1946

From Acheson for Secretary Byrnes. The President has asked me to transmit urgently to you the following message which you may care to discuss with Mr. Bevin:

'Following is the text of a statement which I shall issue at 7:00 p.m. today, simultaneously with the release of the Anglo-American report on Palestine:[8]

"I am very happy that the request which I made for the immediate admission of 100,000 Jews into Palestine has been unanimously endorsed by the Anglo-American Committee of Inquiry. The transference of these unfortunate people should now be accomplished with the greatest dispatch. The protection and safe-guarding of the Holy Places in Palestine sacred to Moslem, Christian and Jew is adequately provided in the report. One of the significant features in the report is that it aims to insure complete protection to the Arab population of Palestine by guaranteeing their civil and religious rights, and by recommending measures for the constant improvement in their cultural, educational and economic position.

I am also pleased that the Committee recommends in effect the abrogation of the White Paper of 1939 including existing

---

[7] Mr. Byrnes was attending the meeting of the Council of Foreign Ministers at Paris. On April 28, in telegram 2025, he advised Mr. Acheson of a communication from Mr. Bevin expressing the hope that the United States would not make a statement of policy on Palestine without consulting with the British Government. Mr. Byrnes noted he was willing to agree but requested Mr. Acheson to apprise President Truman. The President informed Mr. Acheson at their regular meeting on April 29 that he felt it necessary to issue a statement when the report was released on May 1. Subsequently the White House sent the President's proposed statement to Mr. Acheson for communication to Mr. Byrnes. It was done in this telegram. Mr. Byrnes, in a telephone conversation with Mr. Acheson on April 30, stated he did not object to the President's making the statement and that he would mention it to Mr. Bevin.

[8] The report of the Committee, dated April 20, 1946, was released by the Department of State in 1946 as Publication No. 2536.

restrictions on immigration and land acquisition to permit the further development of the Jewish National Home. It is also gratifying that the report envisages the carrying out of large scale economic development projects in Palestine which would facilitate further immigration and be of benefit to the entire population.

In addition to these immediate objectives the report deals with many other questions of long range political policies and questions of international law which require careful study and which I will take under advisement. Harry S. Truman" '.

Repeated to London. Adding following heading 'Urgent repeat of telegram 1970 to Paris which follows should be conveyed at once to Mr. Harriman.'

ACHESON

President Truman to the British Prime Minister (Attlee)[9]

CONFIDENTIAL
US URGENT

WASHINGTON,
October 3, 1946 – 1 p.m.

I deeply regret that it has been found necessary to postpone further meetings of the Palestine Conference in London until Dec 16 and I sincerely hope that it will be found possible in the interim to begin moving on a large scale the 100,000 displaced Jews in Europe who are awaiting admission to Palestine.

In view of the deep sympathy of the American people for these unfortunate victims of Nazi persecution in Europe and of the hopes in this country that a fair and workable solution of the Palestine problem be reached as soon as possible I find it necessary to make a further statement at once on the

[9] Sent to London as Department's telegram 6959, with the instruction: 'Please deliver at earliest possible moment following message from the President to the Prime Minister.' The telegram was repeated to the Secretary of State in Paris.

subject. Attached hereto is a copy of the statement which I am planning to issue tomorrow Oct 4:

'I have learned with deep regret that the meetings of the Palestine Conference in London have been adjourned and are not to be resumed until Dec 16, 1946. In the light of this situation it is appropriate to examine the record of the Administration's efforts in this field, efforts which have been supported in and out of Congress by members of both political parties, and to state my views on the situation as it now exists.

It will be recalled that when Mr. Earl Harrison[10] reported on Sep 29, 1945 concerning the condition of displaced persons in Europe, I immediately urged that steps be taken to relieve the situation of these persons to the extent at least of admitting 100,000 Jews into Palestine. In response to this suggestion the British Government invited the Government of the United States to cooperate in setting up a joint Anglo-American Committee of Inquiry, an invitation which this Government was happy to accept in the hope that its participation would help to alleviate the situation of the displaced Jews in Europe and would assist in finding a solution for the difficult and complex problem of Palestine itself. The urgency with which this Government regarded the matter is reflected in the fact that a 120-day limit was set for the completion of the Committee's task.

The unanimous report of the Anglo-American Committee of Inquiry was made on April 20, 1946, and I was gratified to note that among the recommendations contained in the Report was an endorsement of my previous suggestion that 100,000 Jews be admitted into Palestine. The Administration immediately concerned itself with devising ways and means for transporting the 100,000 and caring for them upon their arrival. With this in mind, experts were sent to London in June 1946 to work out provisionally the actual travel

---

[10] Earl G. Harrison, United States Representative on the Intergovernmental Committee on Refugees.

arrangements. The British Government cooperated with this group, but made it clear that in its view the report must be considered as a whole and that the issue of the 100,000 could not be considered separately.

On June 11 I announced the establishment of a Cabinet Committee on Palestine and Related Problems, composed of the Secretaries of State, War and Treasury, to assist me in considering the recommendations of the Anglo-American Committee of Inquiry. The Alternates of this Cabinet Committee, headed by Ambassador Henry F. Grady, departed for London on July 10, 1946 to discuss with British Government representatives how the Report might best be implemented. The Alternates submitted on July 24, 1946 a report, commonly referred to as the Morrison plan, advocating a scheme of provincial autonomy which might lead ultimately to a binational state or to partition. However, opposition to this plan developed among members of the major political parties in the United States – both in the Congress and throughout the country. In accordance with the principle which I have consistently tried to follow, of having a maximum degree of unity within the country and between the parties on major elements of American foreign policy, I could not give my support to this plan.

I have, nevertheless, maintained my deep interest in the matter and have repeatedly made known and have urged that steps be taken at the earliest possible moment to admit 100,000 Jewish refugees to Palestine.

In the meantime, this Government was informed of the efforts of the British Government to bring to London representatives of the Arabs and Jews, with a view to finding a solution to this distressing problem. I expressed the hope that as a result of these conversations a fair solution of the Palestine problem could be found. While all the parties invited had not found themselves able to attend, I had hoped that there was still a possibility that representatives of the Jewish Agency might take part. If so, the prospect for an agreed and constructive settlement would have been enhanced.

The British Government presented to the Conference the so-called Morrison plan for provincial autonomy and stated that the Conference was open to other proposals. Meanwhile, the Jewish Agency proposed a solution of the Palestine problem by means of the creation of a viable Jewish state in control of its own immigration and economic policies in an adequate area of Palestine instead of in the whole of Palestine. It proposed furthermore the immediate issuance of certificates for 100,000 Jewish immigrants. This proposal received widespread attention in the United States, both in the press and in public forums. From the discussion which has ensued it is my belief that a solution along these lines would command the support of public opinion in the United States. I cannot believe that the gap between the proposals which have been put forward is too great to be bridged by men of reason and goodwill. To such a solution our Government could give its support.

In the light of the situation which has now developed I wish to state my views as succinctly as possible:

1. In view of the fact that winter will come on before the Conference can be resumed I believe and urge that substantial immigration into Palestine cannot await a solution to the Palestine problem and that it should begin at once. Preparations for this movement have already been made by this Government and it is ready to lend its immediate assistance.

2. I state again, as I have on previous occasions, that the immigration laws of other countries, including the United States, should be liberalized with a view to the admission of displaced persons. I am prepared to make such a recommendation to the Congress and to continue as energetically as possible collaboration with other countries on the whole problem of displaced persons.

3. Furthermore, should a workable solution for Palestine be devised, I would be willing to recommend to the Congress a plan for economic assistance for the development of that country.

In the light of the terrible ordeal which the Jewish people

of Europe endured during the recent war and the crisis now existing, I cannot believe that a program of immediate action along the lines suggested above could not be worked out with the cooperation of all people concerned. The Administration will continue to do everything it can to this end.[']

The King of Saudi Arabia (Abdul Aziz Ibn Saud) to President Truman[11]

YOUR EXCELLENCY: In my desire to safeguard and strengthen in every way possible the friendship which binds our two countries together and which existed between the late President Roosevelt and which was renewed with Your Excellency, I reiterate my feelings on every occasion when this friendship between the United States on the one hand, and my country and the other Arab countries on the other hand, is endangered, so that all obstacles in the way of that friendship may be removed.

On previous occasions I wrote to the late President Roosevelt and to Your Excellency, and explained the situation in Palestine: How the natural rights of the Arabs therein go back thousands of years and how the Jews are only aggressors, seeking to perpetrate a monstrous injustice, at the beginning, speaking in the name of humanitarianism, but later openly proclaiming their aggressiveness by force and violence as is not unknown to Your Excellency and the American people. Moreover, the designs of the Jews are not limited to Palestine only, but include the neighboring Arab countries within their scope, not even excluding our holy cities.

I was therefore astonished at the latest announcement issued in your name in support of the Jews in Palestine and its demand that floodgates of immigration be opened in such a way as to alter the basic situation in Palestine in contra-

[11] Transmitted to the Acting Secretary of State by the Saudi Arabian Minister in his note of October 15, 1946, requesting that the message be communicated to President Truman.

diction to previous promises. My astonishment was even greater because the statement ascribed to Your Excellency contradicts the Declaration which the American Legation in Jeddah requested our Foreign Office to publish in the Government's official paper *Omm Al-Qura* in the name of the White House, on August 16, 1946, in which it was stated that the Government of the United States had not made any proposals for the solution of the Palestine problem, and in which you expressed your hope that it would be solved through the conversations between the British Government and the Foreign Ministers of the Arab States, on the one hand, and between the British Government and the third party on the other, and in which you expressed the readiness of the United States to assist the displaced persons among whom are Jews. Hence, my great astonishment when I read your Excellency's statement and my incredulity that it could have come from you, because it contradicts previous promises made by the Government of the United States and statements made from the White House.

I am confident that the American people who spent their blood and their money freely to resist aggression, could not possibly support Zionist aggression against a friendly Arab country which has committed no crime except to believe firmly in those principles of justice and equality, for which the United Nations, including the United States, fought, and for which both your predecessor and you exerted great efforts.

My desire to preserve the friendship of the Arabs and the East towards the United States of America has obliged me to expound to Your Excellency the injustice which would be visited upon the Arabs by any assistance to Zionist aggression.

I am certain that Your Excellency and the American people cannot support right, justice, and equity and fight for them in the rest of the world while denying them to the Arabs in their country, Palestine, which they have inherited from their ancestors from Ancient Times.

With Greetings,   ABDUL AZIZ

President Truman to the King of Saudi Arabia (Abdul Aziz Ibn Saud)[12]

US URGENT   WASHINGTON, October 25, 1946

YOUR MAJESTY: I have just received the letter with regard to Palestine which Your Majesty was good enough to transmit to me through the Saudi Arabian Legation under date of October 15, 1946, and have given careful consideration to the views expressed therein.

I am particularly appreciative of the frank manner in which you expressed yourself in your letter. Your frankness is entirely in keeping with the friendly relations which have long existed between our two countries, and with the personal friendship between Your Majesty and my distinguished predecessor; a friendship which I hope to retain and strengthen. It is precisely the cordial relations between our countries and Your Majesty's own friendly attitude which encourages me to invite your attention to some of the considerations which have prompted my Government to follow the course it has been pursuing with respect to the matter of Palestine and of the displaced Jews in Europe.

[12] Sent to the Legation in Jidda as Department's telegram 266, with the instruction: 'Please transmit urgently through appropriate channels following message from President to King in reply to King's message of Oct 15 on Palestine and confirm immediately by telegram receipt of message and hour of delivery. Message will be made public here in near future since King's letter was made public by Saudi Arabian Govt.'

In telegram 322, October 28, 1946, from Jidda, the Minister reported that the President's message had been delivered to the King by the Legation's interpreter, Mohammed Effendi, presumably on the evening of October 26. According to the interpreter, the King was extremely vexed, observing that the President had expressed an obviously hostile point of view and that his communication was not based on logical grounds. The King stated further that the United States had nothing to do with the Palestine question, a matter which should be settled by the British, who had enticed American involvement in order to prejudice Saudi Arabian friendship with the United States. He concluded that if the United States desired to preserve its relations with the Arabs, it should give up its interest in the Palestine question.

I feel certain that Your Majesty will readily agree that the tragic situation of the surviving victims of Nazi persecution in Europe presents a problem of such magnitude and poignancy that it cannot be ignored by people of good will or humanitarian instincts. This problem is worldwide. It seems to me that all of us have a common responsibility for working out a solution which would permit those unfortunates who must leave Europe to find new homes where they may dwell in peace and security.

Among the survivors in the displaced persons centers in Europe are numbers of Jews, whose plight is particularly tragic in as much as they represent the pitiful remnants of millions who were deliberately selected by the Nazi leaders for annihilation. Many of these persons look to Palestine as a haven where they hope among people of their own faith to find refuge, to begin to lead peaceful and useful lives, and to assist in the further development of the Jewish National Home.

The Government and people of the United States have given support to the concept of a Jewish National Home in Palestine ever since the termination of the first World War, which resulted in the freeing of a large area of the Near East, including Palestine, and the establishment of a number of independent states which are now members of the United Nations. The United States, which contributed its blood and resources to the winning of that war, could not divest itself of a certain responsibility for the manner in which the freed territories were disposed of, or for the fate of the peoples liberated at that time. It took the position, to which it still adheres, that these peoples should be prepared for self-government and also that a national home for the Jewish people should be established in Palestine. I am happy to note that most of the liberated peoples are now citizens of independent countries. The Jewish National Home, however, has not as yet been fully developed.

It is only natural, therefore, that my Government should favor at this time the entry into Palestine of considerable numbers of displaced Jews in Europe, not only that they may find shelter there, but also that they may contribute their talents and energies to the upbuilding of the Jewish National Home.

It was entirely in keeping with the traditional policies of this Government that over a year ago I began to correspond with the Prime Minister of Great Britain in an effort to expedite the solving of the urgent problem of the Jewish survivors in the displaced persons camps by the transfer of a substantial number of them to Palestine. It was my belief, to which I still adhere, and which is widely shared by the people of this country, that nothing would contribute more effectively to the alleviation of the plight of these Jewish survivors than the authorization of the immediate entry of at least 100,000 of them to Palestine. No decision with respect to this proposal has been reached, but my Government is still hopeful that it may be possible to proceed along the lines which I outlined to the Prime Minister.

At the same time there should, of course, be a concerted effort to open the gates of other lands, including the United States, to those unfortunate persons, who are now entering upon their second winter of homelessness subsequent to the termination of hostilities. I, for my part, have made it known that I am prepared to ask the Congress of the United States, whose cooperation must be enlisted under our Constitution, for special legislation admitting to this country additional numbers of these persons, over and above the immigration quotas fixed by our laws. My Government, moreover, has been actively exploring, in conjunction with other governments, the possibilities of settlement in different countries outside Europe for those displaced persons who are obliged to emigrate from that continent. In this connection it has been most heartening to us to note the statements of various Arab leaders as to the willingness of their countries to share in this humanitarian project by taking a certain number of these persons into their own lands.

I sincerely believe that it will prove possible to arrive at a satisfactory settlement of the refugee problem along the lines which I have mentioned above.

With regard to the possibility envisaged by Your Majesty that force and violence may be used by Jews in aggressive schemes against the neighboring Arab countries, I can assure you that this Government stands opposed to aggression of any kind or to the employment of terrorism for political purposes. I may add, moreover, that I am convinced that responsible Jewish leaders do not contemplate a policy of aggression against the Arab countries adjacent to Palestine.

I cannot agree with Your Majesty that my statement of Oct 4 is in any way inconsistent with the position taken in the statement issued on my behalf on Aug 16. In the latter statement the hope was expressed that as a result of the proposed conversations between the British Government and the Jewish and Arab representatives a fair solution of the problem of Palestine could be found and immediate steps could be taken to alleviate the situation of the displaced Jews in Europe. Unfortunately, these hopes have not been realized. The conversations between the British Government and the Arab representatives have, I understand, been adjourned until December without a solution having been found for the problem of Palestine or without any steps having been taken to alleviate the situation of the displaced Jews in Europe.

In this situation it seemed incumbent upon me to state as frankly as possible the urgency of the matter and my views both as to the direction in which a solution based on reason and good will might be reached and the immediate steps which should be taken. This I did in my statement of October 4.

I am at a loss to understand why Your Majesty seems to feel that this statement was in contradiction to previous promises or statements made by this Government. It may be well to recall here that in the past this Government, in outlining its attitude on Palestine, has given assurances that it would not take any action which might prove hostile to the Arab people, and also that in its view there should be no decision with respect to the basic situation in Palestine without prior consultation with both Arabs and Jews.

I do not consider that my urging of the admittance of a

considerable number of displaced Jews into Palestine or my statements with regard to the solution of the problem of Palestine in any sense represent an action hostile to the Arab people. My feelings with regard to the Arabs when I made these statements were, and are at the present time, of the most friendly character. I deplore any kind of conflict between Arabs and Jews, and am convinced that if both peoples approach the problems before them in a spirit of conciliation and moderation these problems can be solved to the lasting benefit of all concerned.

I furthermore do not feel that my statements in any way represent a failure on the part of this Government to lie up to its assurance that in its view there should be no decision with respect to the basic situation in Palestine without consultation with both Arabs and Jews. During the current year there have been a number of consultations with both Arabs and Jews.

Mindful of the great interest which your country, as well as my own, has in the settlement of the various matters which I have set forth above, I take this opportunity to express my earnest hope that Your Majesty, who occupies a position of such eminence in the Arab world, will use the great influence which you possess to assist in the finding in the immediate future of a just and lasting solution. I am anxious to do all that I can to aid in the matter and I can assure Your Majesty that the Government and people of the United States are continuing to be solicitous of the interests and welfare of the Arabs upon whose historic friendship they place great value.

I also take this occasion to convey to Your Majesty my warm personal greetings and my best wishes for the continued health and welfare of Your Majesty and your people.

Very sincerely yours,

HARRY S. TRUMAN

The King of Saudi Arabia (Abdul Aziz Ibn Saud) to President Truman[13]

[Translation]

YOUR EXCELLENCY: I have received with deep appreciation, your message of October 25, 1946 which you sent to me through the American Legation.

I value Your Excellency's friendship and that of the American people to me personally, to my country and to the rest of the Arab countries. In appreciation of the humanitarian spirit which you have shown, I have not objected to any humanitarian assistance which Your Excellency or the United States may give to the displaced Jews, provided that such assistance is not designed to condemn a people living peacefully in their land. But the Zionist Jews have used this humanitarian appeal as an excuse for attaining their own ends of aggression against Palestine: – these aims being to conquer Palestine and by achieving a majority to make it Jewish, to establish a Jewish state in it, to expel its original inhabitants, to use Palestine as a base for aggression against the neighboring Arab states, and to fulfill (other aspects of) their aggressive programs.

The humanitarian and democratic principles on which the foundations of life in the United States have been built are incompatible with enforcement on a peaceful people, living securely in their country, of foreign elements to conquer and expel the native people from their country. In the attainment of their objectives these foreign elements have confused world public opinion by appealing to the principles of humanity and mercy while at the same time resorting to force.

When the first World War was declared not more than 50,000 Jews lived in Palestine. The Arabs took up the fight on the side of Great Britain, its ally the United States and

---

[13] Transmitted to the Secretary of State by the Saudi Arabian Chargé in his note of November 2, 1946, asking that the message be communicated to President Truman.

the other Allies. With the Allies, they fought in support of Arab rights and in support of the principles enunciated by President Wilson – particularly the right of self-determination. Nevertheless Great Britain adopted the Balfour Declaration and in its might embarked upon a policy of admitting Jews into Palestine, in spite of the desires of its preponderantly Arab population and in contradiction to all democratic and human principles. The Arabs protested and rebelled, but they were ever faced with a greater force than they could muster until they were obliged to acquiesce against their wishes.

When this last World War commenced the forces of the enemy were combined and directed against Great Britain. Great Britain stood alone and demonstrated a power and steadfastness which have won for her the admiration of the whole world. Her faith and courage did truly save the world from a grave danger. In those dark days the enemies of Great Britain promised the Arabs to do away with Zionism. Sensing the gravity of England's position at that time, I stood firm by her. I advised all the Arabs to remain quiet and assured them that Britain and her Allies would never betray those principles of humanity and democracy which they entered the war to uphold. The Arabs heeded my counsel and gave whatever assistance to Great Britain and her Allies they could, until victory was attained.

And now in the name of humanity it is proposed to force on the Arab majority of Palestine a people alien to them, to make these new people the majority, thereby rendering the existing majority a minority. Your Excellency will agree with me in the belief that no people on earth would willingly admit into their country a foreign group desiring to become a majority and to establish its rule over that country. And the United States itself will not permit the admission into the United States of that number of Jews which it has proposed for entry into Palestine, as such a measure would be contrary to its laws established for its protection and the safeguarding of its interests.

In your message, Your Excellency mentioned that the

316

United States stands opposed to all forms of aggression or intimidation for the attainment of political objectives, if such measures have been applied by the Jews. You also expressed your conviction that responsible Jewish leaders do not contemplate the pursuit of an antagonistic policy toward the neighboring Arab states. In this connection I would call Your Excellency's attention to the fact that it was the British Government which made the Balfour Declaration, and transported the Jewish immigrants into Palestine under the protection of its bayonets. It was the British Government which gave and still gives shelter to their leaders and accords them its benevolent kindness and care. In spite of all this the British forces in Palestine are being seared by Zionist fire day and night, and the Jewish leaders have been unable to prevent these terroristic attacks. If, therefore, the British Government (the benefactor of the Jews) with all the means at its disposal is unable to prevent the terrorism of the Jews, how can the Arabs feel safe with or trust the Jews either now or in the future!

I believe that after reviewing all the facts Your Excellency will agree with me that the Arabs of Palestine, who form today the majority in their country, can never feel secure after the admission of the Jews into their midst nor can they feel assured about the future of the neighboring states.

Your Excellency also mentioned that you were unable to understand my feeling that your last declaration was inconsistent with previous promises and declarations made by the Government of the United States. Your Excellency also mentioned the assurances which I had received that the United States would not undertake any action modifying the basic situation in Palestine without consulting the two parties. I am confident that Your Excellency does neither intend to break a promise which you have made, nor desire to embark on an act of aggression against the Arabs. For these reasons I take the liberty to express to Your Excellency quite frankly that by an act which renders the Arab majority of Palestine a minority, the basic situation would be changed. This is the fundamental basis of the whole problem. For the principles of democracy dictate that when a majority exists in a country, the government of that country shall be by the majority, and not the minority. And should the Arabs forego the right conferred upon them by their numerical superiority, they would inevitably have to forego their privilege of their own form of government. What change can be considered more fundamental! And would the American people acquiesce in the admission into the United States of foreign elements in sufficient numbers to bring about a new majority? Would such an act be considered consonant with the principles of humanity and democracy?

I am confident that Your Excellency does not intend to antagonize the Arabs, but desires their good and welfare. I also believe that the American people will not agree to acts which are contrary to democratic and human principles. Relying on your desire for frankness and candidness in our relations I am prepared to do my best to remove all sources of misunderstanding by explaining the facts not only for the sake of truth and justice but also to strengthen the bonds of friendship between Your Excellency, the American people and myself.

I trust that Your Excellency will rest assured that my desire to defend the Arabs and their interests is no less than my desire to defend the reputation of the United States, throughout the Moslem and Arab worlds, and the entire world as well. Therefore you will find me extremely eager to persist in my efforts to convince Your Excellency and the American people of the democratic and human principles involved, which the United Nations, Your Excellency and the American people all seek to implement. For this reason I trust that Your Excellency will review the present situation in an effort to find a just solution of the problem – a solution which will ensure life for those displaced persons without threatening a peaceful people living securely in their country.

Kindly accept our salutations.

ABDUL-AZIZ

The dreams

In the winter of 1945, when the Second World War had just ended, I had two dreams within the period of one month. The question of Palestine was coming to a head, and conferences and meetings were constantly being held by the Arab countries, and by the British and their Western allies. The Jews were soliciting support from world Jewry and the Western powers, who were all supporting them without reserve. At this time, things looked as black as they could possibly be. It was during this time that I had the first dream.

As you approach Dhahran coming from Al-Khobar, a wadi descends from the heights of Dhahran. (Dhahran itself means 'prominence'.) Both sides stand on very high ground, with two twin hillocks on the right known as the 'Maiden Bosom'. In my first dream there was a table located between these two hillocks where four men were taking their seats: Mr F. A. Davies, Manager of Aramco at the time; his deputy, Mr Floyd Ohliger; the Saudi government's representative at the oil company, Sheikh Ali Sultan; and myself, sitting as translator amongst them. There were people gathered all around, who seemed to be company workmen and employees; they were all looking down the valley. Suddenly the wadi was filled with two long lines of chairs, the farthest side ending in a horseshoe-shaped circle. As the scene unfolded, heads of states, presidents, kings and many famous men started to assemble and take their seats – men like Churchill, Roosevelt, Hitler, the Shah of Iran and King Farouq of Egypt.

When all of the seats were filled, one chair remained empty at the top of the horseshoe circle. Then suddenly all were transfixed by the brilliance of the scene, as His Majesty King Abdul Aziz Ibn Saud arrived from the open end of the horseshoe. He towered above all with his majestic figure, his resplendent Arab dress of flowing robes studded with gold brocade, and a golden head-dress. He was a truly magnificent sight. As he proceeded towards the top of the horseshoe, everyone remained immobile, overcome by a feeling of honour and esteem. Finally, the King reached the empty chair, where he turned and faced the assembled company before sitting down himself. Then all resumed their seats, and a feeling permeated the assembly that this was the most powerful monarch and the greatest personality of the age. It seems that this prophetic dream is being realized today. Its truth can be judged by the great power accorded to the Saudi dynasty.

In Islam, the whole world is a mosque and there is no priesthood. Anyone can lead the prayers, provided that he can recite some verses from the Koran and believes in all the prophets, including Jesus. When camping or out in the desert, His Majesty used to pray in the open with his followers five times a day without fail. My second dream unfolded with a line of worshippers sitting somewhere in the desert. His Majesty was facing them, sitting at an altar, dressed in his long white robe and a simple white head-dress. This scene remained for a while, then he descended from the altar and advanced towards the line of worshippers, extending his hand in salute to a turbaned sheikh sitting in the middle. The King hauled him to a standing position and everybody watched this turbaned dignitary; it turned out to be the Mufti of Jerusalem. It dawned on all the assembled company that King Abdul Aziz was the great man who would rescue and save Palestine. The dream ended.

Dreams are described as a succession of images, thoughts or emotions passing through the mind in sleep – a means of gaining access to the unconscious mind. Our materialistic, Western friends may not believe in dreams, but we Moslems and Arabs believe and listen. We feel that the unconscious has much to say about the past, present and future. It has been said that 'the truth shall set you free'. The unconscious mind is truth in the telling!

Index

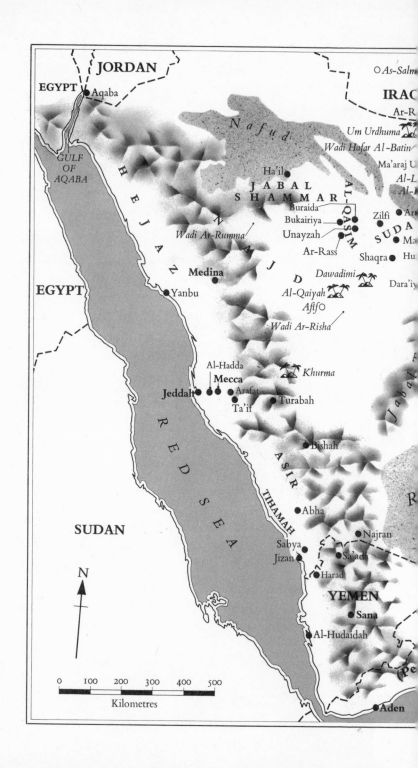